WHEN THE WORLD STOPS WATCHING

WHEN THE WORLD STOPS WATCHING

Life After the Game

DAMIAN LAWLOR

BLACK & WHITE PUBLISHING

First published in 2020
This edition published 2021
by Black & White Publishing Ltd
Nautical House, 104 Commercial Street
Edinburgh EH6 6NF

1 3 5 7 9 10 8 6 4 2   21 22 23 24

ISBN: 978 1 78530 344 9

The publisher has made every reasonable effort to contact copyright holders
of images in the picture section. Any errors are inadvertent and anyone who
for any reason has not been contacted is invited to write to the publisher so
that a full acknowledgement can be made in subsequent editions of this work.

A CIP catalogue record for this book is available from the British Library.

Typeset by Iolaire, Newtonmore
Printed and bound by CPI Group (UK) Ltd, Croydon, CR0 4YY

To my late father, John, who passed away in June 2019.

Thanks for everything, Dad.

CONTENTS

Part 4: Trailblazers Target New Territory

INTRODUCTION
THE FINAL DAY

Most people shop at Woodie's for homeware or garden furniture.

Paul McGee went there for a rope to hang himself with.

Earlier in the day, he'd googled how to tie a knot properly, that was the first part of the job. A visit to the DIY store was next.

Once home he headed for the attic, attached the rope to a beam anchored to the wall and, after firmly fastening it, went back downstairs.

McGee was almost ready to check out. He'd had his fill.

'I was done,' he admits. 'I felt life had turned against me.'

Maybe it had too.

The Dubliner burst on the English football scene in 1989 as a 21-year-old rookie, fleet of foot and happy-go-lucky in possession. He roared to prominence by netting a stylish goal against Arsenal on his top-flight debut, a goal that almost cost the London club the 1988/89 Division One League title.

Lights stayed green as he raced through life and it seemed like only open road lay ahead. Every time he played a game of football he turned more heads, and though he was only at the club a wet week, McGee was already preparing to leave Wimbledon to sign a lucrative top-flight deal elsewhere for £2.5 million.

Premier League football lay just around the corner. Any time whatsoever spent there, playing in one of the world's most lucrative divisions, could have set him up for the next ten years of his life.

Out of nowhere, however, without any flash of amber, the lights abruptly turned red and the soaring trajectory of his career was flattened, forced to a screeching halt.

Everything changed on the day he was meant to sign for his new club.

An offer from Coventry City had been accepted by Wimbledon and only the personal terms and conditions of his new contract needed to be agreed. As he jogged onto the field to go training with his Crazy Gang teammates for the last time, they stopped what they were doing, applauded him out of the dressing room, and gathered around to hug their departing winger.

A quick warm-up then before the coaches called an internal game. McGee said he would join in, just to get a session into his legs. After all, the next few days would be taken up with travelling, paperwork and medical tests. About 20 minutes into the practice session he cut in from his wing, rose high for a cross, fell to the ground and suffered a career-defining injury.

The moment he hit the ground the new contract offer was rendered worthless. McGee was rushed to hospital, operated upon and spent the next two years out of the game, just at a time when money in football was starting to lose the run of itself with new transfer records set every few months. It was a horrific injury and to make it worse he bore a hindered recovery. As if to rub salt on his wounds, on the day of his operation, a letter arrived at the foot of his hospital bed.

'Couldn't make it up,' he smiles ruefully. 'The letter was from Jack Charlton. Calling me up to the Republic of Ireland squad.'

That was as close as McGee would ever get to senior international honours.

When he finally returned from the injury and a string of subsequent complications, he was a Premier League footballer, but in name only. The boyish confidence had eroded, weakened legs meant his pace no longer swept him out of tackles or past opponents. Instead of the dash and dynamism that defined him, every step and sprint was taken with trepidation.

His body knew something wasn't right and while he tried to figure out what was causing breakdown after breakdown, his vitality slowly vaporised.

Life took at him off the field too.

He broke up with his partner and his young son, who he had been living with, left as part of the break-up. 'I was heartbroken,' he remembers. 'I just didn't know what to do anymore.'

As he mounted many comebacks there was this time not a flicker of green, nor a straight road to be seen. Instead every restart was met by an impediment.

Eventually, McGee moved back to Ireland because he needed friends around him. He had stints in leagues both sides of the border, but, as he drifted further away from the game, he became unrecognisable to the player, indeed to the bubbly young lad, he once was.

'When I quit being a professional footballer something inside of me died,' he says. 'The most immediate effect was that I put on weight and stopped looking after myself. But it ran a lot deeper than that.'

He spent the next few years playing football in the Leinster

Senior League, but it was only when he had to leave the game entirely, at all levels, that he spiralled into full depression.

Football was all he knew. He had been a star player from the age of seven. Now he was out at the other side, stones heavier, disillusioned and disoriented. He was totally in on himself and jobs came and went as he struggled to settle.

It was the tail-end of 2011 when McGee made the call to buy the rope. As it hung in the attic, he knew it was there whenever he wanted to use it. Only a few nights after the visit to Woodies, he was down in a local pub when his feelings got the better of him. He started crying.

With that he bade his friends farewell and went home with the intention of taking his own life.

This, he told himself, was his final day.

* * *

Sport is not supposed to be life or death but Paul McGee's experience shows what can happen when it's taken from you. If your identity, purpose and lust for living is completely tied to a game you grew up with, how will you cope without it?

Everyone manages differently. Tommy Bowe's story couldn't be further removed from the upsetting tale outlined above.

Bowe had his own injury worries to contend with as his splendidly successful rugby career drew to a close and three serious setbacks in a row in the autumn of his career robbed him of nearly two full seasons as a professional rugby player.

But by the time he overcame those injuries, and eventually fought back to fitness in 2018, he was ready to walk away.

On his own terms.

Officially, his final game came on 28 April, 2018 when he featured for five minutes at the tail-end of Ulster's 24-apiece draw with Munster.

The previous weekend, at Ravenhill, however, was when Bowe emotionally signed off, the evening he spiritually offered a final salute to Ulster rugby. He was in his own back yard that night, they were up against Glasgow Warriors, and all around the stadium his family, friends, and supporters had gathered to cheer him home. It was a most enjoyable ending. Ulster got a win and Bowe was handed a hero's reception and guard of honour as he strolled off the pitch, his legacy long since assured.

'Yeah, that was the day,' he smiles. 'If I could have gotten away with it, I wouldn't have played in the Munster game at all the following weekend. I only came on in the last five minutes of that derby anyway, but I was half-raging I had to play at all because everything had gone so well against Glasgow. I still hold Ravenhill as my farewell game.'

For years, the same tried and trusted process had acted as Bowe's pre-match northern star.

Pasta. A 40-minute snooze, shower, and then off to collect his packed gear-bag. A coffee, kiss goodbye to his loved ones and then into the car.

It was a surreal feeling as he ticked the boxes for the last time. He was a little emotional but excited, too, about what lay ahead.

'Coming into the stadium, I was aware I would never follow that schedule again, but I was okay with it,' he insists. 'It turned out to be a lovely goodbye and not everyone is lucky enough to have one,' he says.

'We signed off with a win, those close to me were all around, some lovely pictures were taken and it was special. I was ready to move on then.'

He laughs. 'Until the club said, "No, we need you on the bench for Munster."

'So, I togged out again in Thomond. Got a nice reception from the Munster fans but, as I say, I was more than ready to leave rugby by then.'

His body was simply not up to it anymore. Bowe was 34. He'd enjoyed a brilliant innings, winning 69 caps for Ireland, scoring 30 tries, going on two Lions tours and playing a crucial role for the 2009 Grand Slam winning team, including scoring an iconic try at the Millenium Stadium to help Ireland on their way.

After tearing his cruciate, breaking his ankle, and cracking his sternum in consecutive years, the good had been taken out of it.

'I'd spent so long coming back from injury that it was actually mentally draining,' he recollects. 'When you play for Ulster or Ireland you must always be up for it, and you must train so hard to get to that level. With the injuries, I just felt I was starting from rock bottom with every comeback.'

The loop became a familiar one. Bowe would get injured, fight his way to fitness, prove himself all over again in training, bust a gut to get back on the starting team and then suffer another injury soon after.

'It just sapped the life out of me,' he admits. 'That is why I made the decision to retire at the start of the 2018 season. And do you know what? It actually took all the pressure off. I really enjoyed my last year; played some good stuff and got the best injury-free run I had in ages. The shackles came off; there was no fear of playing knowing that Joe Schmidt or the international management team might be there watching and fretting over making a mistake.

'I went back to playing like I did when I was a kid with the very same love and enjoyment for the game that I had then. If I threw a bad pass or took a wrong line, to hell with it, I didn't really care. I enjoyed every last minute that campaign. That was nice.'

Bowe left sport on his own terms. He also had business interests outside of rugby. It looked like plans to work in TV were coming to fruition too.

He was well prepared for what came next.

* * *

The road to retirement, as the McGee and Bowe insights suggest, can lead you to wildly varying places. Athletes can suffer from loss of identity, depression, uncertainty and worthlessness. There is a struggle to fill days once packed with rigorous training, preparation and adrenalin of performance.

But there are just as many who thrive.

In this book, 16 former Irish sportspeople, including some of the country's biggest and most respected names, tell of their experiences in life after sport and explain how their lives changed on the outside.

Niall Quinn is one of those. He charts his retreat from playing in packed 50,000 stadiums to hiding out in deserted golf ranges as he made his transition.

Former Irish rugby international Marcus Horan tells of the last year of his contract with Munster, how he pushed himself harder than he'd ever done in pre-season to try and gain a new deal, only to lose out as a new head coach arrived with a different plan. Horan had to square off that ending with the many glory days the game had given him.

There have been seamless transitions too.

Kevin Doyle left football due to concussion issues and went straight into breeding horses. He has scarcely ever been happier. Donncha O'Callaghan, too, has settled well into life after rugby and is busy carving out a media career across various platforms.

The themes vary from chapter to chapter, linked by insights from some of Ireland's leading sporting professionals, experts and psychologists, well used to dealing with elite stars and their battles after they stop competing.

Every athlete that gives an insight helped transform Irish sport. For so long they thrilled and entertained us.

Somewhere along the way they realised they couldn't stay chasing a sinking sun. This is the story of what happened when the world stopped watching.

PART ONE

LEAVING THE BEAUTIFUL GAME

1

NIALL QUINN

Mighty Quinn and the Gorgeous Gael

BORN: Dublin, 1966.
474 appearances for Arsenal (67), Manchester City (204)
and Sunderland (203). 92 Irish senior caps.
Retired in 2003 aged 37.

Before Niall Quinn left Dublin to join Arsenal his late father, Billy, called him aside and offered a few words of advice.

'Don't be like Jack Doyle,' Billy cautioned.

Quinn smiles as he casts his mind back. 'Dad would often say that,' he remembers. 'He loved Jack Doyle. But he knew the outcome of his story too. And he didn't want me going down the same road.'

Doyle was Ireland's first A-lister. The Gorgeous Gael. A boxer, singer, actor, playboy and heavy drinker. He was born in 1913 in Cobh, Co Cork and his life was a rollercoaster ride from beginning to end.

'From the outside looking in he had everything,' Quinn reckons. 'Champion fighter, married to a millionaire's daughter, Hollywood actor. He was our first superstar in this country.'

But his story, like that of many prize-fighters, ended in desolation. Doyle died on the streets of London. Homeless and penniless.

The second of five children, he grew up on the third floor of a tenement building on Queen Street in Cobh and hauled coal onto ships to make a living.

'Dad said he was a huge man,' says Quinn. 'Around six foot five. When he went into boxing, he won nearly every fight he had.'

Indeed, out of 28 fights that he had upon joining the army, Doyle won them all, 27 by knockout. This prompted a foray into professional life where he won his first ten pro bouts and fought for the British heavyweight boxing title in 1933 in front of 85,000 in White City and subsequently the world title. That British belt fight ended in disaster. Doyle was disqualified for continually hitting low, lost his £3,000 purse and was banned from boxing for six months.

'Then he took up acting,' Quinn continues. 'His social scene was hectic. It featured the cream of celebrity, but that didn't last long either. Down the line it all took a turn for the worse. He died in London without a shilling. I actually went to see the backstreet he died on. Everything he had and yet it all ended in the gutter, he drank himself to death.

'I tell that story because it made a huge impression on me from the moment I left home and, no matter what happened in my career from then on, it was always in the back of my mind.

'Jack Doyle's story was both tragic and surreal but it was movie magic, a Hollywood epic in its own right. And don't get me wrong – at best I would say my journey is about one tenth of the life he had. I played soccer; he was an international

Hollywood actor and fought for world titles. But I was always enthralled by his tale.

'I tell it now to outline the pitfalls of what can happen sports stars when they leave the game they now. You can go into free-fall. I've seen it myself.'

Four years ago, Quinn set up an initiative called 'Catch a Falling Star' to help ex-footballers cope with retirement. He had his reasons for establishing that campaign.

Many of them were personal.

* * *

In 2018, a UK study conducted by the Professional Players' Federation found that more than half of former professional sportspeople had concerns about their mental or emotional wellbeing after retiring.

In the survey, retired athletes testified to losing their identity when they finish playing sport, experiencing loss, regret and devastation in the aftermath. Survey conclusions suggested that a similar number did not feel in control of their lives within two years of ending their careers.

Quinn would concur with all of that.

'The stats show that almost half of professional footballers face the threat of bankruptcy within five years of their retirement,' he states.

'A third will be divorced less than a year after hanging up their boots.

'Most of these lads are not prepared and, once they go, they have little or no support from the game to which they gave their lives.

'Footballers by nature are addicted when they play. Training, recovery, physio and rubs, yoga, diet and nutrition, they spend every waking hour preparing for the next game.

'That obsession has to be replaced when they move on and that's why so many end up addicted to something else, depressed, or living with debilitating illnesses. Gambling and drinking are two of the top issues. And these days they can punt away on the phone without anyone knowing about it. So, help can be hard to find.'

In 2002, Quinn walked away from the game in hasty fashion and for a long time afterwards he carried resentment with him. He's still not sure if that anger was directed towards the game for how it spat him out, or at himself for getting into soccer in the first place.

He was 36 and had been with Sunderland for six years when his career wound up abruptly. By then he had secured his standing as a Black Cats legend, having represented them 222 times, scoring 71 times, and marking his name down, alongside another Irishman Charlie Hurley who starred decades before him, as one of the best players in their history. Like Hurley, Quinn was worshipped by the Sunderland supporters because he cared about the club.

'In the six years I had there, three were brilliant, two were okay, and one was tough going,' he surmises.

It was in late 2002, just as the new season dawned, when Quinn sensed the sun was setting on his playing days. A persistent back injury had dogged him and, upon stepping away from an international career that saw him capped 92 times and which culminated after the 2002 World Cup, his club manager Peter Reid also informed his striker he would be using him sparingly in the coming season. Reid duly appointed Quinn first team coach and the Dubliner was delighted.

'I thought, "Here we go, this is my future in the game sorted".'

Three months into the new season, however, Reid, was sacked by the chairman, Bob Murray. Quinn was deputised to look after the first team on a temporary basis and told he had a chance of becoming the full-time boss. He ended up on a shortlist of two for the vacant position but was ultimately overlooked.

'Instead Howard Wilkinson came in,' Quinn adds, taking up the story. 'In a short space of time I went from being a contracted player, to being told I was being considered for the job as manager, to then not being wanted at all at the club – neither as a player or coach. I was told I had no future there. They said they would let the dust settle for a while and then move me on.'

But trust had left the building and Quinn didn't care for how he'd been treated. He was out the door pretty much there and then.

'I told them not to worry, that I would make it easier on them and leave immediately,' he recalls. 'I left that evening, a Friday. I went back to my wife, Gillian, and told her what had happened.

'We had no plan whatsoever. We just packed as much of our stuff as we could into a horsebox and by the Monday we were back in Ireland, not knowing what was next or what to do. That was my retirement in a nutshell.'

The coldness of that departure belied the family-like spirit that had been fostered in the Sunderland dressing room under Reid. Everyone gelled, they foraged hard for each other, put in some great displays and twice finished seventh in the Premier League, including the 2000 season, the same year that Quinn's strike partner Kevin Phillips won the UEFA Golden Boot award for being the highest scorer in European top-flight football with 30 goals.

By the time he left the club, though, a lot of Quinn's close friends had moved on and the warm glow around the place had cooled.

'My brother-in-law has a pub in Hartlepool and, before I left for Ireland, I told a few of the lads that I was having a few drinks to mark leaving the club. I didn't expect anyone to show but in the end five lads did. I had a few pints with them and moved on. Just like that. Probably angry at the way it had happened but not fully realising that for a while either.'

He returned home to a roaring Celtic Tiger. The Special Olympics was officially launced at Croke Park, the Ryder Cup was on its way to the K Club, and there was even a heatwave to welcome him back. Quinn wondered why he had ever left Ireland in the first place, it was such a natural habitat for a sports-mad native like him.

Schools were full up, but eventually the Quinns managed to get places in Killashee primary school in Naas for their children, Aisling and Mikey, and later at the Gael Cholaiste just outside the Curragh. 'Aisling picked up the Irish language in about six weeks, so no worries there, but I'm not sure if Mikey has it mastered even yet,' he laughs. 'That was a big thing, though, getting the schools sorted.'

And what about himself and Gillian?

'Well, I had a great six weeks upon coming back,' he recounts.

'Golfing every day, racing – all the things I hadn't been able to do. I wondered why I had ever left home. It was brilliant. Then after a few weeks, reality bit.

'The buzz had gone. There were no more pats on the back, the lights had suddenly gone out, no more capacity crowds shouting your name. I had no purpose whatsoever when I woke up every morning.'

He quickly retreated into a shell. Didn't want to be in company, didn't want to talk to anyone, including his family.

'I felt sorry for myself,' he declares. 'And there is nothing as bad as an ex-sports star feeling sympathy for themselves. I was a complete strain on the people around me, that is what I was like. I knew it was related to leaving my old life behind but yet couldn't exactly pinpoint why I was so down. Was it the game? The club? My esteem?

'I'm still not sure of that. It just grabs you and takes hold,' he says.

He wasn't alone in his struggles. Many footballing families that Quinn and Gillian knew began to have issues.

'A lot of friends around us from my time in football saw their marriages collapse and that was on my mind too,' he states.

'Now, Gillian and I held it together, but I know now I was 90 per cent to blame for what happened in that time. I was lost.

'We got through it, though. It certainly helped that the kids had settled, and that Gillian was near her family, which was important for her too. But it was a mad year for us.'

Opportunities were not in short supply during this period of withdrawal, but Quinn had no interest in seizing any of them.

He was forever invited to functions of all types. The media came calling too but he kept everyone at arm's length.

'Geoff Shreeves from Sky Sports rang up a few times,' Quinn says, 'It was, "Come on, get over to us, we would love to have you".'

'But I wouldn't do it. To be fair to Geoff, he kept at me. One day I relented and said I'd go over and analyse a game for them.'

Leaving his Kildare home to head for a flight to London, Quinn was apprehensive. He didn't really want to be in an airport, never mind on TV in front of millions of viewers.

'I was dreading it,' he said. 'I got to Dublin Airport, went in, turned around and came back home again.

'I told Gillian my flight had been cancelled. The truth was I didn't want to go over there and have to face anyone.'

Those words, from someone as personable as Quinn, are difficult to comprehend.

'I think I was bitter without really knowing it,' he explains. 'In the end I think the game had just chewed me up and I wasn't happy with how things ended.'

Shreeves, ever the tenacious sideline reporter, persisted in his pursuit of the Irishman, however, and weeks later the former striker was again booked for another show.

'This time Gillian drove me to the airport herself and actually watched me board the plane. And I got through it,' he says. 'More than that I actually enjoyed it.'

That was the first turn of Quinn's road back navigated.

* * *

Whenever the issue of future plans surfaced, or when Quinn was in conversation with others, there was nearly always a hackneyed attitude from others. The attitude seemed to be, 'Sure, you'll be grand.' After all he had been a professional footballer for 18 years. The assumption was that his money was made. 'The money thing never bothered me,' Quinn shrugs. 'It still doesn't. When I need to make money, I go off and make it. Having a path forward was way more important. For my mental health and my mind,' he insists.

Openings came and went but it took time to get used to being back out and about following his Sunderland exit.

'I stayed in my comfort zone for quite a while, maybe nine months,' he says.

'During that time, if I wanted to go to out, I would just go to a nearby pub where I knew no one would bother me.

'For all those months – and beyond – I was a golf range rat. That was a place where you could be on your own and be left alone. I spent so much time there that my handicap went from 11 down to three.

'That was a positive, at least,' he smiles wryly. 'But at this stage I was very insular, my self-motivation had disappeared. I was all about the negative view as opposed to the positive person I would have been most of my life.'

Even simple things like an incoming phone call could get him worked up.

'I remember people ringing and thinking aloud, "What the fuck is he ringing me for?" Whereas in the past they might have rung for a chat and I would have been delighted to hear from them.

'That was the place I retreated into. And I was there for a while. Definitely.'

From time to time Jack Doyle popped into Quinn's head.

Little alarm bells would sound as the realisation hit home that no plan had been hatched for life beyond the game.

'Most days you're out on the golf range and it's so quiet,' he says.

'Just a few months earlier you were playing in front of 50,000 people, most of them passionate fans who roared you on. Every week we packed the place out in Sunderland.

'The fans ate, slept and breathed the game. If you fought for the shirt, they adored you. You could pull up to a garage, get petrol and someone would try and pay for it. You'd be pulled aside for photographs walking down the streets. Little pats on the back in the supermarket. Now, I never went out looking for all that, but I won't lie – it did boost you having that sort of fuss made and attention given. It affects you to the extent that when it's gone you wonder what has happened. What it is all about now? Who am I?

'I often saw players tell supporters to eff off when asked for a picture, but my outlook was always, "If you are nice to me, I will make time for you".

'So, I stepped in for an awful lot of photos and autographs over the years. Only a small thing but that all went quite quickly too.

'People kept harping on about having no money worries, but I soon copped that it was what you did mentally to prepare for retirement that counted – not money. And sport doesn't do that, it doesn't help you prepare.

'Maybe deep down I was half haunted by the notion of doing a Jack Doyle. The thoughts of being another ex-sports star on skid row.

'For sure, as I look back on my first year in retirement, I can say categorically that I had a prolonged spell where I didn't care about anything I had ever done in the game. Goals, caps, clubs, they meant nothing to me. Gillian would feel it was longer than a year, by the way,' he smiles.

'I felt worthless. Annoyed too that I'd picked this thing as a career and it had brought me to juncture I was at. I resented having been a footballer. Regretted it. I was muddled.'

He pauses for a moment. 'I know there are people out there going through this now. They should talk about it. It's not just sport, it's the same in lots of industries, whether you are on TV or not, whether you are a public figure or not, we can all hit these low spots.'

* * *

Sky used him increasingly and the gig brought him back to the game and across football stadiums in the UK. From time to time he bumped into former teammates who referred to the decline Sunderland experienced following the Reid era. The club had dropped to 17th position the year Quinn left and were later relegated from the Premier League to the Championship. It didn't look like there would be a revival any time soon. Things had fallen well below the standards previously set there, although what passes for normal service at a constantly confounding football club is open to debate.

As they bounced up and down between the divisions over the next number of seasons, Quinn was often asked by the media for his views and he gave straight answers, prompting Sunderland chairman Murray to ask for a meeting over some of his comments. When they sat down, Murray asked Quinn to help his old club.

The ex-striker agreed and spent the next number of months forming the Drumaville Consortium, including Irish businessmen Charlie Chawke, Louis Fitzgerald, Jack Tierney, Paddy

Kelly, John Hays and Patsy Byrne. They bought Sunderland for €12.65 million in 2006.

'I had never gone to college but over the next few months I learned from the university of life,' Quinn smiles. 'I spent every waking hour working on the project, staying awake till 4 a.m. most nights, working on spreadsheets, learning about corporate governance and getting the funds available.

'I went from my own shell to being thrust back out front and centre, immersed in this project. Suddenly that was my purpose in life and there was scarcely any time for looking back.

'Good men backed me,' he says of the consortium. 'They had worked hard for their money and trusted me to invest a large portion of their earnings. That put a different type of pressure on me, it was their money and I was looking after it, but we did things well and I always knew we were on the right track.'

For the next six years Quinn moved back to live in the city, spending six days a week there, rebuilding the club as the new chairman. As they took over, they cleared the club's €40 million debt and hired Roy Keane as manager. Keane went on to deliver promotion to the Premier League in his first season in charge.

'I essentially spent months learning how to buy a football club,' Quinn laughs. 'I didn't even have the Inter Cert from school, but I adapted, and the Sunderland fans accepted me because they knew I loved the club.

'I was back in the game again. Along the way I had learned about regulation and financing. But bringing people together and working on a project in the game I grew up with, well that was the key. Finding something you are good at and aligning it with an area of interest, that's the trick.

'I start enjoying life again. Everything was going well at home with the kids in their routines and I even stayed involved with the club after the consortium pulled out six years on when Ellis Short took over as the new owner.'

After his stint ended, there was little time to reflect on what was achieved in Tyne and Wear. Not long after he left Sunderland, Sky offered him a contract again and he spent the next couple of seasons flying over and back to the UK twice a week.

There were times when both Quinn and Gillian did mull over the dark patch he had gone through and there lingered a curiosity to drill deeper into his mindset to see what had actually triggered the change in his personality.

'Gillian actually made a decision to go to college and study psychology on the back of that,' Quinn says.

'She got her degree with flying colours and is now studying for a doctorate. She was recently approved for a study into footballers in retirement and why three-quarters of their marriages go within three years of quitting.

'Footballers, their wives or families are simply not warned of what the footballer will go through when he stops playing – and the consequences of what that means for the family are huge.

'Gillian is doing a lot of work in this area and is at the interview stage now, then the task will be coming up with findings, making recommendations and putting some educational literature in place so that footballers might have a reference point to examine before they move on.

'The time for looking ahead to this area is when you are 28 or 29, not 33 or 34. Players are making huge money if they are in the top-flight and that's the time to look at things.

'Very few of us have ever done that. It's like, "Retirement talk is not for now – get on that pitch".

'Ultimately, though, the player will have to face the issue head on somewhere down the line.'

Quinn cites Kevin Moran as a great influence in that regard. A good example of a man who did things well and balanced his life.

'A great lad, great player, educated man, and qualified accountant,' Quinn notes. 'Also, the best craic in the dressing room. Then you'd see him after training going back in to meet either the FAI or sponsors to negotiate on the players' behalf. I always took something from that,' he adds. 'Kevin had it both ways and was someone who I felt mixed both worlds – sport and business – so well.

'Half on purpose, I tried to follow that path myself. In other words, there is another world out there but hang onto your football background too.

'To any lad coming out of the game, I would find something that will make you jump out of bed in the morning. If you find that you stand a great chance of having a happier life with your family.

'Don't drift. Those footballers who drift in and out can do some media work but that might only be two days a week. There is lots of spare time – that's when drinking or gambling can become an issue.'

In 2020, Quinn was appointed as interim deputy chief executive of the FAI following a hellish year for the organisation with disaster striking on the administration, public relations and financial side of its affairs. His appointment came after Government funding had been suspended following the revelation that former Chief Executive John Delaney gave a €100,000 loan to the association in 2017. It was revealed in December 2019 that the FAI faced debts of up to €62 million. At one stage the FAI was at risk of insolvency and asked the Irish

Government for a guarantee of €18 million. For a period state funding of the association was cut off before Quinn came into help. Morale was on the floor when he took charge and jobs were at risk. Quinn and his new team of executives had to work hard to restore financial aid from the Government.

'I asked myself did I really need the hassle and the truth is that I didn't,' he says. 'None of the other directors who stepped in needed the hassle either by the way.

'But I want to help clear things up here, lay down better structures. We have a huge job to do here.

'Outside of football I still want to improve and better myself and that's my obsession,' he admits.

'I want to crack the tech company market; I am quietly involved with three companies and I have been addicted to making sure they work.

'People tell me I am mad to be with the FAI, that I have a lovely life and why would I want to get involved? Things are up in the air at the moment but here's the thing – I'd be addicted to getting it right here too.

'It is messed up as an association, and a lot of bad stuff happened, but as long as the pathway is there for me, I am hooked on getting it right.

'I go to bed around midnight and Gillian would tell me to go asleep, but she'll know full well that at 2 a.m. my eyes will still be wide open, thinking about what needs to be done in work the next day. I feel that if you do stuff like that in life, stuff that energises you, makes you feel alive, you're not going to get into too much bother. It might not be easy, but I jump out of bed to come into this job and that is a long way from where I was in the early days of my retirement.'

2

PAUL McGEE

The Way Back

BORN: Dublin, 1968
172 appearances for Bohemians (54), Colchester (3), Wimbledon (60),
Peterborough (6), Linfield (17), St Patrick's Athletic (13) and
Athlone Town (19). 4 Irish under-21 caps.
Retired from top-level football in 1999 aged 31.

It was the winter of 2011 when Paul McGee decided he had had enough.

He was out one night in the Thirsty Bull pub in Dublin City and he'd started crying. The burden on his shoulders was weighing heavier and that last bit of resolve was dissolving. As the night drew to a close, he looked at the drink in front of him, pushed it aside, said goodbye to those in his company and headed for home.

The night winter air was sharp, but it only focused him all the more. He had a single-mindedness about what needed to happen, what he felt needed to be done. Once inside his house, he shut the door and climbed the stairs.

As detailed earlier, McGee sustained an injury just as his top-flight English football career was taking off. He spent two years out injured just as he had been called up to the

Republic of Ireland squad and never regained his best form again.

Years later when McGee, by then a father of two young boys, Ryan and Evan, looked in the mirror, he saw the reflection of a man he no longer knew. The glow of that cheeky, warm-hearted slip of a youngster was no longer looking back. Where was that 21-year-old rookie, happy once he had a ball at his feet? The kid who scored against Arsenal on his English top-flight debut, who was moving closer to breaking into the Irish team? The youngster about to make a three million pound deal to another Division One club?

He was long gone.

Instead, when McGee looked at his reflection, staring back was a middle-aged man, stones heavier than he had been as a player at his peak.

'Unrecognisable,' he says. 'I felt isolated, dark and lonely. I didn't know who I was anymore. I could see no way out.'

A friend, Dave, was one of the lads drinking with him that night and, luckily for McGee, he saw something in his friend's eyes as he left. A kind of glazed look. An emptiness.

Whatever it was, that friend recognised a blankness and it bothered him.

Worried for McGee's welfare, he followed him back to his home, opened the front door and, after scouring downstairs, he also ran up to the attic.

'I forgot to put the latch on the front door from the inside, so while it was closed, it was still unlocked,' McGee says, taking up the story.

'Dave came up the stairs and saw me on the steps of the ladder about to hang myself. He screamed. He got me down, put me sitting on the floor. He was in shock. I was completely gone too. Just gone. Frozen within myself.'

Dave brought McGee straight to his GP and he was checked into Connolly Hospital where he received immediate attention.

And that's what saved his life – his friend's intervention and the medical care he has received since. It would be a long journey back. But nothing could be as traumatic as the one he had been on.

* * *

'As you may have guessed, football was my whole life,' McGee explains, bringing us back to the start.

'I was born in Ballymun, lived in the flats. My father wasn't around, so to make it easier for mam, I went to live in Finglas with my nanny. So, while I am from Ballymun, I spent most of my youth in Finglas.

'I never gave anyone trouble, I never asked my mam, Pat, for anything bar a ball and pair of football boots,' he continues. 'Nothing else mattered to me. I just wanted to be a professional footballer, I knew I was good enough and I was obsessed with making it.

'There were not many jobs around at the time and the economy here was shot. Ballymun had its problems with drugs but I stayed well away from all that and I was left alone too. Football was the only drug I needed.'

He spent his schoolboy years with Tolka Rovers. On days where there were no games, he would jog from Finglas or Ballymun into town, building up his stamina and leg strength all the time.

In 1986, Tolka took part in a prestigious international schoolboy competition, the Pan-Am tournament, and managed to win it. McGee soared like a shooting star in that series and hit 30 goals in six games, he was voted player of the tournament and marked down as one for the future.

Back on home ground, the left winger-cum-striker averaged 60 goals per season in domestic competitions and contributed just as many assists for the club. From seven to seventeen he was Tolka's top scorer and frequent player of the year. Scouts tracked him closely. On a regular basis they got in touch with Pat to see if he was interested in going to the UK for trials. Each offer seemed more enticing than the last. This was understanable – here was a natural talent who was not only a prolfiic striker but could provide assists too.

Pat, however, wouldn't countenance any enquiry. 'Leave him be, he is too young,' she replied more than once, swatting the scouts away.

McGee stuck around Dublin and stayed in school, completed his Group Cert, Inter Cert and Leaving Cert. Once those were in the bag, his mam said he could look further afield.

His first professional deal was in Ireland with Kilkenny outfit, EMFA. While on the books of the south-east club, he went on a three-week trial to Chelsea, but a deal couldn't be arranged as EMFA were looking for more money than Chelsea were willing to fork out.

'During that trial at Chelsea, I scored in every reserve game I played in and I loved it,' McGee says. 'Did really well. The two clubs couldn't agree terms, but I wasn't overly upset. I knew a move would come.'

He was valued highly by the Kilkenny club and fired them to

the League of Ireland shield in 1987, winning the PFAI Young Player of the Year award two seasons later, before the inevitable cross-channel switch ensued. His form was so steady that other clubs aside from Chelsea were on his trail but, surprisingly, McGee opted for humble surrounds when he made his move.

Colchester, rooted in the lower leagues of English football, happened to make contact at a time when EMFA badly needed funds and timing proved to be everything. EMFA needed a cash boost quickly and Colchester's luck was in – a deal was swiftly agreed. Their manager, former Rangers boss Jock Wallace, still wasn't sure if McGee would fancy the switch and said as much on a few occasions during the transfer process

'We are low in the fourth division,' Wallace reminded the young Dubliner, almost as a warning shot.

'Don't worry, Jock, I won't be around for long,' McGee quipped merrily.

Nor was he. Four weeks and three league appearances later he was out the gap. First division Wimbledon, fresh from their famous FA Cup win, had been keen on McGee too and didn't want to wait any longer. Not long after signing for Colchester for £75,000, he went on his way to join the Crazy Gang for double that, £150,000.

* * *

It turned out that Wimbledon's management team, gaffer Bobby Gould, and coach Dave Barnard, had scouted McGee several times and liked what they saw. Yet, when Gould sat down to discuss exact contract terms and conditions and make an offer, the terms didn't exactly bowl McGee over.

'I don't think that's good enough, Bob,' the youngster said after studying the first contract they gave him. 'Those wages are shite and I'm not coming here for that. I'm on more at Colchester. I'll stay here and wait for someone else to call. I'm not having that.'

He shook Gould's hand and left for Liverpool Street station and the train back to Colchester. Before he reached the entrance gates, Gould reappeared, called him back into his office and offered a more attractive deal.

'They just thought I was a bleedin' thick from Dublin,' McGee laughs. 'But that was all part of football. Bob was dead sound, but he was looking out for the club. I was just looking out for myself.

'I shook his hand on the second offer and said, "You know you are signing a very good player?"'

'Yes, and a very clever young boy,' Gould replied.

After scoring 15 goals in the reserves, McGee was promptly called up to the first team squad with just one game left in the season – an away day at Arsenal who were closing in on the League title.

The night before the game, following training, club captain Vinnie Jones offered to keep an eye on McGee and Gould agreed. Jones brought the young Dubliner back to his house, introduced him to his family and then hauled him down to the local pub, The Vulture, for pints.

As for the final game there was little to lose from Wimbledon's point of view. They were perched in mid-table shelter and posed no danger or threat to anyone including themselves. As he supped pints inside The Vultre, McGee hadn't a care in the world. He was fit as a flea and only a squad member who might, at best, get a few minutes near the end. A few pints wouldn't harm anyone. That was the thinking anyway.

'I had a few drinks, sat back and took it all in,' McGee remembers, smiling at the memory.

After breakfast the next morning they went to collect Don Howe at his home. Howe was also coaching Wimbledon at the time and McGee, who was awestruck when they met, puts him down as the best he's ever worked with.

'Inside his house was a footballing wall of fame all the way up the stairs,' he laughs. 'Signed pictures from Pelé and Maradona. Don took me around the house and said, "Son, you are a nice lad and a good player. A very good player. Work hard and take your chance. But this game all comes down to luck, remember that."

'I took in every word. I knew he was a great man.'

At Highbury, a wide-eyed McGee was further enthralled when legendary TV commentator Brian Moore came over for a chat before kick-off. Moore knew all about him – his stats, his weight, height, style of play, everything.

'I told Brian that me and me mam had many a row over him back in Ireland – with mam wanting to watch *Little House on the Prairie* and me looking to watch *The Big Match* at the same time. He laughed away and joked that if he had a pound for each time that he'd heard that story, he'd be a millionaire.'

In the dressing room, McGee broke away to use the toilet and his manager followed him in, enquiring if he'd enjoyed his few pints with Jones. Then he told the youngster he was starting.

'I was in the middle of having a slash,' McGee says, laughing at the absurdity of the moment, 'and I turned around to him in complete shock and said, "What? You are kidding? You know I am 21 today, Bob! And I'm playing against Arsenal on my

21st birthday?" I started to accidentally dribble wee all over his lovely new shoes,' McGee adds, howling with laughter.

'Fucking hell,' Gould shouted, leaping away from the urinal, 'my new shoes! Get out and get changed, son. Go on! Go out enjoy yourself. Be proud.'

McGee did all of that.

'I went out and had a bleedin' ball,' he smiles.

'I walked out the tunnel with Lee Dixon, Tony Adams, David Rocastle, all great players and within a few minutes they were all trying to kick me,' he laughs again.

Dixon marked him tightly, while Rocastle nearly nabbed him with a welcome-to-the-big-time tackle but having dodged a thousand tangles like it in the Superquinn car park in Ballymun, McGee saw it coming and leaped to safety.

He capped an extraordinary day with a sublime volley from outside of the box to earn them a 2–2 draw. The result had a seismic effect on the league table and set up a dramatic final day duel between Arsenal and Liverpool at Anfield that would go down in history. McGee's goal meant that if Arsenal were to clinch the title over Liverpool they would have to win by at least two goals.

McGee soaked up the atmosphere and then hit the dressing room to make sense of what had just happened. He didn't get long to collect his thoughts. As he sat in the bath, in walked Paddy Daly, the FAI's international referee assessor and someone that McGee knew well from his League of Ireland days.

'I just got out of the bath, towelled off, and told Paddy how great it was to see another Irishman. I gave him a big hug.'

Daly was thrilled for his compatriot.

'You deserve it young man,' he said. 'What a goal you got!

33

This will go down in history, no matter what you do for the rest of your life.'

McGee gets emotional as he shifts through the memories. He reckons having Daly with him at that moment was as good as having his family there. 'Paddy was Irish, he knew me and how I had worked. I had no one around me on my debut day because no one knew I was starting, but Paddy definitely eased that loneliness.'

When the 1990–91 season began, McGee was firmly in Wimbledon's first-team plans. He had adjusted well in a dressing room notorious for its machoism and cruel banter. At that time English football environs were not for the faint-hearted and being an Irishman hardly bought McGee any credit either.

'I didn't get much slagging,' he says of the famous Crazy Gang mentality.

'I got the odd bit for being Irish, especially if there had been a bit of sectarian trouble in the north or around the UK. Sometimes I would get looks when I came into the dressing room or something would be said to me.

'But I always said that while I was Irish, I didn't believe in any of the stuff that was going on. Those involved in sectarianism had their own plans, my target was to be a full-time professional player and the lads on the team knew that. They saw that I worked hard, I could have a bit of craic, and also noticed that I helped the younger lads in the academy with extra bits of training, even though I was only 21 myself.'

McGee scored ten goals during that season across the League, League Cup and FA Cup. Spurs took note and club representatives asked to meet him on two occasions.

'I spoke to Terry Venables a few times, but by then Bob Gould had left Wimbledon and was now Coventry manager. Bob wanted me to follow him and I felt I owed him because he had been a father figure. So, I agreed to go to Coventry.'

It was a big-money offer.

McGee had just signed a three-year agreement at Wimbledon but now security for life beckoned with a £2.5 million deal to move to Coventry. The stakes were massive.

'I remember just putting the head down and trying to stay away from the hype,' McGee recollects. 'By now Joe Kinnear was managing Wimbledon, with Terry Burton beside him, and they called me aside one morning when I arrived for training.

'Looking back now, and they say things happen in threes, I feel I shouldn't have gone training at all that day. Firstly, I was late, a half-hour late because of a bad accident on the motorway – and I'm never late for anything. When I arrived, Terry and Joe called me aside and said, "Listen, Bobby came in for you last night. We need the money on the table and that means we have to sell our best players. The deal is done, son. You go up to Coventry and sort your own financial stuff now."

'I thanked them and went over to join training. The Wimbledon lads stopped and gave me a round of applause and after that we broke into a bit of a match.'

If McGee could go back in time and press pause on any passage of his life, he would return to the Wimbledon training ground on that day, he would stop the footage at the point of applause from his teammates and he woud redirect himself back up the M40 to Coventry.

But that's not possible. There was the chance of a kick around that morning and McGee, like he always did, was going to throw himself into it.

Halfway through the internal squad game a cross came in. McGee rose high but collided with goalkeeper Neil Sullivan.

'I came down in a heap and Neil landed on my ankle,' he says.

'And I was never the same after it. That, to me, was the second part of things happening in threes – getting that injury. I have still never got me head around that day. My ankle ligaments were done, and I was in a bad way. It was a freak thing – a total accident. Neil is a great lad and there wasn't a bit of animosity in it. We are still in contact and good friends. He went onto have a stellar career with Scotland and ended up with Spurs too (playing for his country 28 times and 565 for various clubs.) My career went a different way. But this is football; things happen. My only regret is not having gone straight to Coventry after the lads had confirmed the news. I shouldn't have taken part in that training session. It's just that I loved playing so much I wanted to be professional until the very end.'

As he was brought to hospital, McGee remembered what Don Howe had told him the previous season. 'You can do anything you want son; you just need a bit of luck.'

It seemed like fortune had deserted him just when he needed it most. His ankle bone had come through his skin. The deal was gone.

* * *

He was a year and a half out of game and never the same after it.

It felt like vinegar was poured on his open wounds when, on the day after the training ground incident, when he was lying in a hospital bed, McGee was handed a letter.

36

'It was from Jack Charlton inviting me into the Republic of Ireland squad. They were meeting up to play in a testimonial game. To me, that was the final aspect of three things coming at once. Arriving late for training, not going to Coventry after the transfer was agreed, and then the irony of being called up for your country when you were lying on a hospital bed.'

His mam still has Charlton's letter in one of about 20 different scrapbooks she accumulated over the years. Sadly, that was as close as her son got to full international senior honours, having already worn green at under-18 and under-21 level.

Another quirk is that Ireland had no specialist outside left at the time. Tony Galvin had retired and Kevin Sheedy was nearing the end of his international career. Steve Staunton was better known as a full-back but later played left side of midfeld with Terry Phelan filling in behind him. Damien Duff wouldn't arrive on the scene for another few years and McGee feels he would have got opportunities. 'And I can't say for certain, but I think I would have taken them,' he says. 'I had met every challenge put in front of me up to that point.'

Instead he had nearly two years out in the cold. When the initial injury came around things were still not right. The doctors later diagnosed a condensed nerve – the compression of the plaster on his leg had been too tight. That was only discovered two weeks after his operation because his leg was turning purple, there was no circulation and the leg was becoming numb.

Growing completely frustrated, it was clear McGee's career was hanging in the balance. He spent six months at Lilleshall, the English FA's former centre of excellence, alongside now Celtic manager Neil Lennon, who was recovering from a career-threatening back injury. He kept picking up smaller injuries every time he threatened a return to action.

'Ultimately, I had a weakness, whether it was putting weight on my right foot, my standing leg, or picking up hamstring and back injuries. I got back, played a few Premier League games for Wimbledon up to 1995, before being sent to Peterborough on loan.'

Even though he had a contract, he was only being paid week to week by Wimbledon. 'The Bosman ruling hadn't come in and clubs could do what they wanted at that time,' he explains. 'When I was flying it, they all loved me, when I wasn't at the same level post-injury they didn't really want to know. I was just a commodity. A piece of meat.'

When he came back from Peterborough, he sought out Kinnear, told him things weren't working; that he wanted to go home.

'And that's when I knew something changed in me,' he admits.

'Sure, I would never say that if I was right in myself. Being a professional footballer was all I had worked for since I was six. But now I wanted out.

'I needed me home. I needed to be around people I felt wanted me. The arm around the shoulder was not there anymore and I also realised that I couldn't produce what I once did either. My whole psyche changed.'

He came back, joined Irish League outfit Linfield and played 17 times for them. He did okay but they never saw the best of him. 'I had a little weight on, and I didn't have that drive I once did. Something just triggered in me brain and something was gone from me mentally. I changed. "Ah fuck," I would think. "Do I really want this anymore?"'

'I didn't really. I think the arse fell out of me and it was like something had drained. I lost my spirit. Somewhere in 1994 to 1995 I lost my way in life and it continued until I tried to kill myself all those years later.'

Spells in the League of Ireland with Bohemians, St Patrick's Athletic and Athlone followed, and while he spent three years at Athlone, he then made the call to go back to junior football, back to Tolka Rovers, where it had all started.

There he got some respite from his torment.

'This was my home,' he insists. 'I played as if I was 21 again. I was actually 30 then but I was flying and once more clubs from the League of Ireland started knocking on my door again. But I didn't want that anymore. I was back in the Leinster Senior League and happy again.'

McGee spent the next few years there before dipping into over-35 football with clubs like Fingal United, Fingal Athletic and Griffith Rovers where he racked up more trophies, cups and medals than he knew what to do with. Playing kept him energised, the interaction with his friends kept the demons at bay.

It was only when he stopped completely, when injury and age caught up with, that he was hit hard once more.

'After I finished, I put on three stone. I just hid away from everyone,' he reveals.

'I was drinking, eating shite and doing nothing fitness-wise. My self-worth went through the floor. There was no one I wanted to talk to. I didn't say it to mam even though she is my rock. I was trying to protect everyone bar myself.

'For everyone else, it was more like, "Ah, Paul is just a bit depressed. Better leave him alone."

'I didn't know what it was I felt. "What is this?" I would ask. "Why this?" I had never experienced any sort of darkness before the injury. Now at night, instead of being out playing football, I was drinking bottles of wine, ordering in Chinese food and I couldn't get off the pillow. I had so much time to think that all sorts of thoughts came into my head. I was in a hole.'

It culminated in trying to take his own life.

McGee draws a clear comparison between the night his friend Dave followed him up the stairs and the evening in Highbury when Paddy Daly came in to see him after his scoring debut against Arsenal. They were two very different scenarios, one with McGee at his happiest and the other having him at his most vulnerable, but he looks back on both with a degree of spirituality.

'I was frozen when I saw Dave that night,' he says, visibly upset at the recollection. 'But when I saw Dave, even though I was out of it, even though I was cold, I had a vision of Paddy Daly beside me after that game at Highbury. On both occasions with those lads beside me I felt I was safe again. Lads who knew me. Lads who were there when I needed them.'

It took a few years but through a combination of medication, counselling, better diet and fitness work in the gym, McGee has pulled through. He works for himself as a courier now and loves meeting people through the job, often stopping off at businesses and companies to chat football with people he has met and got to know from working his route.

When he's asked what his legacy might have been, had he gone through with his intentions on that troubling night, he is philosophical.

'I'd hope people would remember me as a footballer who put

smiles on faces,' he says. 'Not as a footballer who had taken his own life. That would be all I'd want really.'

McGee hopes people will learn from his story and urges everyone to look out for friends and family.

'The signs are always there – if you look closely enough.'

For years after his injury, supporters came up to him while they watched the Irish soccer team at championships like USA '94. Many of them said McGee could have been out there with the team.

'But I wasn't,' he states, flatly. 'I know I could have been, but it wasn't meant to be. I just needed a bit of luck and obviously I didn't get it. I reckon anyway that life is mapped out from the day you are born until you die. And it doesn't matter if you have millions in bank or are on the street, it's what you make life to be.'

McGee had a front seat on an incredible rollercoaster ride. He took it all in, highs and lows, dealt with every phase as it came. And he's all the stronger for it.

3

SHANE SUPPLE

The Art of the Comeback

BORN: Dublin, 1987
86 appearances for Ipswich (34), Falkirk (4), Oldham (5)
and Bohemians (43). 1 Irish under-21 cap.
Stepped away from top-level football in 2009 aged 22 and,
following a return to play in the League of Ireland,
ended his career in 2018, aged 31.

The conversation between Roy Keane and Shane Supple was respectful and earnest.

Quietly, Supple had been circling the decision, waiting for this moment. His call to quit professional football in 2009 was made on no whim.

He'd spent seven years at Ipswich Town, almost enduring many of them, though there were highlights for his showreel too – including winning the 2005 FA Youth Cup, making his senior debut at 18, dislodging Welsh number one Lewis Price in the process.

Before his second pair of gloves were fully broken in, Supple was already rated as one of the best goalkeepers outside the Premier League. And yet each step of the exciting journey was made with a nagging internal voice hissing at him; one that he couldn't seem to block out. 'You don't belong here. These are not your type of people.' If this was his conscience speaking, Supple found it hard to supress, or even disagree with it.

Perhaps agreeing fully with Supple's views of the modern game, Keane tried dealing a few hands to see if anything would entice the Dubliner to stick.

But to no avail.

The chat lasted no more than five minutes. Supple put forward his reasons for wanting out and Keane engaged with him.

'Do you want to take a couple of weeks off?' the manager asked.

'Or do you want to see a professional about this?' he enquired.

'You can go home and take a break; see how you feel then.'

Supple smiled politely at the thought of seeing a counsellor, or 'professional' as Keane put it. Not that he didn't appreciate the gesture, but he replied that he was fine, and very comfortable about the decision he was making.

Keane took the youngster at his word.

'Okay, what do you need me to do?' the Corkman probed.

'Just get me out of here as quick as you can,' Supple replied.

If that was the end of the journey, Supple had reached a fork in the road two years previously. In June 2007, as Ipswich put in the hard miles for the season ahead, they took on Blue Square Premier side Stevenage Borough in a pre-season friendly they were expected to win easily, especially as they featured quality players like Alan Lee, Jonny Walters, Jason De Vos and Owen Garvan. Instead, they were beaten 3–0 in a humbling loss.

For the last goal that went past him, Supple dived sharply, low to his left, and made an excellent save which caught the eyes of the watching media and was highlighted in subsequent match reports. But to no avail – an incoming Stevenage player tapped in the rebound. Supple slowly hauled himself off the ground and found a grunting, centre-back running at him, gesticulating as he approached. Shouting angrily and pointing a finger as he blathered in the youngster's face.

'Shaper,' Supple surmises of that particular teammate. 'Doing it for show. I didn't rate this lad either as a player, or a person. He was always gesturing with his hands and blaming others. The same fella would be the first to check his own player ratings in the newspapers the following day. I was sick of him and felt he could have done more to help me in that instance, so I just went for him.'

Went for him?

'Yeah. I wanted to hit him a belt. The rest of the lads came over and separated us, and in the dressing room afterwards I got grief from the gaffer (at the time, Jim Magilton). Deep down I knew I was wrong, but I just said: "Boss, you would have done exactly the same thing."

'The next day the gaffer passed by, privately called me to one side, and quipped that I was dead right – he *would* have done the same thing. What your man did on the pitch was just an example of the posturing that goes on. Across my time at Ipswich, I often felt like speaking up in the dressing room and calling lads out for stuff I saw happening, but I was only a young kid who wasn't established. There is a dressing room hierarchy that you have to live by. It wouldn't have been worth my while to talk. There would have been hell to pay for me speaking up. I guess that day it just boiled over.'

And yet to the outsider Supple was living the dream.

Having broken through to the first team at 18, he was

pronounced by the Irish media as Shay Given's likely long-term successor in the national team and he found himself singled out for mention by a plethora of opposing managers who came up against him. No matter who looked in, the tag slapped on Supple was the same – 'one of the best young talents out there.'

The first team environment, however, was not one that held any appeal for him.

He lamented the bunch of decent, hard-working kids he had left behind in the youths and reserves. Not all of his senior teammates irked him, mind, but there were enough to create a culture he couldn't align to.

As he presses rewind on those formative years, he picks another memory from the vaults and, though it is from years back, there is no fuzziness in its outline. The 2004 English Football League Championship play-offs. Ipswich are just a hop and a skip away from the Premier League with Joe Royle this time in charge.

'We had narrowly missed out on automatic promotion,' Supple says. 'We lost to Watford in January and things were so tight for the rest of the season that we actually struggled to make the points difference up after that defeat. Instead, Wigan and Reading went up to the top-flight, we came third in the table and had to be content with West Ham in the play-off semi-finals to see could we go further.

'Some lads were worried,' he recounts. 'But not about the big game coming up – more with how they would have to give up three weeks of their holidays in order to get through the play-off series and get promoted.

'Other lads fretted that, if we did go up, they wouldn't be kept on by the club as they might be deemed not good enough for the Premier League.

'Jesus, I can understand that bit of anxiety about the future, but for fuck sake let's do our best for the club while we were in that position,' he says.

'I saw then that most people there tended to look out for only themselves. Coaches too – they were as bad. They'd tell you one thing and then go behind your back and say another. You couldn't take anything much at face value. It's an absolutely ruthless environment.'

After that failed promotion bid, Magilton took over from Joe Royle, lasting three years before Keane arrived. Once at the helm Keane did a quick stock take and decided to offload as much as he could, almost in flash sale fashion. Thirteen players were out of contract and he offered just three of them new deals. Supple, still only 22, was one of those retained. He took the contract initially but almost in the same breath started making arrangements to sell his house in the locality and began getting his affairs in order.

He wanted out.

'As soon as I did sell up, I was gone,' he says. 'I know I took the contract, but that was only until I got my personal affairs in order. I didn't want to leave the club hanging either. I was straight about it.'

Keane was as good as his word. Supple thinks he was a little taken aback at the decision, but he followed through and a contract to signal the player's departure from the club was drafted.

'And that was it,' Supple shrugs. 'I signed an agreement with the club that I wouldn't sign for another team within the next two years – or if I did, an amount of compensation would have to be paid.

'Roy came through for me. I didn't hear from him again for nine years. That's football.'

* * *

Three years into his spell at the club, Supple's dad, Brendan, had travelled over for a game and they went to dinner afterwards.

'During the meal I remember pleading with him to get me out of there, to get me back home to sign up for the guards,' Supple remembers.

Brendan had given a lifetime's service to An Garda Síochána and would have been proud if his son followed in his steps, but he always supported his sports career too, and he wanted Shane to stay at Ipswich. Or at the very least, move to a different club. That night they agreed to put any move on hold for a while.

But the pendulum swung quickly. The following week Supple was drafted into the first team and went on to clock up 38 appearances for Ipswich in the Championship over the following three seasons. During spells out of the starting 11, loan moves to Falkirk and Oldham Athletic were arranged but they did nothing to rekindle Supple's appetite for the game he once loved.

He just found that, while he was at different clubs, it was the same ethos and not one he could abide by. On 13 August, 2009, Supple played his last professional game in the UK – a Carling Cup tie against Shrewsbury. He did well, saved a penalty, helped Ipswich to a shoot-out win.

After that he was into Keane's office and out the gap.

The English media, especially, struggled to comprehend the call. One *Daily Mirror* journalist questioned how Supple could walk away from what they figured would be potentially €230,312 worth of wages alone on his existing contract. They speculated what walking away from the game might result in over a ten-year career that would most likely have blossomed.

That never worried the strong-minded Castleknock man, however.

'I can tell you now there was no chance I was going to sit around and stay for the money,' Supple insists. 'Anyone who would think that doesn't know me.'

There was no real plan when he made the move back to Dublin, but at his age there didn't need to be either.

One door that opened led right back into the warmth and embrace of his old GAA club. When he came home in 2009, he had no interest in playing soccer again but instead sought out his old Gaelic football mates.

'I won't say I went down to the GAA club straight off the flight from England,' he quips, 'but it was pretty soon afterwards.'

Gaelic football was his first sporting love. Rooted between Blanchardstown and Castleknock, St Brigid's has seen a huge influx in numbers over recent years with the population increase in Dublin 15, though success hasn't always been a near neighbour.

Supple grew up in Roselawn and palled around with players like Mark Cahill, whose brother, Barry, would later win All-Ireland glory with Dublin.

He sussed out the club environment and learned from insiders that they were down on morale and success. He needed something away from sport too. Bills had to be paid. At that stage it had transpired that the Irish economy, despite the hype, had all the substance of a reality TV show. After a few years of Celtic Tiger excess, the country was dragged to its knees at an alarming speed.

Supple had long since identified service with the guards as a future way of life, but a recruitment freeze in An Garda Síochána dashed any long-term employment hopes. It would be four years before he could apply.

'Instead, Gerry McEntee, the former Meath player who was very involved with St Brigid's, arranged for me to work in the Mater Hospital, initially as a care attendant in the wards and then as a physio's assistant for two and a half years which was very enjoyable. I didn't see it as long-term but every day you were trying to make a difference to the patients and help them get better.

'I came across some characters in there. You would get chatting to them about all sorts and one lad, who hurled with Kilkenny in the 1930s and 40s, still stands out to me as being a great character. Eventually, after a while some of them figured out my background, not that you would ever be harping on about it or anything.'

He threw himself into Gaelic football while sorting work matters out. He met the Cahill brothers one evening in the 12th Lock Hotel in Blanchardstown to get a deeper insight into what he was facing with Brigid's. The club had been locked in a relegation battle earlier in the year and upon his first championship game back in the red and white against St Jude's, they suffered defeat.

Soon after there was an ill-tempered game with St Vincent's where five players were sent off. Supple himself got booked for a tackle on Dublin forward Mossy Quinn and following that game he remembers wondering; 'This is a shit show, what have I gotten myself into?'

They trudged through until the tail end of the year when the gloom lifted a little with the news that the popular Mark Byrne was stepping up as manager of the second team alongside McEntee. They would take the Brigid's seniors for 2010.

'The impact was immediate,' Supple says. 'We won promotion from the second division, won all of our championship games, and got to the final against Kilmacud Crokes.

'The spirit Mark and Gerry brought into club was just incredible. Suddenly, fellas were just fighting for each other. We had good lads at the helm previously, but we just needed a structure. A lot of it was that you just don't say no to Gerry McEntee. He would do anything for you and in return he got it all back in spades.'

He was appointed team captain in January 2011 and took the mantle with huge pride. From 4 January to 18 December the Brigid's team beat all before them until they fell to Westmeath's Garrycastle in the Leinster final at Tullamore. The hurt of that day still pierces like a spear.

He had found a second family within that dressing room. Brigid's had only won two Dublin senior football titles in 80 years but not long after coming home from Ipswich, Supple had led them to a third. A considerable achievement. There were no shapers or posers in that set-up, Supple could look them all in the eye and be confident that they were united. In a way this later helped rekindle his passion for soccer; a lust that had been lost in England.

'We had players in that dressing room that would look out for you, they would have run through a wall for you, and when you get that spirit anything is possible,' he reasons.

'No one really backed us on the way to the county final and

when we got there to play Oliver Plunkett's it was all about the Brogan brothers, Alan and Bernard, who were stars of the game at inter-county level, never mind club level. So much so that Gerry had our dressing room plastered in newspaper articles and cuttings – every article centred on the Brogans. If we needed any extra incentive, we got it from seeing those clippings on the wall.'

He remained at the coalface for the next six years, and, down the line, when he was asked to return to play soccer, it was only on the proviso that he could continue to play Gaelic football.

In 2013, the management team stepped away and the following year saw a raft of retirements. The club's underage production line had ceased to move with proficiency, and whilst Ballymun, Kilmacud Crokes and Plunkett's came to the fore, Brigid's regressed.

Supple was busy helping underage teams but his own form was so impressive that, in 2010, he received a call from Dublin football manager Pat Gilroy to come in and train.

'I always felt Pat was a little wary of me because of walking away from soccer and the stuff around that. Maybe he felt I might be an issue in the dressing room, but nonetheless he called me in. After a while we played Cork in a challenge game in Portlaoise. Stephen Cluxton and Michael Savage were the two other keepers and I didn't get much game time. I played one O'Byrne Cup game afterwards but that was all I got.'

He rang Gilroy and said he just wanted to play, that there wasn't much point in him being there getting no action and made the decision to stay with his club.

'I didn't have a go or anything over not getting a run with

Dublin,' he says. 'I wanted to play, but I knew I would be sitting behind Stephen in any case.

'And when he kicked that famous free to win the 2011 All-Ireland against Kerry he went into a different stratosphere.

'Jim Gavin took over in 2013, so I went back into the set-up. I got a few league games, and but I was never going to dislodge Stephen.'

Supple ended the year with an All-Ireland medal but saw no game time, as Cluxton's grip on the number one shirt only tightened. 'I could just see how he went about his business every night at training, how involved he was and how big he was within the set-up. He was so important that unless he got injured, I felt I would never really dislodge him.'

The pair trained hard together and Supple says he picked up a lot off the Parnells star, while Cluxton pressed him on more technical aspects of goalkeeping.

'I got on really well with Stephen. As much as I could anyway when I was looking for his jersey,' he says.

'I found him a very nice guy, fiercely determined and driven. He looked after himself really well, though we had a couple of nights out too. There was mutual respect there, I think. Hopefully, I went in and raised his game a little bit and maybe we both picked up stuff from each other and benefited that way.'

Supple expands by saying that goalkeeping in Gaelic is completely different to soccer.

'Stephen is a quarterback – a good shot stopper too, but in terms of the goalkeeping coaching I got when I was younger all the way up, I would be more technically minded.

'I learned loads from him as well. But after we won the All-Ireland, I didn't have much ambition to go back in 2014 and be a sub again. I rang Jim and said I would leave it go. Thank God I didn't hang around too long. I'd still be waiting for a game.'

* * *

Before he knew it six years had passed without kicking a soccer ball in anger.

As time ebbed away, however, he noticed a shift in his mindset, a mellowing of his scepticism of the game.

'Initially after leaving Ipswich I felt I'd fallen out of love with football but maybe as the years passed, I discovered that I actually still held a flame for it, and I loved the technicalities of being a goalkeeper. It was some of the people involved, I guess, who had left me disheartened,' he explains.

The cross-channel culture, as he remembered it, was primarily about self-preservation, both for players and the coaching staff. Back home, the ethos was very much centred around a love of grassroots and community.

Along with business partner, Darren Kelly, Supple co-founded the Irish Pro Keeper (IPK) Academy, which offered specialised coaching and they ran their sessions at Crumlin United. In return for use of the grounds they coached the club's keepers.

Crumlin were a non-league intermediate club and regular first choice keeper David Meehan had opted to take a break in 2015, leaving manager, Martin Loughran, in something of a quandary. So good was Meehan in goal that several other keepers had turned down the chance to join Crumlin because they knew they'd never get a game.

During the odd session, Supple had been known to hop into

goals and Loughran felt it was worth chasing him up to see if he'd put in a shift for them.

Loughran was told 'no chance' on several occasions but, desperate to replace Meehan, he managed to get Supple to sign an 'option to play' form.

In Ireland, contracts are sometimes only as binding as people need them to be. Equally, there are times where if you lend your name to anything you could spend years trying to get out of it. Supple initially agreed to line out for one match and his presence caused an immediate stir in the Leinster Senior League. It raised standards in Crumlin too, to such an extent that Loughran recalls having to ask his new number one to let in a few goals during training so as 'not to destroy the strikers' confidence levels.

Predictably, Supple spent the rest of the season with Crumlin, losing the league on the last day, but winning the 2016 FAI Intermediate Cup final, thrashing Letterkenny Rovers 5–0 in the Aviva Stadium.

Before the kick-off he looked into the stands and saw his St Brigid's teammates there to support. They had brought the club flag with them with the message 'Our spirit will never be broken' proudly over the hoardings. It meant a huge amount to him.

Inevitably, Supple's soccer retirement was now firmly set in the direction of a U-turn, inescapably veering down a road back to playing full-time. Following just one season at intermediate level, one of Irish soccer's traditional teams, Bohemians, came calling.

After weighing up his options Supple agreed to join the Phibsboro crew – only on the basis that he could keep playing Gaelic football with St Brigid's.

It was an exceptionally busy time. He looked at enrolling in

Dublin Business School and later took a degree in Human Resources Management there. He also started with Legacy Consulting, an agency co-founded by Dublin football legend, Bernard Brogan.

Supple took to the club instantly, first signing as a semi-pro. That deal only lasted a year – a demanding League of Ireland schedule meant he went full-time when offered a new contract in late 2016. It was a perfect fit for both parties.

Supple gained that 'community' feel he always craved. As part of the Bohemian Foundation, an independent non-profit organisation intent on improving the health and wellbeing of its North Dublin community, he and teammate Oscar Brennan began branching out, working with locals.

Part of the programme involved visiting Mountjoy Prison every week to coach the inmates. Actor and stand-up John Colleary ran a comedy club there too and from time to time special guests would be invited in.

The two footballers trained the inmates for months, leading up to the Conway Cup final, a game between inmates, played in the prison yard.

'All the prison governors were there to watch, it was a brilliant day,' Supple recalls.

'I was wary that some of the lads would try to burst each other as the game was played on the yard itself, but there was none of that. They were very disciplined and actually called fouls on themselves. It was fascinating to watch.

'That evening we had a reception where the comedian Tommy Tiernan came in and did a version of his RTÉ show (where he interviews guests with no advance notice of them being on his couch). He held those chats in the prison chapel. I was first up, he didn't know me or my background at all, but he got some great stuff out of me. He loved talking about Roy Keane and hearing all about him.

'After I finished one of the prisoners went up and told Tommy his life story. You could hear a pin drop when Tommy asked him about his background, how he ended up where he did, what he had learned from prison, and the education program that he was now on. The silence was unreal.

'I could see many lads in Mountjoy who wanted to turn things around, but there were others, who had done some serious stuff, and maybe they weren't helping themselves either. Some guys would near the end of their sentence and would be caught with a mobile phone in their possession on the day before they were due to get out. That was frustrating to see. At the time I did a life coaching course as well and I was allowed to go into Mountjoy and do some course work there too, pro bono. It was massive for me to be involved in a program like that and to see how it has since developed.'

On the field Bohs had also demonstrated a huge level of respect to Supple by making him their highest paid player and still allowing him to play Gaelic football. In turn, Supple was happy to sign a waiver to forego his wages if he received an injury playing GAA. 'I threw myself into the club. When you are paid well, you have to back it up and I wanted the players' respect. I got it because I drove standards along with the others.'

* * *

He gradually let his GAA career go, devoted two full seasons to Bohs and played some of the best football of his life, before his body gradually started to break down.

His second and final retirement took much more out of him than his first ever did. Anyone who read Supple's emotional love letter to Bohemians in late 2018 will have been struck by the warmth of his words. It is hard to reconcile that well-worded and heartfelt farewell with the departure of a detached, disenchanted youngster from Ipswich Town a decade earlier.

'A couple of things on that,' he notes. 'Firstly, I had matured more as a bloke and, secondly, I really enjoyed the dressing rooms in Bohs. It was a GAA club for all intents and purposes. I mean that in the sense that, at St Brigid's, I had two managers, Gerry McEntee and Mark Byrne, who created an unbreakable bond.

'And I got that feeling when I went to Bohs too.

'Keith Long was the reason for that. He was some manager. A brilliant man. He actually gave a shit about people. He actually cared about you.

'He looked after us as people and, in the process, he developed as a manager himself. He brought in Trevor Croly as coach and assistant manager and it was the best thing he could have done for the club. People felt Keith was taking a risk bringing him in because Trevor is so talented that he could have been lined up for the managerial job himself. But the way they worked was incredible.

'They trusted the experienced players to run the dressing room for them and, unlike the way it was cross-channel, no one got away with anything. Lads who didn't put it in were pulled up on everything. Derek Pender, Ian Morris and myself were his men in there and it was important for me to get an environment like that. We definitely created something special.'

It was in the summer of 2018, with May winding to a cheerful end, when Supple received that call up for the Republic of Ireland senior squad. He had just been named on the PFAI Team of the Year but while he had forged his own path back to competitive sport, his body was starting to ache by then. Throughout 2018, now 31, when he kicked the ball, his hips burned. Club captain Pender noticed that Supple's kickouts didn't carry the same distance and asked if he was okay. He told the skipper of his concerns, but few others knew. Instead he played it down and worked even harder with the club physio to get some freedom and respite.

Anyway, in keeping with Supple's phlegmatic approach, when he first got wind of his Irish senior call up, he wasn't even sure if he would accept the invitation. Instead he wondered if it was merely a token gesture towards the League of Ireland.

'Eventually, I said I couldn't turn it down because I would be seen as an arsehole by all and sundry if I did,' he insists.

'After weighing it up, I went in. I had two games to play with Bohs in between the two Irish games, so I was in and out of camp. I hung around with guys that I had played under-21 with, Seamus Coleman, Shane Long. Both good lads.

'When I was at Ipswich Town, Jonny Walters had lived with me for a few months and he is just the best I've ever come across over. A decent bloke and a great friend. I would fully trust Jonny, there's not many other footballers I could say that about, and it was great to see him again and catch up.

'Likewise, Seamus is always actually genuinely interested in you and what you are doing. Most of time footballers want to tell you what they are doing. Whereas Seamus was asking about my GAA career and he was telling me about the modern-day dressing room and the environment cross-channel. What he was telling me justified my decision to walk away from that all that, if it needed justifying.'

Supple was not called upon for either fixture, France or the USA, and missed out on a full international cap to go with his Under 21 honours, but he remains unfazed about it.

Upon his return to domestic duties he recounted his experiences in the media and recalled how his eyebrows were raised when he saw the Irish kitman go around to players rooms and pick up dirty laundry that they had placed outside.

In an interview with the *Sunday Times* he highlighted how the England team had developed a new identity under manager Gareth Southgate where self-regulation had been introduced. Supple reckoned a parallel approach would greatly help the Irish camp.

'Something similar enough to the mobile phones at the dinner table and bringing your laundry down to the laundry room. Bits and pieces like that,' he said.

His words didn't go down well with Martin O'Neill when they were put to the Irish manager.

'Martin kind of responded with a "Shane Who?" type of quip,' the Dubliner adds. 'I didn't think I had said all that much wrong, and maybe with the way the Irish results subsequently went I may have been proved right.'

When the dust had settled, he looked back on his senior international call-up almost as an underwhelming experience. That unshakeable sense of being a token domestic league player, not picking up a cap, some coaches wondering why he wouldn't go back to the UK again, the players having their laundry collected. It reminded him of a life he had long since left.

If that was the dream as a pro footballer, he was happy to stare at the ceiling each night and let his mind wander elsewhere.

* * *

In the end injury ensured the time had finally come to look beyond sport.

He doesn't miss the acute pain that playing brought and he was in such trouble with his hips that he was barely training anyway so there is complete ease with the second decision to step aside just months after his international call-up.

'Ah scans don't lie,' he states matter-of-factly. 'The implications of playing on would have been too serious, and it was far too early for me to be looking at a hip replacement.

'Had it been seven years earlier, I would actually have done all I could to stay playing, or turn to coaching, but, beyond playing, Irish football is not big enough as an industry to let many athletes sustain a career within the organisation. You would be better off coaching in the GAA really because it is more lucrative with expenses that are offered.

'I knew it was time to try something new again. This time when I retired, though, I was more experienced, more mature. But I did have a period of reflection.

'Could I have achieved more? Possibly. Could I have played Premier League? Possibly. Would I have carved out a career for myself at Championship level at the very least? I think I definitely would have.

'Now, I was still uncertain about what lay ahead, where I would fit into the real world, but I just knew I would cope. This time around I had things behind me, a few qualifications.'

These days he works with a recruitment company in Dublin and is learning his trade there as he bids to climb the ladder of the organisation.

'I am taking it all in,' he smiles. 'It can be bad for the ego at times because I left school at 15 for football, didn't go to college when everyone else did and, therefore, I miss out on certain things. Business is tough but I am learning and the one thing I have is communication skills. I have resilience too. I learned both of those from sport.

'My family, my girlfriend, they are all there to help. My network through sport has already helped in business.

'I will find my way on the road ahead. I would have a lot to offer sporting organisations and feel I could make a big difference with the new plans that will be implemented at the FAI, for instance.'

Supple wants to focus primarily on building a stable career in business before he looks any further.

'Ah I do, I have to prioritise that.

'I probably don't sit down and reflect on what has happened in the past, but I guess not many have taken path I've taken.'

Understatement of the year. He did things his way. Stayed true to himself.

4

KEVIN DOYLE

From Pitch to Paddock

BORN: Wexford, 1983
490 appearances for St Patrick's Athletic (10), Cork City (76),
Reading (157), Wolves (164), QPR (9), Crystal Palace (3)
and Colorado Rapids (71). 64 Irish senior caps.
Stepped away from top-level football in 2017, aged 34.

Early in his career, Kevin Doyle decided he needed to do more than other players if he wanted to get to the top.

Bread roll? Scoop the dough out first and that was before he gave it up altogether. Extra training? Every single day. Always staying back or getting in early.

Summer holidays were cut short. He would come home to Wexford and run the sand dunes in Curracloe Beach to return to pre-season training sharper than everyone else.

At the peak of his powers Doyle was so lean that his body fat went down to 7.5 per cent but with that came constant and chronic sore throats, flus and feeling rundown.

'The body's way of telling me I'd probably gone too far,' he muses.

He loved it, though, and misses the intense drive to get on the field. The Christmas games especially. He relished the frost, festive atmosphere and fierce rivalries. The colder the day and surroundings, the warmer Doyle felt inside.

It took time to foster that affection, however. When he first docked in Berkshire, outside London, that inital holiday season away from Wexford was the loneliest he ever put down. If it's not of your choosing, Christmas can be a challenging time, especially if you are separated from the harmony of life back home. That was how it was for Doyle in 2005.

On Christmas morning, Doyle trained before taking a break for a few hours and that evening heading on a bus to the north east of England to prepare for a game with Wolves the next day, which they lost 2–0. He would have spent the afternoon by himself until fate, or faith in this instance, intervened and Rev Fr Michael Hore, a Wexford native and the local parish priest in Reading, invited him and teammate Stephen Hunt to dinner with him.

'That was such a nice gesture and it made me forget about being alone on a day like that,' Doyle says. 'We became good friends with Fr Hore after that and he ended up marrying Jenny and I years later. It was so thoughtful offering to look after us on Christmas Day because, while I was never homesick, that occasion was the most depressed I ever was. I knew all my family were in Wexford together, and spending that day alone wouldn't have been ideal.'

Tough days like that were worth it, though. After all he was a professional footballer, earning good money, playing for a classy Championship club, Reading, and they had a cultured and caring manager in Steve Coppell at the helm.

Having battled so hard to climb the ranks of football, from Wexford junior level to sign for Reading, he wasn't going to let his big opportunity pass. Instead he maintained a relentless work ethic and went onto play Premier League for six seasons and represent the Republic of Ireland senior side on 62 occasions.

One of the great things about Doyle is that he never lost the run of himself while his career soared. He stayed grounded, kept coming home, held onto interests outside of football and that, he reckons, helped hugely when he emptied his dressing room locker for the last time, following months of headaches and increased concerns about concussion and its symptoms in 2017.

* * *

In late September of that year, Doyle was in his second season with Colorado Rapids in America's Major League Soccer.

After training one day he mentioned to Jenny that he was suffering with headaches, especially after heading the ball. It had been going on a while, for the guts of maybe six months.

He was almost coercing himself through sessions and games. He was getting by, but it was becoming harder to hide. At the end of regular training, he would dodge heading practice by light-heartedly explaining that he was 34 and his legs needed rest. Joking aside, though, the truth was he couldn't head a ball anymore without a reaction. Jenny urged him to go to a neurologist and tell all.

'Initially the plan was to get through to the end of that season and consider our future,' Doyle says. 'I was in talks with the club over another contract and we would probably would have gone with it.

'But when I went in to see the neurologist and did the tests, all that changed. I explained how I'd been having headaches for the last six months to a year, and he wasn't impressed that I hadn't mentioned that in a previous meeting we had.'

The consultant did a series of further tests and advised that if Doyle could manage to play without heading the ball, he would be fine. He could continue for one more year. But if he was going to keep heading the ball, he should not play anymore.

For a man who had made a living from backing into grizzled, hardened defenders, soaring into the clouds, and thundering headers into nets, this was not good news. The notion of not being able to meet a ball head-on was as likely as a surgeon being able to operate with one hand behind their back.

Typical sportsman, though, all Doyle took from the consultation were the words 'could be fine' and 'play'.

'It was only when I went home that I said, "Jenny, I think the professor just told me to retire," that it sunk in a little,' he says. 'But Jenny was brilliant. She told me to get out of the game there and then.

'I remember her exact words, "Kevin, if you have to retire, we are fine with that. You have done great."'

They had three children by then so it was important to flesh out any decision that would impact on their long-term future.

'I actually rung the neurologist back as I had been in there with him on my own and there was no one from the club with me,' he remembers.

When Doyle got the professor on the phone, he said, "Just to be sure, did you actually say I should retire?"

'"I would if I were you," came the reply.'

Reality hit home then. The life he had known for so long, that demanding, breath-taking, rewarding and downright vexing sport he loved, was gone from him.

The next day he went into the club, reported the diagnosis to his manager and executives, and they did what many clubs do – agreed that he should seek a second opinion with another neurologist.

But the verdict was no different when Doyle attended a different specialist, although the latest consultant offered a slight chink of light, however, by advising that he might be able to play again provided he took one year out. But if he couldn't do that, then he should retire.

At 34, Doyle couldn't countenance any time away from the game. His body needed constant oiling for him to power at the highest level of the MLS. To stop for any length of time would only result in a gradual, grinding rigidity in his game.

There was no room left for manoeuvre.

He contacted his manager, club officials, and told a few family members. He distinctly remembers ringing his dad, Paddy.

'What are you waiting for?' Paddy demanded to know.

It was a good question. Despite life as he knew it coming to an abrupt end, Doyle didn't exactly feel the weight of the world pressed on his shoulders either. He wondered why that was. Surely, he should be more down about things?

That night at home he undertook a self-audit. First there had been the graft with St Patrick's Athletic and then Cork City to actually get noticed. He wasn't long on the radar before Reading came calling and that was like a marriage made in heaven for all parties. Wolves nabbed him at a time when he was being courted by Spurs, Aston Villa and Everton. Across it all he'd enjoyed 16 years as a footballer in Ireland, England and the US.

He was Ireland's Young Player of the Year in 2006 and Senior Player of the Year in 2009. There were 63 senior international caps, 14 goals and a Euro 2012 campaign to look back upon.

Memories in the vault, money in the bank. Future financially secured. What was there to be sad about?

'If I was 27, I would have taken that second bit of advice, tried to take a break, take a year away and see how I was,' he admits, 'but I was seven years older. I'd done a lot in the game and I was happy. Simple enough really.'

There was no dallying in Denver.

Once his contract had terminated, so too had his visa. The Doyles had to be out of the country by 31st December. Within a couple of days of releasing his retirement statement, they were back in Wexford, their furniture and belongings transported back to the house they had built some years previously, and just three days after landing, their kids were enrolled in the local primary school.

'We just threw ourselves back into it,' he says. 'And how bad? That was the plan anyway, we had a house built and always saw ourselves settling here. I always wanted to get stuck into the farm and working with horses. It just happened a bit earlier than we anticipated.'

* * *

The sporting obituary section threw him, though. Before he could move on, he had to take all the tributes that came his way. Bowled over by the response to his announcement, he felt awkward with so many people talking about him in the past tense.

'It was like being alive for your own funeral, that's probably the best way I could describe it,' he laughs.

'That's something I found a bit mad,' he admits. 'It was nice, but strange too. You'd scroll down on your phone to find some lovely message from a former teammate and it was nearly like you had died. I found that very weird. I was embarrassed to be honest.'

Aside from sorting out the logistics of moving home, various media outlets called too, looking for him to shine a light on his retirement from successive head injuries, a taboo area in so many sports.

Concussion is a live, burning issue, but not everyone wants to talk about it. In Ireland, a 2018 study conducted by researchers from UCD found that more than 15 per cent of players in the top two divisions of the League of Ireland suffered from concussion during the 2014 season. The paper found that rates were higher among defenders, and that 40 per cent of those who suffered a trauma were not stopped from training or playing in a competitive match.

In the past, players who suffered from concussion attempted to hide it, or had it brushed over when they did report it. Further studies have tried to put a stop to that dinosaur-age approach and now we have a glimpse into the long-term health implications that head injuries can lead to.

International research has found that concussion accounts for a quarter of all injuries among elite footballers. There have been high profile examples and three of England's World Cup-winning team of 1966 – Martin Peters, Nobby Stiles and Ray Wilson – all later suffered from dementia.

Data also shows that 22 per cent of Premier League goals come from headers, and while the dynamics of the game means it is very unlikely that heading will ever be outlawed in the sport, there are calls from some quarters to implement that ruling.

'Heading was a key part of my game, one of the things I was best at,' Doyle elaborates. 'I didn't have absolute blistering pace, and there were better footballers out there than me, but I was determined. I had a great engine and could keep going, pulling defenders apart and running at them with a more continuous high speed rather than an all-out sprint. But heading was my game and it was what I was known for.

'By backing into defenders and competing in the air, I picked up belts and bangs in nearly every game I played in. I remember being knocked out on the pitch one afternoon at Reading. I was out cold but got up after a few minutes and played on. Went training the next day, probably heading the ball over and over again with a bruised brain. But concussion wasn't a thing then. We didn't know about it then like we do now.'

It took years for any of Doyle's head injuries to be officially recorded as concussion. Going into the 2018 pre-season, however, he was fairly sure he had endured a number of concussions over the past decade. In one friendly game he collided with a goalkeeper, harmless in the scheme of the batterings he had previously endured, but he was concussed all the same.

'I shouldn't have been for a small bang like that,' he said. 'The club doctor had to send me to a neurologist, and I was given two weeks off.'

With each concussion sustained, his recovery time was longer. He returned to play the first game of the 2018 season but couldn't head a ball without feeling unwell. When he finally told the medical staff the full story, they pulled him out of the squad straight away.

'I suppose as I look back on it my tolerance levels for shipping a blow, or heading, were getting lower and lower. But by the end any little knock was leaving me concussed and it was taking a lengthier amount of time to get over it.'

He touches wood when asked if headaches have persisted.

'No, thank God,' he says. 'I've been good. The first three to four months in retirement were basically spent still getting over the last concussion, not the pre-season one. The neurologist told me that this was more than likely down to a concussion I had sustained against LA Galaxy during the previous season when I was knocked out with the last kick of ball trying to close Ashley Cole down. The more concussions you had, the longer they lasted.

'This is how I look on it. Without my heading ability, I wouldn't have had half the career I did. But there are bigger things out there outside of sport and now the only headache I get is if I have a few pints of Guinness. And thank God they go away.'

He is glad too that he and Jenny tried something different. They loved Denver.

The move came about in 2015 with his Wolves contract at an end. He went on to score 16 goals in 71 games at Rapids whilst continuing to be available for Ireland.

The club's general manager is Irishman, Padraig Smith, and after some persuasion he got Doyle to fly out on a two-day recce and eventually sold the club to him.

Ahead of the 2017 season, the MLS's annual release of players' wage details put Doyle down as the 26th highest paid footballer in the MLS with a 'guaranteed compensation' of $1,045,000 (€960,000). He was happy there from the start.

'I am lucky in that the moves I made in my career worked but this one was really a shot in the dark because we knew no one out there. We could easily have stayed in the UK. Jenny was pregnant with our second child and we knew lots of people and I knew the English game inside out by then.

'When the club said they would fly me over, that I could bring my brother or someone with me, I felt I should give them the respect to at least go and have a look.'

Doyle jokes that he got the 'nice' tour. The club is owned by Stan Kroenke of Kroenke Sports & Entertainment, the holding company of Arsenal FC, and they have all sorts of delights to share around the Denver area. They are the owners of the Denver Nuggets of the NBA and Colorado Avalanche of the NHL and also own NFL franchise the Los Angeles Rams.

'I just came back and told Jenny how lovely it was. It was countryside in the city, and we agreed to give it a shot.

'I could have stayed in England, but would it have been with a top club? I kind of felt I had done everything I could do in England. I needed a test – not just in football but something to get me out of life's comfort zone. And if someone was willing to pay me to go to the US, why not?'

They never looked back. They took a house near the mountains and enjoyed snowy rambles in the winter and peaceful walks in the summertime. They made great friends and found the country to be nothing like what they imagined.

In 2019, two years after he left the club, a group of 60 Americans came to Wexford where two close Denver friends chose to celebrate their big day.

'They'd already come to visit us in Ireland and loved Wexford so much that they had their wedding here in the Talbot Hotel in

2019. We had four mad days with them. We made great friends completely away from football and going to Colorado opened up a whole new branch of our life. We made some friends for life and we've been back there twice since which shows what we think of it.'

* * *

The good thing about coming home to Killurin was there was no glare of an interrogation lamp upon their return. Having served their pre-school and Montessori education in Denver, Jenny and Kevin's two eldest kids, Benneth and Arriane, went straight to the local primary school once home and from then onwards he was just like any other father. Drops and collections, school plays. The odd run-out as a coach.

'As moving home and retiring go, I think I had it as good as you possibly can have it. It was just fine.'

The first real adjustment he noticed was a sudden aversion to exercise, a mood that would have been alien to him for the previous 20 years. Though he had planned the design of his house to feature a gym and swimming pool, Doyle had no inclination to build up a sweat.

'What did take my interest instead was a few pints of Guinness in a bar called Declan's just a five-minute walk away,' he laughs. 'That's my local and I head down there one evening a week, have a few pints, let the world go by.

'I had always been super-fit, but then again it was my job to be. I didn't have to do that work now so the first year was a beautiful release.

'Now it didn't last. Two years on and I'm back three nights a week, just doing a few five-, six-kilometre runs, doing core work in the gym, some press ups and that to keep in shape. But it's nothing taxing.

'I like going out for an early run now. It clears the head and it's great for the mind but it's just as nice to pop down to Declan's once a week. I feel at ease there, they all know me, so it's no bother.'

The burning cauldron of elite sport can be overwhelming, and one issue Doyle did have to deal with was something that cropped up again and again in conversations post-retirement. His identity.

'What's the plan?'

'It was the first thing people would ask. They would be very direct. Some randomer you didn't know would come up and say, "Well, what do you do with yourself now?"'

'I wouldn't ask them what they did, so that annoyed me.

'The truth is that I've always had other stuff going on. While I was a footballer, I was always investing in property and horses. When I was with Cork City, only my second club, I bought an apartment down there. I never made a big deal of the horses because people were only interested in talking football to me, but horses have always been a big thing. And they are even bigger now.'

Horse breeding in the Doyle family is something of a ritual. Both his father and grandfather were involved before him.

'Luckily, when I came home, I had that to keep me busy. Slowly, people who stop and chat to me are more interested in horses than soccer. That's fantastic.'

Just before Christmas 2019 he made his first marquee investment, buying a half-brother to winning machine Altior for

€155,000. Altior was unbeaten in his previous 19 races, and his sire is dual Derby winner Camelot, which bodes well for his prospects. Doyle is hoping that the investment will pay off.

'Well, it's a hobby and a passion but it's a business too,' he insists.

It more than fills his days and will continue to for a long time to come. 'You could spend 12 hours a day on the farm looking after them if you wanted. I'd be up at 7 a.m. feeding them, back again at 10 a.m., walking the horses after the kids had been dropped off at school. But how great is that? If I still lived in the UK or the US, I'd be sitting down having breakfast with nothing to do for the rest of the day and that would worry me. Whereas back here, my dad helps, and we take it in turns to look after each other's horses.

'I have five mares at the moment, but I will probably cut that back to three or four because this business is all about quality not quantity and it can all go out of hand quickly. The quality can go down.

'Each of them has a personality as well. You get very attached to them. We brought one for sale lately and Jenny was in tears bringing the horse into the stall. I can understand that but I'm a horse breeder, not a horse collector,' he laughs. 'Ah, I suppose the great thing as a breeder is that we can track them and see what they are at later in their careers. The first I bred went to England and won five times and it gave great satisfaction for me to be able to keep an eye on that. There are lots of negatives to the business, they need constant feeding, they have to be wormed and during pregnancy they have to be constantly monitored. We are due to have 12 mares foaling next year and five of them are mine. During this time vets would be coming and going every day for the bones of three months, from February to the end of June. We have to have cameras on them and alarms monitoring them. But my dad did it and his dad did it.'

When Doyle was younger, the family had a truck haulage business which ran for 20 years across Spain and Italy.

'My oldest brother was due to take that over from dad then, but he passed away and once he did, Dad totally lost interest in it. He sold the business and went back to horses and farming.'

When Bernard died at the age of 21 it left the family with huge sadness. With the haulage business gone, they bought a pub and Kevin worked there as a kid. It was character-forming as much as anything else. He was quiet, but, in the bar, he learned to look out for himself.

'First job, a fiver a day stacking shelves,' he says. 'By the time I was 14, for one summer at least, I was closing up on my own.

'Stocking shelves, doing the bottle bins, cleaning glasses and then serving. You'd have these lads in, and they wouldn't give you an inch. Give them their drink and they'd reply, "Are you going to give me a flake with that pint?"

'And the fact that I was a stickler for time didn't make me any more popular in there. Once it came to midnight that was it – last orders. They'd look for another drink, I'd refuse. "Put us onto your boss," they'd insist.

'"I am the boss."

'"You're not. Ring Paddy."

'"I won't ring him."'

And the good thing was even if they did ring Paddy, he would ignore them, because once he left Kevin in charge, he fully trusted him to call things as he saw fit. It toughened him.

Luckily, though, for the night-thirsty locals, he wasn't there for too long.

'I was a terrible barman,' he laughs. 'My personality was not there at that stage, but I was just a kid who wanted to be out with his friends, anywhere than having to spend the summer evenings and nights in a bar.

'But that summer job meant that when I did get into a senior dressing room, I was able for any stick and hardship that I got. The guff I got closing up prepared me for that.'

Doyle always had that steel. He came to prominence in Wexford football circles and was first spotted by local football enthusiast and future TD, Mick Wallace. At 15, upon seeing him play, Wallace remarked that he would walk a hundred miles to watch the youngster play again. Later, Wallace signed Doyle for junior teams he managed before a move was made to St Patrick's Athletic in Dublin and later Cork City. On both occasions Doyle was signed by Pat Dolan.

Both Wallace and Dolan cast a protective arm around the youngster's shoulder as he made his way in the game, signing for Reading for £78,000 in 2005 before moving to Wolves for £6.5 million just four seasons later. Across 12 seasons and five clubs in the UK and US, Doyle made 437 professional appearances, scoring 109 goals.

During his time at Cork City he acquired tunnel vision. While the rest of his friends enjoyed the Cork nightlife, he ended up locking them out of his apartment so he could sleep properly. He doesn't know if he was dedicated or boring, but he locked the bedroom door at night to keep the carnage outside.

In any case, City boss Dolan kept a close eye on his players too and Doyle recalled how there were numerous nights when there'd be a knock on the door at 12.30 a.m. and Pat would come in and check on him.

'He was very good for me,' Doyle says of his old manager and advisor. 'You'd be scared shitless down in Cork because he knew everything. He knew every bouncer so that kept me on the straight and narrow. There were lads more skilful than me, but I had perseverance.'

* * *

And life now?

'I'm peaceful,' he says.

'I play five-a-side once a week in the winter with a bunch of GAA lads who want to keep fit and we rent a pitch at North End FC for an hour and that's enough for me. I play with my son out on the lawn at home and that's great too.

'I think I played soccer for so long that I don't have the bug for it anymore although when I go working with RTÉ as an analyst, I get a buzz from that.'

One of his first experiences as an analyst was working with Eamon Dunphy, the outspoken pundit and journalist whose on-screen bullishness set headlines for decades.

'I like him,' Doyle said. 'But he never had a real cut at me either when I was a player so that helps,' he laughs. 'Some of the stuff he said over the years was outlandish but more of it also made sense. Working with him was a great experience and now, if I am not with RTÉ, I go to Ireland matches with my wife. We might go to dinner first so it would be more of a social occasion.

'Yeah, the odd time I miss the adrenalin buzz, I miss winning,

I miss being a good player on the pitch but I don't miss the endless video meetings, or losing on a Saturday and having the next week dominated by fear and being told we were useless.

'Nor do I miss being told what to wear and when, or being fined for being late, being treated like a schoolboy. Don't get me wrong, some lads I played with needed that discipline, but it annoyed me.'

At various junctures of his journey he could have veered off to purer footballing teams where precision passes were routinely played into the feet of strikers. Arsenal, Aston Villa, Spurs, Everton and even Fulham the year they reached the Europa Cup final, were all after him. There is a slight tinge of regret in not closing out at least one of those deals, but Doyle says that it would have meant forsaking principles.

Each time Doyle told Reading that if they wanted to sell him, grand, but, if not, that was grand too. He was in no rush. Reading never wanted him to go. They appreciated the role he had played for them in securing promotion to the Premier League with 56 goals in 153 games over four seasons.

'I never got too upset that the big, big move didn't come,' he reflects. 'Looking back, if I had a bit more experience maybe I would have pushed harder for those moves like others did. They put up a lot of money and Reading would have made a massive profit by selling me but Reading always looked after me, contract-wise, and I never once felt short-changed by them. It wasn't my style to push hard. They were loyal to me.'

As for the footballers themselves, they are ships passing in the night, he reckons. He has retained a couple of friends from every club he was with, from Liam Kearney in Cork to a few guys from the Colorado Rapids. Months could go by without him ringing any of them but if he picked up the phone to Shane Long or Stephen Hunt in the morning, they'd just pick up from where they last left off.

While he is not necessarily in touch with former teammates on a regular basis Doyle doesn't agree with the stereotype of being greedy, precious divas that has been bestowed on modern day footballers.

'I would say that 99 per cent of lads are sound,' he reckons. 'It's like everywhere, you will have a few dickheads in a dressing room, but they will be in offices and factories too. You will have had teams where things could have gone better but the whole image that is portrayed is off. People see a guy do something mad on or off a pitch and say what a clown, but that is just one per cent of the pool.

'This tag of "you're a thick footballer" is way off. They get a bad press. I saw a story of a rugby player pissing in a bar during the year – imagine if that was a soccer player? There would be uproar. The perception is out there but from my experience 95 per cent of staff and players are dead on.

'They are paid a lot of money, but they're cooped up for 11 months of the year and go crazy in their time off. Take Wayne Rooney. He has been a millionaire since he was 16 and a multi-millionaire for most of his life. What would you do in his shoes? When he hit the bigtime the normal person his age was probably in college doing crazy stuff without anyone knowing it.'

With a wife and three young kids, Doyle says not one day has dragged since he retired.

There was speculation that he would stand for the 2020 General Election and that he was being lined up to contest the seat vacated by Mick Wallace, who left Dail Eireann for the European Parliament. But Doyle has no interest in that walk of life.

He has already dabbled in coaching, firstly with the Wexford under-20 Gaelic footballers and, currently, with the Republic of Ireland under-17s where his motive is ostensibly to help develop young strikers coming through the ranks.

'I'd just tell any young Irish guy to hang around at home a bit, play League of Ireland and, if they are good enough, they will get a move over anyway,' he says. 'Parents ring me saying little Johnny is getting trials with Man City and asking what they should do,' he says. 'It's a waste of time. Little Johnny will be sent back home in a few years, broken and not knowing where to go next. Let them stay here, let them finish school, most of the League of Ireland clubs play proper football now, the coaches have the UEFA B licence and while the facilities are not brilliant, they don't need to be. You don't need a gym; you just need yourself to be a proper person. Get out and run, do core work, get all the coaching you can.

'Soccer can be great. Without it I couldn't have the horses or my house in Ireland. Without it I'd have nothing. But lots of people work really hard and don't get the rewards. I just think I got a bit of luck and when it arrived, I was ready for it.'

5

CUT FROM THE HERD

When it comes to understanding the needs of elite sportspeople, Gary Keegan stands out from the crowd.

Keegan is principally known for his ground-breaking term as high-performance manager with the Irish Amateur Boxing Association (IABA) and his overhaul of the sport in this country.

Under Keegan and head coach Billy Walsh, the boxing team almost doubled its tally of Olympic medals, winning three at Beijing 2008 and four more at London 2012. Multiple successes were also recorded at European and World Championships.

Aside from that, Keegan helped Leinster rugby in their clinching of both the Champions Cup and the PRO14 titles, and sailor Annalise Murphy, who claimed a silver medal at the Rio Olympics.

He played a subtle but significant part in the Dublin footballers' historic five All-Ireland titles in a row and, in 2019, he also worked with the victorious Tipperary hurlers. With that double, Keegan became the first person to play a role in two successful All-Ireland backroom teams in the same season.

Few know how to challenge and facilitate Ireland's elite sportspeople better than him.

'The environment that athletes who operate at the highest level inhabit is a very special one,' he testifies. 'People are very driven by the achievements of the group. That becomes their environment and learning to contain that energy can be a very intense thing. It is a heavily structured, process-driven setting, and all mistakes are public within that space. People see and observe everything, and it is a constant challenge for the athlete to find a better self.

'It is only afterwards, I think, that athletes truly recognise that the sacrifice made by their families, partners, children and friends was just as big,' he suggests. 'Those people lost a son, brother, husband, friend along the way because the athlete had committed to this particular world. People rarely think about any of this until they step away. That's one issue right there.'

Another is how athletes themselves cope when they leave that intense bubble. Keegan believes few of them want to entertain the notion of retiring while they are still competing.

'So, when they are cut from the herd, of course they are going to find it difficult to adjust. Why wouldn't they?

'People suffer so much in retirement because they have moved beyond the last stage of their playing careers without having stopped to consider what comes next. Within a sporting organisation, retirement is almost a taboo subject. Then you are cut loose and feel much less valuable than you once were; that's where the pain is.

'It's got to stop,' he warns. 'From the moment an athlete goes into a sporting environment, elite or amateur, they need to realise that they are simply moving and transitioning through three phases. Retirement needs to be just another juncture.'

The first two stages Keegan refers to are development and leadership. The last phase is more complex.

'At the finish they should be looking ahead but instead they invest almost everything into getting back into the middle phase,' he says. 'One last push to get back to where they once were, digging deeper to find an inch, working harder than ever to see if they can remain part of the scene. Very few are looking ahead. They are too busy trying to restore what they once had.

'But we all move on in life,' he counters. 'If you don't keep looking ahead, you effectively hand over control to a manager or an organisation at the end.'

Red flags have been identified for those struggling with retirement including withdrawing from friends, family, and activities, excessive time spent on social media and the internet, alcohol and drug use and over-eating, or binging on junk food.

Maybe these patterns emerge because the athletes are finally off a leash. Or have no structure anymore.

'That purpose they hold in sport, that rhythm they move to, that self-discipline they hold themselves to account to, those extremes are not typically demanded and required in the real world,' Keegan explains.

'The real world is a bit messier. A lot of issues can suddenly manifest themselves when the athlete is on the outside. And many sportspeople don't know how to transition.'

Former Galway hurler Tony Óg Regan is now one of the country's leading sports psychologists and concedes that, initially, he didn't know how to handle life on the outside either.

He was culled twice from the county senior hurling squad. The first time at the end of 2008 when he received a letter in the post from the county chairman, telling him he was gone.

'There was no discussion regarding what I needed to improve on. Nothing,' he recalls. 'I was 24 and had devoted the previous eight years to competing for All-Irelands with Galway. Suddenly then it was, "Thanks and goodbye."'

An abrupt end.

Off the field life had changed too. After leaving NUI Galway with an honours commerce degree and a post-grad in Economic Science, Regan had entered the world of chartered accountancy and was in the process of completing professional exams and qualifying fully.

'I tried to give up a hundred times,' he reveals.

'I found the professional exams ten times harder than college exams.

'Looking back, I was probably spending around 40 hours a week training and preparing, I was giving 31 hours a week to working full-time and trying to find time to prepare for professional exams outside of that.'

But there were no concessions made for his academic commitments.

'No wonder my form with Galway dipped,' he says, shrugging his shoulders. 'Sure, I was fucking exhausted with life. Ger Loughnane was our manager and we over-trained under him, in my opinion. He had us doing hard running for months, trying to break half the panel but only two of us dropped out.'

Three times a week Regan would leave work in Connemara at 4 p.m. to make Ennis for a running session at 7 p.m., have the legs ran off him, before returning home at midnight, totally burnt out.

'I lost a stone and a half. And I had exams on top of that,' he recalls.

'Ger and the others in his management set-up never asked how we were. They never saw the bigger picture. They were decent fellas, but not approachable. I didn't ever feel that any of the backroom cared how I was going off the field. It was more like, "Why are you underperforming? Are you mentally weak?"

'I felt like replying, "No, I'm fucking exhausted because all I'm doing is training, running, working and studying."'

Something had to give. His temporary contract as a trainee accountant ran its course and, having failed two exams, he wasn't offered a new one. Around the same time that he was culled as a county hurler he was made unemployed too.

He had no work. And no inter-county career anymore.

'Unemployment assistance was all I had,' he says. '€190 every Wednesday – that was it.'

Three years previously, in the lead up to the 2005 All-Ireland final, the cream of the banking sector and chartered accountancy practices were trying to seduce him with appealing offers of work.

'But in 2008 no one was ringing me,' he declares.

His self-esteem and confidence took serious hits. Each Wednesday, he went to the local post office to collect his dole, peaked cap on, head trained downwards for fear someone would stop him.

'Going in afraid who might see you,' he adds. 'Shoving your social welfare card on the desk and getting out as quickly as possible. Sometimes even the person behind the counter, their body language, would tell a lot. They would shoot you a "why are you not working?" look.

'And you wonder are you contributing to society at all? Do you place a value on yourself?

'There you are collecting money and you haven't done anything all week to justify it. But there's more,' he adds. 'You also fret, "Will I get work again? Will I ever earn at a high level? Will I ever pass my bloody exams?"'

While self-doubt gnawed away, Regan's resilience didn't allow the situation to fester for long either. He started to control only what he could.

He picked up part-time work around home, just to get an extra few bob and feel worthwhile. Gardening, painting, whatever. At night, Regan was back at the books, getting ready for the next exams. In the gym, he was upping the ante too, lifting more than he ever had. Mobilising his body again. Strengthening. Watching his nutrition.

'I leaned on people close to me, hurling coaches, sports psychologists and I worked relentlessly for eight months after being dropped,' he remembers.

Regan was recalled the next season and started all of Galway's league and championship matches, ended the season with a nomination for his first All Star and was appointed vice-captain of the team. He passed all his exams too.

Five years down the road, however, the axe fell on him again.

At just 29, only a year after playing in the 2012 All-Ireland finals and being nominated for another All Star, he was released from the squad for a second and final time.

Anthony Cunningham was manager by then and he rang with the news. While Regan disagreed with the call, he just didn't have the appetite to live like a monk anymore, nor train like an ironman to get back in. That was what had been required the first time he was dropped.

Two years on Cunningham guided Galway to the 2015

All-Ireland final against Kilkenny and at that stage Regan was working as a sports psychologist with the county minors. The youngsters won their All-Ireland title and a delighted Regan took his place with the squad in the lower Hogan Stand, settling down to watch the senior showpiece.

At half-time the Galway seniors sprinted like cougars to their dressing room, storming past where Regan was sitting, the crowd erupting with tribal ferocity to greet them as they raced into the tunnel to reset. It seemed like his old team was poised to end a near three-decade famine and put Kilkenny away.

That's when a cloud descended and perched right above.

'I suddenly felt I had to get out of there,' he explains. 'In less than an hour's time there was a chance the Liam MacCarthy Cup would be presented 50 yards away from where I was sitting, and I didn't know if I would be able to handle that without losing it.'

Regan thought he had dealt well with being left aside but had clearly misjudged how he really felt.

'When I sat back and thought further about it, I realised that I hadn't attended a Galway senior game in two years before that final. I didn't go to Blackrock (a popular swimming spot on the Salthill promenade) anymore for fear of meeting my former teammates and not knowing what to say.

'I was afraid to go into certain coffee shops around town in case I'd meet the lads. I missed it very badly, still felt I could be in there helping them. But the truth is I didn't know if I would break down if I met them.'

At the interval of that 2015 decider he came pretty close to doing just that.

He skimmed his surroundings for an escape, attempted to flee the stadium and head down the M9 to Waterford where he was studying, but two of the minor selectors began chatting to him and, as he tried to shuffle past, they stayed chatting and deflected his attention. Before he knew it, the Galway team was back on the field again, well ahead of their Kilkenny counterparts.

'I had to stay then. When Kilkenny eventually came out, they turned the screw and we weren't able to respond or adjust.

'Afterwards I was so upset with the thoughts in my head. I wasn't ready to contemplate my old teammates winning and not being part of it and that experience was like a death inside my soul. My spirit sank. A 30-second pitch of darkness. There were 82,000 people packed inside that stadium, and I have never felt so alone, so sad and isolated.

'This voice inside my head saying, "I hope they lose this; I can't bear this."

'I knew that was totally wrong. I was so embarrassed for thinking like that and I realised it was my shit to deal with.'

Regan has since gained serious perspective from that period mourning the player he used to be. He understood never to load all his eggs in the one basket again.

He also realised that life outside of sport was actually more important than what he achieved on a pitch. And appreciating that accountancy, his first chosen profession, was never going to sustain his lust for a career to be passionate about, he made a professional change too.

After undertaking a sports psychology introductory course, he qualified with a Masters in Applied Sports and Exercise Psychology from WIT, and now his days are spent helping individuals and teams in sports, schools and business.

As a professional he wants to see managers and organisations show more humanity before they release players into the afterlife.

'I don't say this lightly, but the grief of being dropped is akin to having a loved one leave you. That grief you feel at having your whole world taken away is traumatic.'

His message?

'Don't let someone dictate your own future. Don't lie down if you feel there's more in the tank. Get on the road you feel is the right one and stay the course. Stay focused. Keep the goals in mind every day. Shit does happen but you can still change things,' he says.

When Kevin Doyle, Niall Quinn and Shane Supple finished as professional footballers they at least had opportunities to stay in the game through coaching, media work or administration. As Regan states, many sportspeople don't have that luxury – instead they can be completely cut from the herd.

In rugby, a concerted effort has been made to get players to switch onto the notion of planning for their future from a long way out. A 2019 Players Association report in England revealed that 95 per cent of retired players need a second career, with salaries nowhere near what professional footballers, for instance, earn.

That survey also showed that 52 per cent of respondents didn't feel in control of their lives two years after they retire, 62 per cent experienced some sort of mental health issue and nearly 50 per cent had financial difficulty in the first five years.

Four former Irish rugby internationals now take us on their journey from rucks and red zones into retirement. They each played for their country, enjoyed highly successful careers, but how did they fare beyond the tunnel?

PART TWO

RUGBY'S RENEWABLE ENERGY

6

MARCUS HORAN

Front Row Seat for Final Whistle

BORN: Clare, 1977.
224 appearances for Munster and 67 Irish senior caps.
Stepped away from top-level rugby in 2013, aged 35,
following a Grand Slam and 2 Heineken Cup wins.

'Well, what are you doing with yourself now?'

Before it frightened Marcus Horan, that question downright annoyed him. Like Kevin Doyle, Horan found the inquisition invasive.

'People almost demanded an answer off you,' he says, scratching his head. 'If you were caught on the hop the first few times you might mention that you were coaching Garryowen or off trying to find the next batch of Munster rugby props, but they'd nearly raise an eyebrow in front of you. It would be like, "Yeah, but what are you really doing?"'

When his own days with Munster rugby ended, there was not a trace of bitterness to be found, but Horan was laid bare all the same.

Identity is a big thing in sport and in the parochial, passionate hotbed of Munster rugby it is simply everything. There is an earthy, man of the land, feel to those born in the province who are lucky enough to wear red. The DNA of the club pulses through their veins and, even for those brought in from the outside, it's not long before they, too, have their deepest emotions stirred by the family-like culture there. Munster days may not be as rewarding nor heady as they once were, but in a game now dominated by sugar daddies, the club always seeks players of Horan's ilk; the embodiment of the stand up and fight spirit.

It begs the question, though, what happens when they move on and leave that unique identity behind? For some, there is a real fear they will lose their way in the world.

'First up is uncertainty over who they are,' Horan says. 'Supporters mean well when they enquire how retirement is going, but the hardest thing for players is how they almost have to justify themselves.

'I know of at least two fellas, recently retired, who have dropped out of social scenes simply because they didn't have an answer to that question, "What are you doing now?"'

He adds: 'In their own minds these guys want to be able to say, "I am Marcus Horan and I am a player development manager" or "I am X and I'm an accountant" or whatever.

'But not everyone earns the status they want straight away. Even guys who quickly find jobs are not sure if the role will be long-term. So, they don't respond to that question with any great certainty. They don't own it; they don't feel confident with the reply.'

Horan is now in the business of helping players to plan ahead. In his professional role working for Rugby Players Ireland as Munster player development manager, he is intent on highlighting the challenges that come with retirement.

For him, they all came earlier than he expected.

He was nowhere near ready.

* * *

Heading into 2013, Horan was looking forward to a ripe season in red and had no clue that there were only barren months ahead.

Having been wrapped tightly in the embrace of Munster since 1999, developing quickly to make the Irish team, life tended to look after itself. Once Horan and his teammates fronted up on the training paddock, in the gym, and learned from video analysis, they were largely left to get on with it. The various teams he played on were close-knit but ruthless, with no room for weakness. It was an environment where calling out another player was deemed beneficial, not damaging.

As the start of the 2013 season loomed, he was nearing his 35th birthday and knew a career conclusion wasn't far off. Still, the body was holding firm, he felt as mobile as ever, and his form was steady. He intended going for another two seasons if he could manage it.

New coach Rod Penney had other ideas, however.

News of Penney's appointment as head coach of Munster rugby first emerged in May 2012 and at that stage Horan had one year left on his contract. With his deal winding towards an end, the prop took his summer holidays – but in name only. In that period, he trained incessantly to be at peak for the new campaign. Power runs, stamina programmes, stretching and conditioning; Horan was super-fit coming back.

'I just worked my ass off,' he states, 'I knew Kilcoyne (David) and others were coming up behind me, so I slogged harder than I ever did.'

Age was against him, however. There was a new boss in town. And Kilcoyne's reputation was growing by the year. There were a lot of variables to consider before a contract extension could be secured.

'Rod actually arrived when we had most of the pre-season training done,' Horan says. 'He didn't get to see the fruits of the work I had put in and that was a pity.

'We went to France for some games and I didn't get a start in any of them. Your man didn't even look at me,' he says, referring to his new coach. 'He was talking to senior players alright – but not me.

'The gas thing about Rod was you might bump into him and he would say, "We must meet for a coffee." I could meet him now, years later, and he would repeat it again. We never did meet for the coffee,' Horan smiles.

'I spent most of those warm-up games coming off the bench, getting ten minutes at the end. By Christmas, I knew it was over at Munster.

'And that was fucking frightening.'

Rugby was his life.

There was no degree. He had a diploma from Limerick IT, but that was it. The irony was that he had been forever championing the Irish Rugby Union Players Association (or IRUPA as it was previously known), serving as the Munster rep for seven years before taking the role of chairman for three, and pushing guys to look after their welfare outside of rugby, to put steps in place for retirement.

'But I never did anything for myself,' he counters.

When it was clear no new contract would be put on the table, he wondered what the future held. His roots had been firmly cemented in a club he had represented 224 times, becoming their most capped forward at one time and winning two Heineken Cups in 2006 and 2008. His progress there led to playing 67 times for Ireland and being part of the famous Grand Slam winning team in 2009.

Reaching such highs again would be impossible.

'It scared the shit out of me,' he admits. 'My wife, Kate, wondered if I wanted to go abroad to stay playing but, for the position I play in and for the size of me, I was never going to go to, say, France, and be the kind of prop that the game there demands.

'I could have gone somewhere else and prolonged my career for another while, but that wasn't right for me or the family. I knew for definite I was done – I just didn't know what lay ahead.'

There was no immediate pressure to make a call either. That summer the British and Irish Lions toured Australia and Horan was invited to line out with the Lions Legends team, alongside his great friend and mentor, the late Anthony Foley. They played two tests against a veteran Australian side and that jolly shoved reality back down the road a bit.

'Kept the dream going on a while longer,' he laughs. 'I was playing rugby again, back in hotels, dressing rooms, with load of lads around you – it was fucking great. But then came this nagging awareness that there would be no pay cheque coming in over the summer. That was a new one for me.

'At that stage we had the three kids at home so I knew there would be no more perks or luxuries from rugby when I got home. I had to act quickly.'

* * *

Initially, he spent the early days of retirement packing the kids off to school, filling time in between, then collecting them in the afternoon.

'It was hard to keep the head straight at that particular time,' he admits. 'The walls would close in on you pretty quickly if you let them.

'The realisation had really rammed home that we had responsibilties and, that with the help of God, full lives ahead of us.

'Don't get me wrong, I was very active as a parent anyway, but I was still able to train, prepare, travel and play matches without distraction. And the rugby bubble was all-consuming,' he continues.

'Even when I got married, the whole week still revolved around Saturday. When the kids came along, if they were keeping us up at night, I went to the spare room because I needed my sleep to be right for the game and I wouldn't apologise for that either.'

Once the roar of the crowd died down, however, and the epic battles in a packed Thomond arena slipped further to the back of the mind, Horan fretted about looking after those who mattered most – Kate and the kids.

'The responsibilities flooded in on top of me,' he reflects.

'Again, it's not like I neglected them before, but the family had to be provided for all the way down the line and, playing rugby, you don't think much about these things because everything is taken care of.'

In comparison to professional football, rugby players do not have anything like the salaries or luxuries available and, when they retire, most concentrate on finding careers and work prospects outside of sport.

Horan took an opportunity that arose early in his retirement; working for an insurance firm. It effectively involved going to his contacts, asking if they wanted to link in for certain products and policies. One day, he found himself scrolling through his phonebook, looking to see who he could ring to discuss insurance policies, before putting it down despairingly. Whatever life held in store for him after rugby, this wouldn't be it.

He was grateful for the chance to start a new career, but after some months he handed in his notice.

'All the time I was cursing myself, "Why didn't I think about retirement while I was still playing?"' he reveals.

Especially since a pathway to further education had been signposted by former coach, Declan Kidney. Horan wonders if he should have tread further down that trail.

He recalls: 'Deccy arranged for a group of us at Munster to take a business and sports management course. Every week we would sit munching our lunch under the old stand in Thomond, myself, Anthony Foley, Mossie Lawlor and Martin Cahill. All the other lads would have gone home. We'd be there with the books out, eating away, and the lecturer would come in and spend two hours with us. That was well before any player development stuff, but it just shows you how far ahead Deccy was. You think you are bullet proof when you are playing – that's the truth. Deccy was thinking down the line.'

Soon after leaving the insurance business, a vacancy came up as player development manager for the Munster branch of

Rugby Players Ireland. One of the staff was out on maternity leave and Horan was originally brought in to cover. He did a good job, to such an extent that the administration offered a position to him on a permanent basis. Initially he accepted it, but soon realised he couldn't hold that role – and complete the strength and conditioning masters he'd commenced at Setanta College so he focused solely on his studies.

This job seemed destined for him, however. After graduating from Setanta, the players' body came calling again and this time he took the role which sees him liaise with youngsters in the Munster academy, fully contracted professionals and retired players.

'Like me, lads do not think about this aspect of professional rugby until they are out the other side,' he says.

'Then they say, "Fuck it, I should have engaged with ye earlier."'

Horan reckons that realisation makes those recently retired angry with themselves that they didn't do more when they still could.

'But I really feel these lads are a huge asset to us. For some of them to go back into a dressing room and tell the current group they should use the services that we provide – well that's the most powerful tool you can have.

'Trying to convince the current crop to do something in that space is the big challenge. The Munster players, for example, are really focused on achieving something on the pitch. All that absorbs them is the playing stuff and I get that. We chased an elusive Heineken Cup for years and the present team don't want anything to get in way of their pursuit either.

'I try to emphasise that you can also fit other stuff in. It's not easy – if I go to some lads with an idea early in the week of a match, they will just say, "I can't do this now – we have a big game at the weekend."

'I remind them they can still do other stuff which will be beneficial both now and when they do retire. I know because I didn't do it.

'They have to be ready for all eventualities,' he cautions. 'So that when they are asked the question, "What are you at now?" they will have a solid reply. Or at least engage rather than being uncomfortable.'

* * *

Horan appreciates that retirement doesn't faze everyone either.

'You see Claw who went off and managed to get the buzz back,' he laughs, referring to his old teammate, the man whose Munster shirt he took, Peter Clohessy.

'I think Claw definitely missed the thrill of being hit and taking tackles, so he took up hunting – the horse-riding kind! One particular day Claw took a jump over a hedge and had a fall. Everyone else was looking on worried for him and went to see how he was but seemingly Claw was smiling on the ground, absolutely delighted to have taken a hit. That's how he gets his buzz now.'

As for Horan, he now gets his kick from helping others.

'I've altered the dial,' he explains. 'My week is different. You check in on fellas constantly and try to change the culture. If we can get in there with young Munster players early, it will be a big thing for us. In Connacht, I would say the union is probably more ingrained and is part of the actual staff there, because of the great work Dee (Dr Deirdre Lyons, the Connacht Rugby players' development manager) is doing.

'Dee built up great connections with players when they were in the academy and now, as senior players, going to speak with her is part of their weekly routine. I hope to have that scenario in Munster too.'

The players' union has a five-pillar template for their members' financial needs, education, careers, mental health and branding. The latter covers everything from community engagement to being active in a responsible way on social media and learning how to manage themselves in that space.

'Lads have different requirements,' he says. 'No two are the same. One might say, "I don't need go back to college as I already have a degree."

'Another might come to me with, "I want sort out my finances because I have no pension, I just bought a house and I want to manage my money so that in ten years' time my mortgage is paid off."

'We work on individual strategies and, as I am not an expert in finance, we bring in specialists to help. It's working well.'

Along with ex-pros from the other provinces, they have formed a group called 'The Clubhouse' that meets in cities all over Ireland, with Cork and Limerick being the obvious focal points for the Munster players.

Denis Fogarty chairs the Cork branch while recently retired Mike Sherry is at the helm in Limerick. The Clubhouse connects former players with each other and there's a big social element to it too.

'When Munster played Saracens in 2019, a load of us met up and while it was a social event, it was a networking event as well,'

Horan points out. 'Lots of our players stretching right back to the 1990s were there, many of them are in business themselves or with links to companies. These people were ready to link each other up with good connections, and what we found is that we can get fellas jobs just through our own players. Our network is real and it's important to us.

'And the message to companies is simple; our players haven't changed. In the workplace they will be similar to what they were on the pitch – determined, great communicators, with a huge work ethic.'

The union is steadily impacting on players' lives. Before one Munster game in 2019, Horan sat down with Mike Sherry for a Q&A with supporters. Unprompted, Sherry described the road he was on post-retirement and thanked his old teammate for looking out for him.

'You get very emotionally attached to lads and their situations,' Horan concedes, 'but the lovely thing about what Mike said was that there were a couple of injured Munster players in the room, guys Mike would have played with, and it's really important as well that they hear his message.

'Because the problem is that men, by and large, don't talk. It's the natural Irish male thing – they just don't talk.'

Another part of Horan's job specification is to set up members for a professional referral. Here, they are entitled to six free sessions with a counsellor for whatever reason they desire, whether it be low level anxiety right up to suicidal tendencies.

'The beauty of it,' he says, 'is that I get more and more referrals through the door than ever. The generation coming through find it easier to talk feelings than we did, and they are more in tune with that aspect.

'As private and confidential as this all is, guys still go to their mates and explain where they got the help from. So, guys are coaxing each other to come to us if they feel shitty. That word of mouth is a big development. A big shift.

'Take my generation. We didn't talk about anything to do with feelings. When John Hayes left Munster, he told us all he was deleting our phone numbers. And he most likely did. We have a past players WhatsApp and Hayes keeps trying to leave it. We keep putting his number back in, but a few days later you see the icon *John Hayes has left*. Again. It's not that he doesn't still love us,' Horan laughs. 'It's just the way.

'Even when I retired and left the current Munster boys WhatsApp, I felt so awkward when I met them a few weeks later. They actually see you differently then, you're an ex-player. When a guy you used to play with walks by and says hello, you see it differently too. Why did he not stop there for a chat? Stupid stuff like, "What did he mean by hello?"

'I'll tell you one thing; Munster is tough in that regard. We had a tight bunch when we played but once you are gone, you're really gone. Many lads haven't been back to Thomond since they finished up. We are poor in that way. I would feel that our ex-players are massive assets that could be used so much better.'

* * *

It's fulfilling when people see the road to Damascus. There was one specific Munster player that Horan pestered to finish a degree he had started nine years earlier.

The player had started college just before professional sport came calling but, almost a decade on, the degree was incomplete.

'There would be nothing unusual about that,' Horan argues, 'that is the nature of elite sport. Lads tend to put these things on hold.'

But when the player sustained a serious injury, Horan got quickly on his case. Why not finish off that degree?

'Fuck it, this injury – I need to get it right,' the player argued.

'No, get this done – it will be over quicker than you think,' Horan responded. 'And you can rehab throughout.'

When the full diagnosis of the injury, a very serious one, was revealed, Horan was subtle in his next approach. 'The lad was distraught so you couldn't even ring him for a while. Imagine getting a phone call from me while he was coming to terms, "Hey, do you want to finish that degree?"

'But when the time was right, I pushed him again, and eventually he finished it out. On his graduation day I asked if he could send me a photograph so I could put it out there in public what he had achieved.

'"Jesus no way," the player responded. "The *Limerick Leader* came up to me at the graduation ceremony and asked for a picture and I said no too."'

Horan was perplexed. 'Fucking hell, man, you need to tell people about this. But he wanted no fuss. It's the old school way and we have to change that,' he stresses.

'Some fellas say absolutely nothing full stop. They look to get a mortgage, we try to line them up with Ulster Bank, who partner us, but they won't share that with anyone else because they don't want anyone knowing their private business in case that information is known when it comes to signing a contract with Munster. If it was known that a player had bought a house in the area, there might be a perception that he was going nowhere anytime soon. Players don't want any shred of information going public when they are in negotiations for a contract.

'It's the same with players' children being born. A lot of the time we mightn't even know guys and their partners were expecting until a birth took place – and for the very same reason.

'That's where my confidentiality with the boys comes in. I am not employed by Munster Rugby, I work for Rugby Players Ireland, and that helps them open up to me. Any issue they discuss with me is completely private; I don't even discuss scenarios with my colleagues. It's one on one, it's completely confidential.

'It's taking time, but we are making progress.'

Currently, there are 40 senior players in the Munster squad, on top of those academy players and past players who also have to be regularly communicated with. Rugby Players Ireland also has an overseas group to keep track of Irish players abroad, particularly in the lower regions of French rugby where there is little or no player development support. Down the divisions, Horan says, players are not even guaranteed to be paid all the time, so his organisation keeps tabs on these exiles and lets them know they have a support framework.

The holistic spirt displayed by his organisation makes it an uplifting role. The case of John Quill epitomises that sense. Quill, a Corkman, played for USA in the 2019 World Cup, and was sent off for a heavy tackle on England's Owen Farrell. The USA management had an agreement that any player who was red carded would leave the squad. Two days after receiving the line in Japan, Quill, who was retiring post-tournament anyway, was back home in Cork.

He scarcely had time to brew a cup of Barry's Tea before Horan was onto him, offering support. Quill was delighted with the gesture.

'Within 24 hours John was back in Cork having said all his goodbyes to his US teammates,' Horan says. 'He flew back in Cork Airport, went through immigration and stopped to have his passport checked when the fella behind the counter openly wondered how he recognised Quill's name.

'"Are you the guy who hit Owen Farrell?" asked the official.

'John replied it was him.

'"You didn't hit him hard enough," quipped the man behind the desk. "Welcome home!"'

And with that, Horan laughs, Quill was back in Cork. Back to reality.

'Luckily for John, in terms of the transition, he had a family business to get back into. That helps with everything, including identity. He knows now who he is again. It's great to have that because leaving a World Cup in such circumstances and retiring would be hard for anyone.'

While Quill and ex-players like him are firmly fixed on Horan's radar, he also has an exceptionally keen focus on the younger breed coming through. He wants them to forge good habits early.

'Some of them come straight into the Munster academy system and life is great. They have played Irish under-20 and people are telling them they are the dog's bollocks. When you first start wearing that green jersey, everyone loves you. The senior players want to talk to you. People who know the game mention you and it's very exciting.

'But in year two of the academy you might be overage for the

Irish under-20s and opportunities don't come as generously as they did a year earlier. It's second season syndrome and maybe no one is talking about you anymore. Instead there's a younger guy coming in and all the hype is around him.

'You get caught in the middle then – do you go back to play with the club to get games? Or does your rugby career stagnate?

'I say to these guys who experience that: "Okay, things aren't flowing exactly perfectly at this moment but take a breath. Would you go back to college and nail year two of your degree? Or get your co-op done? Could you start eating into the little goals that you have outside of rugby. Finish your education when that time is there?"

'The ideal pathway would be boys coming into the academy in three-year cycles – or four-years if they come through the sub-academy. These guys have a great chance to finish their degrees and have that much done for themselves. What a help that will be down the line. Then they can fully focus on being a pro.

'Come in and train hard but nail your degree too. In my experience guys who split their year and put their education on hold never tend to go back to college.

'That happened to Paul O'Connell who did put his degree on hold and never went back. But that fecker ended up getting a doctorate years later from UL, he was grand!'

As he builds a similar culture at Munster, Horan seems to be excelling at breaking challenges and goals down for his members.

'I give them a booklet on how to transition when they retire, but I know they won't even look at it for weeks. It will sit on a coffee table for a while until some evening they will read it and find something that might help.'

When they are ready for meaningful development, Horan works on getting their CV formatted and updated.

He sets them up on the business networking site LinkedIn and asks them to form relationships with six people every day, to actively share content on their page to attract discussion. Maybe provide insights.

He hands them practical tasks like contacting business community members they could potentially match with.

'Put yourself out there and build the confidence up slowly,' he says. 'Lads leave this sport and they feel useless. We link people together. Some of our fellas have already been snapped up by companies impressed with their insight and outlook on LinkedIn. To get the current group of players thinking like that is one of my goals.'

They could do worse than heed the advice of a man who has been there, won the lot, and seen it all.

7

TOMMY BOWE

Many Strings to His Bowe

BORN: Monaghan, 1984.
245 appearances for Ulster (168) and Ospreys (77).
69 Irish senior caps. 5 test caps British & Irish Lions.
Stepped away from top-level rugby in 2018, aged 33,
following a Grand Slam and 2 Pro12 titles.

As Tommy Bowe's rugby prowess heightened so too did his business interests.

In the midst of clocking up 168 appearances for Ulster, 77 for Ospreys and 69 for Ireland, Bowe's entrepreneurial streak also flourished.

In 2010, he set up Lloyd & Pryce, a shoe brand that he and business partners, Jim and Barry McArdle, two brothers from Monaghan, launched. A couple of years later they entered the clothing business with a new menswear brand – XV Kings.

While Bowe's primary focus during that time was always rugby, he worked exceptionally hard on the business side of things. All aspects of his interest in the clothing market were carefully considered from design, fabrication to sourcing, and he used gaps in his rugby schedule to allow him compete in two different terrains.

'The work it took to implement the shoes and clothing lines was huge,' he says.

'Here's the thing – when you are a rugby player, people are very quick to say yes to you. With the first collection of clothing, we started it two years after the shoes were on the market and I was expecting the shops to immediately take the clothes too, but it wasn't the case. I went around to retailers with samples and after chatting to some shop-owners they looked me in eye and said, "No it's not good enough yet."

'These are people I thought would have taken the chance, gambled and supported us, but I learned that when you deal with people's livelihoods, it's completely different. Just because you are a rugby player doesn't mean that it will open gates for you.'

That experience gave Bowe a real taste of the business world. Undeterred, he soaked up the feedback, went back, made some adjustments, and duly launched a range that enjoys prominence on shelves of retailers all over Ireland; one that has become hugely popular with customers.

'I also learned that a lot of rugby players are caught up in bubble,' he says. 'What we do is not real work, it's only when you step out of the environment that you get a taste of the business world.

'You could be anyone,' he maintains. 'You could be an NBA superstar, but if it means people might lose their business, they are not going to back you or your product just because of who you are.'

With a fine foothold long since gained in the market, Bowe is not content just to sit back and watch his products fly off the shelves. He is constantly looking for ways to launch new designs, from polo shirts to chinos to dressy jackets.

'Well, we are creative,' he nods. 'We aim for the 25- to 45-year-old market but, that said, I see some of my dad's friends wearing our range of shoes and I also see lads a lot younger than 25 wearing our shirts. We don't try to stereotype it; the stuff is for anyone.

'This business is like sport – you evolve or die.'

He offers an example of Brian O'Driscoll at 19.

'At that age Brian made his name on the national stage as an unbelievable outside centre who could burst through a gap anywhere, make breaks from anywhere.

'In the next phase of his career he became the best number 13 defender in the world. And he then as he progressed further he developed into one of the best poachers in rugby – almost like a back row. Brian kept with the times.

'We look to do the same. If we came out with a checked shirt, blue jeans and brown shoes every year people wouldn't be long getting sick of us. You are constantly trying to evolve it – with the clothing in particular – you are out there taking on Tommy Hilfiger, Gant, Superdry, G-star – all these big brands and the challenge laid down is massive.

'But it's such an opportunity to take them on and beat them and outsell them and I love that – I get a buzz from that.'

By his own admission, Bowe was no fashionista when a friend first put him in touch with the McArdles but it was clear that a collaboration could work. Ten years on, both brands are successful, and Bowe speaks to the Castleblayney siblings almost on a daily basis.

The footwear brand became synonymous with a host of Ireland's leading celebrities and sports stars and Bowe says that as the business evolved it helped balance his life better.

'Especially during times when I was injured or out of the Irish team,' he notes. 'Having something away from sport was important and it helped my rugby too, kept me more focused. Sharper.

'If things are not going well for you in sport, and you are recovering quickly or not getting picked, I think you need to have a distraction and get some other work done. When you are injured, there is only so much to do bar rehab, so I threw myself into those ventures. We're ten years on now with the shoes, and the clothes range came a few years after, so I'm very proud of them both.'

Bowe has also learned that, no matter how intense challenges were in either discipline, being able to compartmentalise is crucial.

There was a big onus on him to achieve with the Irish, Ulster and Ospreys teams he played on and equal pressure to be associated with brands that worked too. Failure to make a dent in the market was not something he would countenance.

'Yeah, there was that pressure,' he admits. 'When I first got involved with the brothers, I didn't know much about shoes and that was a drawback. But footwear factories were always a big thing in Monaghan, so I had an awareness of the area and what was going on around me. The two lads, though, were really well versed with the scene.

'It was a time when people were trying things too. I looked around at the guys on the Irish team and Jamie Heaslip had opened a restaurant. Ronan O'Gara had an involvement in a bar. A lot of rugby players seemed to be focused on getting involved in bars, cafés, or restaurants.'

That wasn't for Bowe, however. He has always tried to plough his own furrow.

'I went to play for Ospreys in Wales when no one else in Ireland was leaving to play,' he says of his four-year stint cross-channel, which yielded 77 appearances, in between 163 caps for Ulster.

'And I went into the shoe business when no one else in sport was looking at it.

'That's the way I do things. Later on, then, it was the same with TV presenting. I find it very exciting and challenging to go off on a different road. But starting out with the shoes was very much a learning curve. The biggest thing for me was getting the shops onside.'

Bowe enjoyed the graft he put in, travelling the length and breadth of the country and taking time to meet retailers on an individual basis, soaking up their opinions and bringing it all back to the design process.

The way he looked at it, getting out to meet shop-owners and others in the trade provided some of the best empirical research in the marketplace. If that's what it took to get the business line to succeed, so be it.

* * *

In many ways, that approach and work ethic mirrored his rugby trajectory.

His career developed almost independently of traditional production lines, the schools and academy systems that develop so many representative and international players. Like business, there was no straight entry into the market he wanted.

As a kid Bowe was an all-rounder, excelling at sports from athletics, tennis and Gaelic football to golf and rugby. He was proficient in so many codes that there came a point when he needed to make a call on what to stick with. He chose rugby but there was no overnight elevation through the ranks.

'I was playing schools' rugby in Armagh and didn't even get picked on the Irish schools' team,' he recalls. 'I did later play for Ulster schools, but I didn't make the Irish academy from there either, so I was wondering if it would ever happen for me.'

A door eventually opened, however, when he was selected for the Ulster Academy as a wildcard and developed sufficiently to make the Ireland under-21 team. From there he was contracted to Ulster and later selected for the Irish senior squad.

In 2008, with 170 points scored in 91 appearances for Ulster and most likely ten years of his career still to play out, Bowe could have settled for permanent residency in Belfast. Instead he made a trademark brave call to try something new, moved to Wales and developed into one of the best wingers in the world at Ospreys.

He managed 185 points in just 77 games there, a rate of one try every two outings and maintained that prolific form when he returned to Belfast in 2012, scoring 140 points in 77 appearances.

Throughout this period, he racked up the caps and tries for Ireland. He made 69 international appearances and, with 30 tries, is the country's second leading try scorer behind Brian O'Driscoll.

His brilliant strike rate over 14 years has him right up there as Ireland's number one winger and the Monaghan man will be remembered most for 2009, when he set Ireland on their way to the Grand Slam with an iconic catch on the run from Ronan O'Gara's cross-field kick in Cardiff.

Bowe remains the PRO14's all-time leading try scorer, with 67 in 169 games, and his 29 tries in 66 European Cup games leaves him fourth in that all-time list too.

He also managed five tries in ten games on the Lions tours of 2009 to South Africa, when he was one of the most impressive players, and the 2013 trip to Australia.

Clearly, rugby was his number one priority, but downtime and spells out injured allowed him plenty of time to devote to those growing business interests.

In 2015, Bowe, who already had an engineering degree, returned to academia to earn a postgraduate diploma in Business through the University of London.

Somehow, he managed to keep all balls in the air and that ability stood to him towards the end of his career when he was decimated by injuries and was left with a lot of time to fill.

The 2015 season was the start of an injury-plagued run. That campaign saw him sidelined with cruciate ligament damage to his knee.

When he recovered from that he endured an ankle break. Both of those injuries occurred in Cardiff's Millennium Stadium and on each occasion, he was carted off the field by the same medical buggy.

The second time it happened – against Wales in the 2017 Six Nations – he smiled as he was driven off.

'I grinned because you'd either laugh or you'd cry and I didn't want to cry in front of 80,000 people,' he smiles. 'I couldn't believe it, really. Fifteen months before it was that same buggy that took me off in the Argentina match,' he said, referring to Ireland's World Cup quarter-final defeat to the Pumas.

'The second time I just I sat there on the buggy in disbelief.'

Next came a broken sternum at the start of 2018. By then he'd already decided to walk away.

Just as well, then, that Bowe had long since charted a career outside of the game. He had a couple of attractive propositions and TV was one of them.

In 2013, he had presented a documentary for RTÉ, *Tommy Bowe's Bodycheck*, which explored the science and physiology of his make-up, how he dealt with injury and elite sport.

Five years later, as his rugby career entered its final stage, he presented 'Endgame', a program that saw him meet a number of leading Irish sports figures who had gone into retirement, tracing their experiences in the aftermath of competing.

Both shows went down well, and Bowe mentioned to his agent, Ryan Constable, that TV was an area of increasing interest to him. They threw around the idea of doing some punditry, but it didn't really appeal to the Monaghan man.

He watched a lot of rugby but never felt he was the best analyst of the sport.

'I knew my role on the teams I played in and I knew what I was doing,' he says. 'But instead of giving opinions, I loved asking questions. "Why do you do that?" Instead of telling people what to do, I would ask them why they made a certain move or play.

'I most definitely was not the lad in a team meeting, sitting down having a discussion with Jonny Sexton, thrashing out some aspect of a game plan. I didn't feel that was important to my position nor did I think it was natural for me either,' he elaborates.

So, when it came to the possibility of working on TV, Bowe fancied that maybe he could be the one asking the questions.

'There were other angles to it as well,' he continues. 'Once I retired as a rugby player, I knew it might be hard for the business, to keep the shoes and clothing well promoted, so I felt I had to keep myself out there.

'I felt that a role as a pundit would only have a certain shelf life. And actually I love to learn about people and ask them questions, so, yeah, I thought, "Why not go the direction of being a presenter? See can I crack that?"'

Doors opened pretty quickly. Constable is friends with Bryn Cunningham, the operations director at Ulster rugby, and Bryn's wife, Veronica, works as a producer with a TV company in Belfast. She sat down for a coffee with Bowe to chat about the road ahead.

Two months later, Bowe received a call from a production company looking for him to audition as a presenter for a holiday show called *Getaways* which would be screened on both RTÉ and BBC Northern Ireland.

He was duly sent five different scripts and spent a day in Holywood, County Down, filming and doing pieces to camera on the main street and its surrounds, creating content that would attract tourists to the area.

Bowe researched the topic and locality well, highlighted homegrown shops and businesses of particular interest, and, after a second meeting with the production company, he was offered the gig.

The only drawback was it would involve being away for a period of three to four weeks.

'And that posed its own challenges,' he chuckles. 'My wife, Lucy, was expecting our first baby, Emma, around that time. I had to say it to Lucy and see what she thought. We knew if

I took the role, I might not be around a lot at a time when I would be needed most. But Lucy felt it was a great opportunity and encouraged me to take it.

'On 2nd April, Emma was born. Three weeks later, I went to film for a week in Ibiza with Vogue Williams and a TV crew.'

The following week he was off to Lanzarote with Mairead Ronan and a crew to film another segment.

'It was lucky for me that I had an understanding and supportive wife,' he laughs.

Quite so.

'There was another side of it. We only had four weeks summer holidays from Ulster rugby,' he adds, 'and I was filming for three of those, so Lucy didn't get a holiday that year either. It was a big commitment on her part.'

But it was on that show where Bowe grew comfortable in front of a lens, doing pieces to camera with that personable, laid-back style of his.

'Now, it might have taken a hundred takes walking down a beach trying to remember all my lines, but once I could make the link sound interesting and was able to speak into the camera at the same time I was happy,' he states.

'The crew on that show were brilliant which is key. Any presenter must look relaxed and they helped me. Mairead and Vogue too.'

Bowe was well out of his comfort zone but relished the challenge of having to adapt to new environs.

'On the rugby pitch I was always so confident,' he says. 'With the TV I was right back to square one, not knowing what to do. I'd look over at Vogue and Mairead and wonder how the hell they remembered all their lines and still look so natural. But everyone realised that I was learning, and they were keen to take me on board and help.'

The door into a TV career was ajar. It wasn't long before Bowe burst through and took it completely off its hinges.

* * *

In August 2018, only five months retired from the game, the former flying winger was officially unveiled as the frontman for Eir Sport's PRO14's coverage.

It was a daunting task to switch the right wing for the presenter's chair, but he seized the chance and quickly took to it. He immediately discovered that live TV gave him a similar buzz to the one he received from rugby.

It was nice to get the buzz back and he was reminded of a chat he had with former champion jockey AP McCoy for that 'Endgame' documentary. McCoy spoke openly of the frustration of never being able to replicate the kick that racing gave him. The adrenalin rush he had as the fear of hurting himself loomed over every fence or hurdle. McCoy missed that spark so much.

'I soon realised that I don't have to worry about missing it,' Bowe laughs. 'For me, any time you "go live" in front of the cameras that's when the tingle will emerge, so I don't have to worry about losing that.

'Live TV is so different and more difficult than pre-recorded shows and that's why you need a good team around you,' he adds.

The team environment is something he loves working with Eir. 'I can have the craic with the analysts, Peter Stringer, Donnacha

O'Callaghan, and all the other analysts. I can be part of that team, operate in a live environment, and link up with the producers, directors and editors who work in the office,' he says.

'Those fellas are more important than anyone and it probably puts a bit more pressure on me because, as presenter, I represent them and all the hard work they put in during the week.

'And I don't want to be the one to cock up the show.'

And live sports programming can be so unpredictable. Bowe chuckles when he recalls a PRO14 game at the start of 2019. Munster and Dragons at Rodney Parade. One for the purists.

'It was the first time that the live feed went down on us, so there was just Strings and I in the studio. Now, a Munster and Dragons game at Rodney Parade at that time of year, well it's not going to bring the country to a standstill, and also it was played with the Six Nations on the horizon so both teams had some untried players.

'Still, in the build-up, Peter and I were really trying hard to drum up some enthusiasm for a game that wasn't really a big deal and featured some unknown players. We managed to get to throw in and we were delighted then to be able to tuck into a Camile Thai takeaway that we had ordered.

'I forget but I'm sure Strings probably ordered the turkey stir fry with salad, and most likely spent about 15 minutes draining any sauce from it, such is the temple-like shape he is in. Meanwhile, I was stuffing my face with chicken when suddenly the lights in the studio flared up again and all the TV screens lit up.

'The director came in my ear and said, "Tommy, get ready! We're going back live in seconds; the pictures have dropped from Rodney Parade."

'I had to gulp down the Thai chicken, chuck it off the table, wipe my face and try to make some sense of the first six minutes of the game, minutes that neither of us had seen all that closely because we were eating like hounds.'

But he did it.

'Well Peter, that's been an exciting six minutes so far?'

'And then I left Strings at it,' he laughs.

The next few minutes were spent updating the viewer with latest plays from Rodney Parade, filling in until the feed was finally restored – and the chicken too.

Such experiences are part and parcel of every channel's coverage and Bowe has learned to expect the unexpected. He fared so well on that PRO14 campaign that the station offered him the chief presenting role for the 2019 World Cup where he led the coverage for 38 of the 48 games on view.

Four years earlier he had been a starting winger for Ireland in the previous World Cup – now he was fronting live coverage for the latest one. It was a huge switch to make, following the likes of his former Irish teammate and roommate, rugby union and rugby league dual international, Brian Carney, who presents rugby league and GAA coverage for Sky Sports.

Carney is knowledgeable, polished and well-researched. Bowe has a stellar career behind him and now, in front of the camera, is proving to be just as adept.

'My job is to bring the good stuff out of the people in the seats opposite me,' he says. 'And it's brilliant to have something that I am passionate about. Like, I'm 36. Unfortunately, I was not a professional footballer which means I have to keep working and I have had to challenge myself in life after rugby. I felt like that could be a great thing too, trying new things and keeping myself busy.

'The best part is that I have an incredibly supportive wife who deals with me being away from home a lot. We have two children (Jamie arrived in March 2020) and it's not easy for Lucy. She's a nurse so she is very much dealing with proper things, life and life-threatening conditions. I come home sometimes and tell her that I'm a bit disappointed or upset with myself because I fluffed an opening line, or whatever.

'She looks at me as then as if I have ten heads! And that keeps me grounded.'

Not that he needs it. Bowe is as unassuming as they come. A success not just on the field, but in every area of his life.

8

TREVOR HOGAN

Road Less Travelled

BORN: Nenagh, 1979.
116 appearances for Munster (57) and Leinster (59).
4 Irish senior caps.
Stepped away from top-level rugby in 2011, aged 31, following
Heineken Cup and Magners League success with Leinster.

History and English had always consumed Trevor Hogan,
right from his days at Nenagh CBS, where his teacher, Danny
Grace, would sit on a desk at the top of the class, hold court
with his students and cheerily engage, rather than dictate to
them. Grace had a hearty laugh and a hunger to impart every
bit of knowledge he had to his students. His way was inclusive
and informal, he encouraged debate and discussion. Hogan was
captivated. Likewise, with Jimmy Minogue's free-spirited style
of teaching English.

'Jimmy would often bring up the meaning of "Esprit de
l'escalier",' he recalls. 'The expression captures that Eureka
moment when you find the answer to a problem, or the perfect
phrase for an essay – but it comes too late. You head down the
stairs after handing in the essay and only then it strikes you
what you should've written. That's the Spirit of the Stairway.

I've thought of it many times since I left Nenagh CBS.'

From school, Hogan headed for Dublin City University (DCU), graduating in time with an honours degree in journalism. It was his first experience away from home and Hogan remembers his brother, Mark, accompanying him to Dublin on the first day, settling him into his digs, showing him how to cook one meal – spaghetti bolognese – before heading back down the N7 again.

Hogan was alone, but it didn't bother him. He had never been afraid to find his own way, forsaking the dominant local religion of hurling for soccer, before he discovered rugby and the glorious physicality it offered.

Donnacha Ryan's house was four fields over. Ryan also came late to rugby but, once he dropped the camán, he would go on to have a stellar career with Munster, Ireland and French giants Racing 92.

Two miles further north was Barry Everitt's place. Everitt played fly-half for both Munster and Leinster before moving to London Irish where he won a Powergen Cup title and was also the top scorer in the English Rugby Premiership in his time with the Exiles.

Closer still to home, this time under the same roof, his brother, Ray, forged a decent career too, playing prop for Bristol, Connacht and Ireland 'A' before injury brought his run to a halt.

All around them was rich hurling heartland, bordered by Nenagh, Kilruane and Toomevara where celtic crosses and All-Ireland medals hung on the walls of houses close by.

But at different junctures all four players flourished under the guidance of local coaches, Seamie Harty and Pat Whelan, two custodians of Nenagh Ormond rugby club who nurtured their potential. When Hogan left the town for college, he was trim, square, healthy and muscular and needed no one's praise either; he was self-sufficient and keen to improve all the time. Harty and Whelan were both confident he would bloom if given the chance.

That was the start of a winding road. A DCU placement sent him to the Irish News in Belfast where his highlight was delivering a front-page story, an interview with a member of the Orange Order, during his time there. He was well-versed in affairs of the north of Ireland, and keen to learn more about the history of conflict in general.

Like the situation in the north, he also read deeper and deeper into the Israeli–Palestinian saga, known to many as the world's 'most intractable conflict', with the ongoing Israeli occupation of the West Bank and the Gaza Strip now reaching 53 years. Since 1967, Israel have demolished more than 50,000 Palestinian homes and Hogan followed events there closely as he went through school and college.

'It just always struck me as a tragedy that has worsened year after year,' he states. 'The Palestinians are totally isolated, further adrift than ever right now and the whole thing has become more overwhelming. I suppose, being Irish, there are parallels with us.'

Hogan shakes his head as he details the onslaught and destruction. A million and a half people under siege, most of them relying on aid to live. Mass unemployment. No trade. No fishing or farming. After he retired, he had an insatiable urge to do something to help. He wasn't sure what he could do to actually make a difference, but he simply knew he had to try.

He was only weeks retired from professional rugby when,

in June 2011, he and 13 other Irish citizens boarded the *MV Saoirse*, an Irish ship which was to bring aid to Gaza.

'Usually, I speak to my wife, Claire, about everything I am going to do but this time there was no conversation to be had,' he recalls. 'It happened quickly. I was on the boat before I knew it.'

More than bringing aid to Gaza, the principal mission of the Freedom Flotilla was to raise awareness of the conflict. Those on board understood they would be stopped by the Israelis, and while docked in Greece, saw the first signs of hostility when their ship was sabotaged and damaged. Undeterred, they switched ships and steeled themselves for the remainder of the journey.

They expected more Israeli intimidation and certainly got plenty of that. At one stage the flotilla was completely surrounded by Israeli navy – warships, smaller gunships out the side, inflatable boats with a clutch of balaclava-wearing soldiers. They got as far as 38 miles out from port and started to imagine they might actually break the blockade, but all hope was quickly abandoned when battleships came on their radar.

The Israelis were antagonistic and roared at them through megaphones. They unleashed water cannons to literally rock the boat. They shut the flotilla down, cut the power. At that stage Hogan admits to feeling tense, but only because he couldn't swim. The flotilla's captain began screaming at the volunteers that the Israelis were trying to sink their boat.

'Still, I was confident they wouldn't hurt us,' Hogan says. 'We were a group of white Europeans and unless you got a young, inexperienced soldier who could have lost the plot we would be okay, I felt. Now that had happened before, with a young soldier, but I always felt we would be alright despite the intimidation.

'We explained that we were on a humanitarian mission, that we were not anti-Israel but had an issue with the policies of their government. But they weren't listening to anything,' he remembers.

Instead, around 20 commandos, all with balaclavas on, came on board, the whites of their eyes glaring wildly. They had rifles, knives, handguns and tasers.

'They broke windows, shouted at us, but we stayed calm, formed a circle,' Hogan recalls.

The aggro went on for hours. The size and physicality of Hogan meant that the commandos took particular interest in him, before the group was eventually hauled into the port of Ashdod.

Despite efforts by the Irish consul to diffuse the situation, the crew were then taken to a detention centre and imprisoned. Their belongings were seized, and they were interrogated. Hogan still sees the hatred in their eyes.

They enquired about his size. Standing at six foot six and weighing 113 kilos, he was built like a brickhouse and when he told them of his profession, they scoffed that there was no rugby in Gaza and no need for him there. Hogan replied that they might have an interest in sport if only they were allowed to move around.

'I didn't want to antagonise them much further,' he says. 'So, I mostly stayed quiet.'

At 4 a.m. they were sent to their cells with the bright lights switched on through the night. There they were detained for six days, only being allowed out for half an hour twice a day. From the Thursday of his imprisonment to the following Sunday they were out of contact with home but late on Sunday afternoon they were allowed one three-minute phone call.

Hogan rang Claire but the call went straight to voice mail. 'The prison warden was right beside me, listening, and she said that if I left a voice mail it would count as a phone call,' he remembers. 'She was a real bitter woman. She said a lot more besides that.

'Instead, I rang my mam (Nancy) and, looking back she must have been worried because I hadn't even told her I was going either. But she was delighted to hear from me. All Nancy was concerned about was what were they giving me to eat,' he laughs.

'Pure Tipperary, pure Irish mam,' he chuckles. "Are they feeding you there?"

'I told her we were grand; that they were giving us bacon and cabbage. Not to worry.'

Truth was Hogan and his group lost a lot of weight over the week. That happens when all you get is a few slices of cucumber in the morning and again in the evening. If they were lucky, they got a bit of hummus to go with it. That was that.

They tried to break him; he doesn't doubt that for a second.

'They were at us all the time, but I think it only made us stronger,' he says.

Eventually, diplomatic pressure from home shores told and their release was sanctioned – but only after several disruptions and delays.

'They were persistent,' he says. 'Right until the moment we left they kept trying to crack us.'

On the way home Hogan wondered if anything had been achieved but when they finally returned to Dublin airport and saw their families and the support for their efforts the reception lifted them considerably. A tricolour they brought to Gaza with them had been seized by the commandos on the boat, but the group grasped it back and raised it aloft in the arrivals hall. A symbol of defiance. But more importantly, a symbol of solidarity.

Deep down Hogan hoped his profile had helped raise awareness of the conflict – he spent the next few days recounting his story in the media. He'd seen first-hand what the Palestinians were facing. He would never forget it.

* * *

Injury terminated his playing days. And when that happened, he explored a few different outlets. He returned to college life, qualified as a teacher, worked as a rugby analyst, became Claire's husband and father to Pearse, Eve and Rosie. He'd love to have played on and achieved more, but that was not the script handed to him.

From 2004 to 2007, Hogan really stepped up as a professional rugby player. In 2005, he played twice for the Ireland senior team against Japan and came off the bench against Italy in the 2007 Six Nations before picking up his fourth cap on that summer's tour to Argentina.

He was a mobile second-row who mixed physicality with athleticism; perfect for the modern game, but a 2008 fixture for Leinster against Welsh side Scarlets saw him tear the cartilage in his right knee. Doctors said there was a 1 in 10,000 chance of the knee getting infected after surgery but, incredibly, that's exactly what happened.

He remembers being in Santry on a drip for nine days after the initial procedure and losing a huge amount of weight during his stay there. When they let him out, they sent him off with a drip that had to be changed every four hours in a 24-hour cycle.

Hogan was down about it, but knew others were fighting much bigger battles and retained perspective. Upon his release home, his sister, a doctor, helped change his drip at the allotted times, but it wasn't always pretty. He was rushed to a clinic one night around 1.30 a.m. when the line going into his vein blocked. Blood pumped and flowed down his arm.

There were many other rough nights through to January 2011 when he finally stepped away, aged just 31, having spent three years between the pitch and treatment table trying to coax a busted knee back into life.

It cut him down in his prime. Hogan wanted to add to his four Irish caps, and further build his career with Leinster. There was no doubting his pedigree, he had represented Munster on 57 occasions and Leinster on 59, but Paul O'Connell, Donnacha O'Callaghan and Mick O'Driscoll, who amassed 225 Irish senior caps between them, were all ahead of him in the international pecking order.

Game time was hard to come by, but he was up for the fight.

At the club he was part of a Magners League and two Heineken Cup successes and Joe Schmidt, his coach at Leinster, would later go on to take the Irish team. As he ponders what might have been, Hogan felt that, under Schmidt, there might have been hope of gaining more Irish caps but there was a caveat – you had to be on the pitch to stay in Schmidt's mind.

Through the 2010–11 season, however, Hogan's field time was lessening. He spent more time in and out of Dr Ray Moran's surgery than on the paddock.

'Ray was always so positive,' he says. 'There was always

something else he could look at to get me back on the pitch. He'd hit me a shoulder, full of optimism, and say, "Don't worry, we'll get you back on the field again."

'But when I went into him at the end of 2010, his body language was less positive. This time there was nothing more he could do for me.'

His last professional game was against the Dragons in November 2010. After officially retiring he returned to Nenagh, popped out home to Knockalton, and talked things over with his family. Nancy had kept scrapbooks with articles going right back to when he played for Nenagh Ormond, Trinity College, Shannon, Blackrock and then hit the big time with Munster, Leinster and Ireland.

She had held onto the Dragons match report too, perhaps sensing it would be the last, and when Hogan read it, he gathered the scrapbooks, put them in a box and threw them up in the attic.

'It was time for a new life there and then,' he says. 'I wasn't bitter because I saw some of the big names in Irish rugby who also had to retire through injury around the same time and I was not at their level. So, all I felt was gratitude to even have had the chance to play with those guys. And it wasn't as if it all came on me overnight. I had three years to almost get used to the idea.'

He lived in an apartment in Dublin with his then girlfriend and now wife, journalist and broadcaster, Claire Brock, and lifelong friend, Noel Fox, from Mullinahone in Tipperary. In the apartment a poster from IRUPA, the rugby players' body, was pinned to the wall, outlining all the various stages of retirement. Denial. Depression. Anger. Space. The future.

'Claire and Noel would come home after work each evening and ask what stage I was at that day?' he laughs. 'The truth is I skipped them all. I had lots of stuff to do after rugby – the trick was finding something I was just as passionate about.'

He didn't have long to wait to find that.

* * *

Thanks mainly to the insurance policy he had taken out, he had breathing space and the payment allowed him to go back to college. He picked up on his two main interests and, after coming back from Gaza, started a degree in English and history in University College Dublin (UCD). He coached Nenagh Ormond in the All-Ireland League. His days quickly filled.

The only thing close to his love for rugby was history and English and at UCD, and his curiosity in both disciplines grew. He puts it down to Paul Rouse and Diarmaid Ferriter, two brilliant lecturers who helped feed that passion.

'I put a huge amount of time and effort into studying, preparing my essays. So much that Claire would remark how I spent more time editing assignments than I did preparing for a match.'

He doesn't say it, and wouldn't anyway, but he left UCD with a first-class degree and then pondered what to do with it. He chose teaching and took on a two-year education masters, teaching in two schools along the way as part of his positioning.

He spent one year at Willow Park in Dublin and one year at St Gerald's in Wicklow and reckons they were the two most contrasting schools you could find to Nenagh CBS.

'They were obsessed with rugby whereas I had the non-traditional rugby upbringing at my school at home,' he smiles.

'But it gave me huge insight into what life was like for those who come through the schools' system and then I had my own experience of the club and youths' pathway. That was an invaluable insight.

'Kids, though, are the same, no matter what school they attend. They have the same worries, interests and challenges.'

He set his sights on a career educating others and, drawing from his experience of Grace and Minogue, his old teachers back home, set out on a new way of life.

'I'd have been happy to stick at teaching, that was the plan, and I had a good base to build upon,' he says.

A phone call one evening, however, from Noel Fox, a first cousin of Tipperary hurling icon, Eoin Kelly, set Hogan's radar on another trail. Fox was someone Hogan frequently turned to for counsel.

'By then I was coaching at Blackrock along with Emmet Farrell and at the end of the season I just checked in with Noel to see whether he felt I should stay with Blackrock.

'Noel mentioned an advert for a role in the IRFU as talent coach with the Leinster Academy and reckoned I should go for it. It was pure luck I rang him because I hadn't even seen the ad.'

Hogan duly put together a presentation and, after three rounds of interviews, he got the job. The Leinster Academy is the envy of European rugby due to the quality players it has developed, and their output shows no sign of relenting as their faith in youth has been rewarded tenfold.

In the past few years alone, players like Will Connors, Max Deegan, Ross Byrne, Joey Carbery and Rory O'Loughlin all graduated with distinction while Josh van der Flier, Peter Dooley, Jack Conan, Adam Byrne and Dan Leavy went on to earn senior contracts before them.

Hogan is at the coalface of the whole thing and, by his own admission, happy to stay there for as long as he is welcome.

'I love it,' he says. 'It's relentless and I don't mean that in a cut-throat way, but the culture and what we do here is just so interesting,' he says.

'Once the Leaving Cert finishes, we have a new crop of guys who are coming here to start from scratch.

'In fact, we first touch base with them as transition years and that's where it starts really. People talk about our success but there is no danger of getting complacent because we're always looking three to four years ahead.

'People once eulogised a Leinster backrow of Jamie Heaslip, Sean O'Brien and Jack Conan and probably felt they would be there for years, but very quickly two of those three were gone and we had to have the next lad ready to step up.

'We don't entertain the outside talk, really. We know it could only take a few bad years and we would be in trouble.'

Once the youths graduate, they go under the wing of Leo Cullen, Stuart Lancaster and the senior management.

'We have a totally new cycle to focus on every year,' he explains. 'I am currently looking at kids who were born in 2003 and soon enough I will be dealing with those born in 2010.

'Kids these days have to deal with the immediacy of every-thing. I see it from my own children if they are watching cartoons, Room on the Broom, or whatever, everything is on demand and kids can't understand when it's not. They have no patience and that tests your resilience too. Down the line it leads to stress – kids need something, and they want it there and then whereas we had to wait for something, build up anticipation and that made it more meaningful long-term.

'So, it's harder for them now, they have to generate that ability to work for things and be patient.

'We have to be there with a connection so they can trust us but at the end of day we cannot be their best friends either. There is still a coach-player dynamic to consider. It's important this stage of their development that there are areas in which we hold them back too and it's all about getting that balance right.

'They are operating in a pressure cooker window to get a contract and we try to keep the door open for them for as long as possible, knowing lads develop at a different rate. But it's a dream to be here, still involved with rugby. As long as this job is here, I think I will be too.'

* * *

Perhaps what hit Hogan hardest in retirement was losing the bond with former teammates. With the passing of every season, the link they once had loosens. It saddens him.

'Maybe it's a mid-life crisis or something but some of us met over Christmas of last year and it was so bloody hard to arrange,' he recalls. 'It shouldn't have been. My wife seems to meet up her pals a lot easier than I do. Even on that particular night some lads couldn't make it in. Maybe it was only then that I realised the group is never going to be as tight as it used to be. I had always thought we would remain close as the years went on but that is not the reality. The reality is that it's gone.

'In a rugby sense, I only have a small group of friends and that is not necessarily the healthiest scenario. Like Claire, I've thrown myself into looking after our kids but it's probably better for the children if I have more friends that I meet regularly,' he laughs.

'Is that a bloke thing or a sport thing that you just move on over time?' he asks. He reckons the ongoing development of the iPhone, social media apps and phone technology has killed personal contact.

'Before you know it, so much time has passed and it's hard to get back to where you once were. The phone has been a killer in lots of ways. Yea, everyone is connected on a load of social platforms, and we are all on WhatsApp groups, but it is easy to be attached to some group and yet not actually be connected with people. That's what social media is – you can send a message but it's not proper communication. You don't meet up.

'Realistically, we had great times with the Leinster team I played on but what we had has passed and what has probably hit me most in retirement is that I need to keep a healthy circle of friends. Thing is, when I get home from work, we get the kids sorted, off to bed, and I'm wrecked. Where do you ever get time to do anything?

'My motivation now is what can I do for the kids, what can help our family lives be better. The family has moved into the centre of our lives but, for me, rugby is still orbiting the whole lot and that's great.'

In 2015, their son Pearse arrived on the scene. Eve is three now and Ruby is at toddler stage. Hogan is besotted with them.

'Claire and my sisters say it's important to take a step back from them too,' he laughs, 'but I don't know. Pearse has a good left foot on him and that's something to be working away on, getting him up to speed with his right foot too.

'Ah look, everything else has just taken a back seat.'

Almost ten years have passed since he gave up the game and it's like things have come full circle. As we chat, he says he's due to see Dr Ray Moran again for a check-up.

'It's a decade on and I'm happy I got so long out of this knee, but now anytime I jog or hold a pad it starts to creak,' he says. 'In my head I was hoping I could get to 50 before I needed it replaced but if it comes sooner rather than later, then so be it.'

Before family life took over, Hogan took on some media roles, working as a rugby pundit for Off The Ball and also featuring on RTÉ's *Today with Sean O'Rourke*.

'I found it a big commitment,' he says. 'I wanted to watch every game properly to be confident in what I was talking about. Not just a Leinster or Munster game but the other fixtures in their pool too so I could give a rounded view. I sense there may be people in punditry who don't watch every game.

'I feel pundits should also be able to say they don't know the answer to a question if that is the case. For everyone to know everything about everything requires a lot of time!

'Then the other thing I always struggle with is doubt. The imposter syndrome always hanging over me.'

Really? Capped for Leinster, Munster, Irish Youths, Ireland. Highly qualified academically and in a top job – how can that be the case?

Hogan thinks about it.

'Not sure, but maybe coming from Nenagh, a town that was

not fully steeped in rugby, had something to do with it. I always had that feeling – 'You are not supposed to be here.'

'That hung over me all the way through. I had the same mindset with punditry and, to counter that, I wanted to watch every game so I could give a proper insight. But I definitely had that syndrome playing. And everywhere else I went.'

After ceasing media work there were approaches from political figures to link up. Around 2015, Richard Boyd Barrett from the People Before Profit movement asked him to join their effort.

'The water charges were a big thing then and I was quite active in terms of highlighting what has happening in Palestine too. I was definitely tempted, I always told my students it was so important for people to be involved in things, to take a stand and make their voice heard around what is happening in the world.

'I was close to putting my hand up for local election here in Dublin with them. There was a window, I felt, that could have been capitalised upon. We were in the middle of austerity and there was more optimism, I felt, for a different way forward. But by the next election that had evaporated.

'I still feel that the inequality is as bad as ever. You pay up to €600,000 for a house in Dublin that may not even suit your family needs. I thought when Richard contacted me that there could be another way of trying things, but then Pearse arrived and with the 24/7 nature of politics, Claire was very reluctant for me to get involved and wasn't sure if she could support me on that one, and she supports me on everything!'

Political beliefs and activism took a back seat as he got to grips with becoming a parent.

It's not something he laments but he does look back with regret for not continuing to lead the charge in raising awareness of the Palestinian conflict.

'To this day I feel a lot of guilt that I am not as active as I was. I experienced just a fraction of what the Palestinians did, but it always stuck with me. We wanted to raise awareness, but I was never naïve enough to feel that we could end the Siege of Gaza or anything. Never did I think that we could affect change over just a few days.

'You would be overwhelmed with some of the shit that is going on in the world but do you decide it's too much to take on any cause? Or do you continue to try and change one small thing and hope that it will lead to something?

'I've left that one unanswered. Some days I wonder if our trip made any difference. The reality is no it didn't and that's demoralising. You get near the stage in life then when you wonder what's the point in doing anything?'

There is one memory from the trip that Hogan particularly struggles with. He recounts how warm most Palestinians were when the group arrived to help. Others, though, were cynical.

'They had seen so many try do something and then disappear,' he says. 'One girl stands out. She said, "Don't just go back to Ireland and forget about us."'

Hogan takes a few seconds to ponder those words.

'That's what has happened,' he says, softly.

'Lads sometimes slag me about it. "You went mad for a while there, Trev." But it was not just a mad thing that happened. Fair enough, if someone looks at my trajectory of life they can say, "Well, that girl was right. You didn't really care, or do anything, because you went back to Ireland and did nothing else."

'And I couldn't counter that,' he accepts. 'Instead I threw myself into my family life. I know that I want to do something again, but I do struggle with the whole thing. Like, what could I actually change?'

Few would criticise Hogan for focusing solely on his job and family and he remains adamant that his best achievement in life is being a father and trying to be a good one.

'I have plenty of stuff to think back on, to reflect upon, but the main message for me is I am grateful to have had the life I've had. I don't necessarily see that I achieved anything apart from being a dad and that is the primary focus for me. I look at what's next rather than look back and even when I was playing, I never looked back either.'

9

DONNCHA O'CALLAGHAN

No Long Goodbye

BORN: Cork, 1979.
331 professional appearances for Munster (268) and Worcester
Warriors (63). 94 Irish senior caps. 4 British & Irish Lions caps.
Stepped away from top-level rugby in 2018, aged 39,
following Grand Slam, Heineken Cup (2), Triple Crown and
3 PRO14 successes with Munster.

Donncha O'Callaghan wasn't up for a long goodbye. The farewell came at the end of April 2018 in the West Midlands of England and by the turn of evening he was back in Cork. That was just how he wanted it.

O'Callaghan spent the final three seasons of his career at Worcester Warriors, playing 63 times and, to mark his impact there, the club put together a tribute video which featured contributions from his children, wife and a selection of former teammates. But that was the extent of the emotional stuff.

'I played the game, we beat Harlequins, got the result we wanted, and I jumped on a 5 p.m. flight back home,' he says.

'My housemate, friend and teammate, Matt Cox brought some of my stuff back over to Cork a while after, but it was a straightforward departure. The act of stepping away wasn't too tough on anyone because of the age I was at [38] and the generational divide there too; I was nearly twice the age of some players,' he laughs. 'There would have been a much greater wrench leaving Munster a few years earlier because my identity was wrapped up with them.'

It helped greatly that O'Callaghan had lots of stuff lined up outside of the game. A newspaper column with *The Times (Ireland edition)*, a coaching role on the RTÉ show *Ireland's Fittest Family*, and many other endorsements and opportunities to consider.

One of those was a documentary for Virgin Media called *Game Over*, a look at how sportspeople coped with retirement, an idea that was seeded in conversations with Mairéad, one of the Fittest Family producers.

'We'd be on the set, after filming a challenge with one of the families, and I'd enquire if there was any lunch going,' he laughs.

'Mairead would reply, "We just ate two and a half hours ago."

'Yeah, but I have to eat every three hours,' I'd explain.

'She found it fascinating to hear that stuff, how I had to take in 6,000 calories on the day after a game. And that's where the idea for the documentary came from.'

First on his interviewee wish-list was Roy Keane. Former captain of Manchester United, Ireland, and serial winner. Keane obliged.

'Roy was important to meet, both personally and for the documentary,' O'Callaghan says. 'He was a hero for me because he became the standard setter for a group of us rugby lads. He introduced us to that winning mentality – "don't just be happy to tog out". Before he came to prominence, I have to be honest, my goal was to play for Ireland. But after seeing what he did and how he achieved it my goal changed to winning with Ireland.'

Keane was a dream to deal with, O'Callaghan says, and great craic too. Various Irish rugby coaches had summoned him to talk to squads over the years, but still the two Corkmen didn't know each other that well.

'There was one flight to New Zealand that we were on, heading down to play a test series, and Roy was going to spend some time with the All Blacks in their training camp. He was sitting two seats across from me, but I never picked up the balls to go over and chat. I had too much respect to pothole him. Unlike Quinny (Alan Quinlan) and Rog (Ronan O'Gara) who potholed him for the rest of the journey.

'While we filmed for the documentary, we broke away a few times to have the chats. I was only out of Worcester and was starting to fall into the victim stage. "Oh God love me, what will I do now?"

'I told him that when it came to my exit medical at Worcester, I had been asked to list my occupation and that I had to pause as I didn't know what to write down.

'I didn't even get to finish the sentence,' he recalls.

Instead Keane cut across him.

'Unemployed,' Keane proclaimed.

'There's nothing wrong with you writing down that you are unemployed on that form. Don't identify yourself as an ex-rugby player, you are unemployed right now and it's fine to say that. To say you are an ex-rugby player is not. That's done man,' Keane told him. 'Slam the door on that and get going again.'

In that moment O'Callaghan remembered again why he loved Keane.

'Sure, in one second he was honest enough to tell me what he felt. Imagine having a captain like that in a dressing room, someone who gave enough of a shit about you personally to tell you straight out what he thought.

'That doesn't happen too often. I was lucky to have had it growing up with Munster and Ireland, but that culture is not everywhere. I went into hundreds of review rooms, dissecting games with our coaches. A missed tackle of mine might have been pointed out, but from the back of the room there would always be, "Donners, why has that lad got three metres on you? Because you haven't pushed up quick enough. That's twice in a row you have done that now."

'And each time I heard something like that,' O'Callaghan adds, 'I would turn to whoever said it and say, "You're right. Thanks a million."

'Because it was always for your betterment that they said it.

'And that's what Roy has. In spades. He basically got me to wake up and stop feeling sorry for myself for leaving sport, told me not to fall into that trap, to set new standards elsewhere and not become the victim. Even if I never did the documentary with him, he was so sound to me personally.'

As retirements went, O'Callaghan's was manageable, but there was still huge adjustment required.

'I was in a spin for little bit.'

A spin?

'Well, I had things lined up, but days were filled with uncertainty too. The other players I soldiered with egged me along. They just gave me their own experiences. One lad said to me, "Donners, I'm 18 months out and I still don't have a clue what to do."

'That was actually good to hear. I felt under pressure to have plans in place quickly but it's not always the way.'

He rang around a lot, called guys who were thriving and others that hadn't fully found their feet yet. He gleaned little gems from all conversations, especially from those ex-teammates who had delved too quickly into something and had not found fulfilment. He also listened intently as other friends revealed how they were content to think bigger picture, to knock on one door in the hope that it would open another down the line.

'When I was playing with Munster and it came to contracts, we chatted amongst each other and that helped. People think professionals don't chat about that – but the gang I was with did. Brilliant. I would ask what terms and conditions I should be seeking, and they would tell me about their own situation.

'They were still the same when I retired. They kept on advising and helping. Decent lads.'

Back to the spin.

'Lack of routine, that's what it was for me,' he states emphatically.

'Lack of purpose? I was actually fine with that. It was the routine I was missing. I'll give an example. One Monday evening, not long after I came back from England, my wife, Jenny, said that her mom had invited us down to dinner on the Thursday night.

'I showed Jenny my weekly plan, showed her where I had food laid out, the calorie intake already counted, and asked did she mind if I brought my own food down to her mam's house?

'Jenny looked at me in bewilderment and sighed, "Will you just come for some fecking dinner?"'

It made no difference whatsoever whether O'Callaghan

tucked away a tuna salad or a whopping beefburger dripping in gravy – he had no call to be forensic anymore. There were no more games left to play.

'No, but I still wanted to scratch that little itch,' he explains.

'As a player I knew I had to max out in my preparation and application to make it. I was not the most talented player in the room, so I had to work very hard. For 20 years I had a routine of watching every morsel of food I ate, solely to get an edge, and I couldn't just let it go like that.

'But the whole thing of stopping playing was nuts – I remember the first weekend as an ex-rugby player, going to the toilet at home and having my first dehydrated piss in about 17 years. I was there, "Oh my God, I'm dehydrated! It's yellow! This is mad!"

'That's the environment you had created.'

Another day stands out. He went training with his old Munster colleague and former All Black Dougie Howlett. The two of them were doing interval sessions and, boys being boys, they were trying to reach times of yore when they were at their peak.

O'Callaghan's target was to come in under 30 seconds for a particular run, but he missed that goal. He was devastated.

'I was a nerd when I was playing, I loved setting out measurements and targets. Always trying to meet them. They made things more attainable for me.

'And then it was like, "What the fuck? I didn't make the time!" Unthinkable.

'Later on, I got thinking more about it. I was nearly over a year in post-retirement by then. I was no longer accountable to anyone. And I was 40 for Christ's sake! Yet, there I was still judging myself for a time I had clocked about ten years earlier and still dealing with that competitive edge, probably because Dougie had made his time! It takes an awful lot to shed that.

'For 20 years, my life was all about inches and gains. All to reach the level I wanted to be at. You will definitely miss that. I was a pure routine man. On the first Monday morning of my retirement I got up and didn't have to follow a dress code. I didn't have to worry about leaving out slips, vests, tracksuits, and following them to a tee. But I found it unusual not having to do that.'

A big help early in O'Callaghan's retirement was former Irish hurdler Derval O'Rourke who spent time working with Munster Rugby as player development manager.

She asked her fellow Cork native for one of his old rugby schedules.

Then she turned it upside down.

During his playing days his schedule was loaded with red. Red meant rugby. There was red everywhere. It was the most important thing in O'Callaghan's week. Strength and conditioning sessions were yellow, and so on.

'Derval got hold of it, changed the variables around and said, "This colour is for meetings, that colour is preparation for meetings. This is for research, etc."

'She saw I was trying to fill every minute of every day. Instead, she just blocked out a huge section and covered that with red. "That's for time with your family," she insisted. "You have earned that now."'

He had. Though it took a long time to grasp.

'Look, you lose a part of your identity when you step away – not from everyone else's perspective, but from your own,' he says. 'As a sports person and a rugby player I was just a bit of a bollox to be honest with you. I was so selfish and so driven.

'Personally, I didn't like that side of me. Then when I retired, I didn't know how to find myself again, how to pull myself back from that.

'To give you an insight, there was always massive competition in Munster. People saw us mostly only on game days, but we were 100 per cent competing with each other every day before then, competing on every rep we did in the gym.

'I was up against the likes of Paulie (Paul O'Connell) Micko (Mick O'Driscoll) and Trev (Trevor Hogan) for a long time and my battles would be fought the entire week of a game. If Micko went into the gym on a Monday morning and threw on an extra 15 kilos on the squat, then it was alarm bells for me.

'Out on the field, if Trevor made a brilliant pass in front of everyone and people remarked how his skill levels had gone through the roof, I would have to react to that then. I had to be the best every minute of the week. It was so relentless and, suddenly, I didn't have that quest anymore.

'The good thing is that when I was researching for the documentary, I realised the rugby person, that character I played, really wasn't me. I looked back at footage of me in action and wondered, "Who is that lad? He's a psychopath. I didn't know that lad at all."'

He's more at ease with himself now, though from time to time the competitive beast roars again.

'I do sometimes still get the itch to fly into it again,' he admits.

'Some days I see people coming towards me on bikes and my eyes instantly narrow in on them. I look at them cycling towards me and start thinking that I'd love to weld them out of it with a shoulder. As they get closer, I start imagining that if I hit them hard in a certain spot, I would wind them, drive them back. And then I cop on and remember that they are just cyclists on the way into work and not some big monster tearing at me. I shiver about the way I think sometimes.

'But I was a product of what I was around. All of those influences? They made me into who I was.'

* * *

Even though his thirties were in the rearview mirror, O'Callaghan could well have played on into his forties.

He was still in excellent shape and two other Premiership clubs had enquired about taking him on after his Worcester contract ended. Little wonder they were interested. Over an 11-year period he played in Ireland's three Triple Crown successes and was on the field for every minute of their 2009 Grand Slam winning campaign. He'd featured in three World Cups, represented the Lions on two series (2005 and 2009), and captained the side to victory over the Southern Kings in Port Elizabeth in 2009. With 94 Irish caps and all that experience behind him, the clubs chasing him clearly felt he could still perform and raise standards in tandem.

Back in Cork, however, O'Callaghan saw there were other, more pressing and important values that needed to be addressed.

'We were sitting down one evening and Jake, our youngest son, was a little worked up and he was getting impatient. He was talking away, repeating the same words all the time. I couldn't really make out what he was saying but it sounded like "Dodiedownda, dodiedownda."

'I was perplexed myself and I tried to make out what he was saying.

'"What?" I asked a few times. But the two of us only grew more distressed each time he repeated himself.'

Eventually, his sisters and Jenny turned around and, in one voice, said, 'His dodie is down the back of the couch and he wants you to get it.'

O'Callaghan stooped down behind the couch and retrieved the soother. But he was rattled.

'Ah, that hit me hard,' he accepts. 'The writing was on the wall then. I was near the end of my third season with Worcester, and Jake was only two and a half, he hadn't seen as much of me as I would have liked.

'I couldn't understand that simple request from him. It was the greatest kick in the stones I ever got in my life. Everyone else in the house could understand him but there I was, I felt like I didn't know my own little boy.

'Don't get me wrong, the life of a professional sportsperson is a selfish life, but I was sucking the marrow out of it at that stage. I always knew that I would have to make sacrifices for my sport, that's what you do and that's what actually fuels you. I have missed family holidays, friends' weddings, all of that but this was different. My young family was in its formative stage while I was away in another country.

'I decided that night that I had my run, it was brilliant but realised that I was nearly doing it for myself. The game was up.'

Initially, Jenny and the kids tried to stay put in England when he first signed for Worcester. The locals were friendly, but they never settled and decided to go back to Cork with O'Callaghan flying over and back as often as possible.

There is a deeper context to this. When he was just five, O'Callaghan lost his dad, Hughie. His mother, Marie, did a fantastic job in raising the family and his older brothers, who could all have achieved highly in the Leaving Cert and at college, selflessly left school to support the family, against the wishes of their mum who wanted them to continue their studies.

O'Callaghan's brothers became father figures and still are. He often thinks how he would give anything to spend even one day with his dad. He remembers hundreds of games down through the years when he has asked himself if his dad would have been proud of him.

Rugby took him places he could only have dreamed of, thrust him to the floor with some gut-wrenching lows and then lifted him with mind-blowing highs. It handed him a stellar career, close friendships, and a privileged existence in many ways. But, increasingly, the game was keeping him and his family apart. He thought of missing Hughie, thought of Jake wanting his dodie picked up. And of the dressing rooms he had recently shared with young men half his age, with whom he had nothing in common bar the pursuit of points.

Goodbye to all that.

* * *

In the end the age gap was proving awkward.

When he arrived at Worcester and met the players in the changing room he was introduced to Ted Hill – then a raw 17-year-old bursting with promise and now an English senior squad member. It took O'Callaghan some time to adjust to his new environment.

'Why wouldn't it?' he laughs. 'Ted's little sister was the same age as my daughter, Sophie!

'Actually, Ted's dad came in for lunch one day and we had a great chat altogether. He had served with the police service in the north of Ireland and had some unbelievable stories. But I could see Ted and he was almost like, "This is so embarrassing,"' O'Callaghan laughs.

'So, when I did make the call to retire, I guess that made the wrench to leave a lot easier – I was a different generation to most of the lads.

'Maybe I lost a little bit of something along the way myself because by the end of it I was probably asking people to do stuff I wasn't prepared to do myself and in sports circles you are not credible if that's the type of person you are.

'You live on reputation but it's all about your actions every day isn't it – not just what you did years back. I was lucky in that Worcester saw a leadership style in me although I wonder was it more that we were short a few leaders in the first place. Anyway they saw what I stood for and gave me that tag based on where I had come from.'

In July 2017, the Warriors announced that they had signed O'Callaghan's old friend, his former Munster and Irish teammate, Peter Stringer, on a six-month contract to cover Francois Hougaard while he was on international duty.

O'Callaghan didn't know whether to punch the air or breathe a sigh of relief when he heard the news. He thinks he may have done both.

'I was delighted, just absolutely thrilled,' he recalls. 'I was so sick of banging the drum every day, trying to point out small things to the rest, that I was actually starting to fall into trap of having standards drop myself. Small things like the ball being allowed hit the ground in training and no one going after it.

'Jesus, if that ever happened in Munster it was like a grenade had fallen and fellas were coming from everywhere, diving on the floor, to try and trap it before it landed, to try and kill it before it went off. Over there, though, a dropped ball was just another dropped ball.

'Until Stringer came in and it happened in front of him one day in a session. He went ape. "Kill that ball, kill that ball," he roared at them.

'I just smiled and said to myself, "Ah yes, someone else to pick up the slack for a while."'

It was a complete culture change at the start. Coming from a club where he had won two Heineken Cups, the expectation was that he would have to maybe compromise on certain standards when he travelled to England.

'It was anything but,' he says. 'They have the best of everything at Worcester – altitude training systems, cryotherapy chambers, Alter G (anti-gravity) treadmills. If our lads in Munster needed that we had to go to Naas or Santry to avail of those services.'

In Worcester they were all on site. A wellness test each morning, assessments on his core strength, hip mobility, sit and reaches, shoulder rotations, lactic acid tests via a prick of the finger, and then saliva tests to determine fatigue levels. In terms of being fit to play at the weekend there was no hiding place. On the day after games he would have to consume those 6,000 calories to restore levels again.

'To be fair at the start you embrace all of that and you are well up for it,' O'Callaghan reasons. 'But near the end maybe you realise that, even though you are an asset for the club, they are maybe looking for ways to leave you out [if the club didn't want to offer a new contract]. That applies to all rugby clubs. It's a ruthless game.'

That he always knew.

In 2015, he took the long-pondered decision to write himself out of his contract with Munster. A year before, O'Callaghan had become the province's most capped player when he made his 241st appearance against Zebre, going on to represent them on 268 occasions over 17 seasons. His time there was filled with heartbreak at first before great success ensued. In all he had a Celtic Cup in 2005, landed two Heineken Cups, in 2006 and 2008, then won Celtic League titles in 2003, 2009 and 2011 respectively.

By the time he made the call to leave he knew his game time was limited and still felt capable of performing to the highest standards. The fact that his old teammate, the late Anthony Foley, was head coach made it harder for everyone, but O'Callaghan respected the position the management was in when it came to his future.

'I was always questioning do I just walk away, or do I play elsewhere?' he remembers.

'Sure, look at my identity. I was a Munster man. I knew it, everyone knew it. But towards the end I also knew my game time would be limited. The last thing I wanted was to turn around and be resentful. I didn't want to dislike the place because I loved it too much.'

Again, there was no chance of a long goodbye.

'For me there had to be an absolute full stop so that's why I wrote myself out of a contract and joined Worcester. It was a dagger in the heart to leave but it was my call. I loved it so much there that I just knew I'd grow to be aggrieved at not playing and I'd hate not to love the place.'

The bonds he had spent years forming and locking tightly were, in some ways, broken instantly. In other ways there had been links formed that could never be broken.

One player O'Callaghan speaks highly of throughout is the former prop who told his story two chapters back, Marcus Horan. In many ways their relationship is indicative of what Munster was all about – blood brothers in many ways.

'We couldn't be tighter, Marcus and I,' he says. 'We even shared and split a contract when we came in first.'

'We joined at the same time and we split a €30,000 contract between us. €15,000 each. We halved it.'

Where did that idea come from?

'Deccy,' he says, smiling, 'That was typical Declan Kidney.'

'A great way of getting two eager young players on board,' he laughs. 'The following year I went to Deccy, explained how I had subbed in the 2000 Heineken Cup final and asked could I be brought up in terms of salary.'

Kidney looked him in the eye and in a flash responded, 'So, what do you want? For me to give you €20,000 and Marcus €10,000 – is that it?

O'Callaghan's face flushed. 'Jesus no. Sorry, Deccy.'

And that was it. End of conversation until O'Callaghan's status soared significantly soon after.

'Imagine having that scenario in the modern game,' O'Callaghan scoffs. 'Nowadays it would probably now be something like, 'Give Marcus €3,000 and €27,000 to me.

'But that is what makes a bond for life.'

Equally, though, within the environment, O'Callaghan and

his teammates learned to weed out colleagues who weren't up to the pressure. And there was no sympathy when glitches were discovered.

'I was the biggest driver of that,' he says, 'when they were gone, they were gone. My attitude was, "get them out of our bubble or they could harm the whole thing". That applied to myself as I left Munster. I worried I could become a distraction. I had been ruthless myself in that regard – "These lads are gone, fuck them off the bus. They are dead weight to us now."

'That was the attitude. I know it sounds awful but that's the competitive nature of what we grew up with, the environment we wanted. When my own time was up, I wanted to be thrown off the bus. I wanted no pity or anything to be softened just because I was leaving the club I loved.

'If a lad was training poorly, I nearly had to be the one who ran over him to get him out. We couldn't take the chance that an opponent wouldn't find the weak link in a huge game and that would be the end of us.

'Again, this just highlights the environment I operated in for so long. Is it any wonder I was so astonished when I saw that my wee was yellow after I finished up?'

* * *

Every so often he and Jenny take the kids out for an ice cream. He's hardly ever gone to the counter and not heard the refrain, 'Jaysus, don't you be eating too much of that now!'

The public still see him as a rugby player – even though he's two years out the gap.

'I can't blame them,' he says. 'Jenny and I sat down one

night lately to watch Netflix and she passed me popcorn and minstrels. I thought, "Wow, this is just unreal," as I dug into both. "Erm, it's just normal," Jenny replied, shaking her head quizzically.

'The bottom line is I will always be known as a rugby player,' he states, 'but if you came to me in 20 years and that's all I had to look back upon I would be very disappointed too. I'd hope to have a bit more going on.'

He already does. Aside from the other gigs already mentioned he is co-presenter of 2FM's *Game On* show, alongside Marie Crowe and Ruby Walsh, and has a role as a children's TV host for RTÉ too.

He blended back into Cork life with ease. No one bats an eyelid when they see him on the school runs.

'In Cork, rugby is a poor fourth behind hurling, football and soccer.

'If you have any sort of an ego or notions, they would be knocked out you quickly enough. When my late nan was alive, she was half-embarrassed over me playing rugby and didn't tell anyone,' he laughs. 'She reckoned if you didn't play hurling it wasn't worth talking about. I remember Wayne Sherlock, the former Cork hurler, was down at the local club one evening with the Liam MacCarthy Cup and Nan rang, asking if I wanted to go down and get a photo with him. I was like, "Eh, Nan I'm actually trying to get ready for a Heineken Cup final here?"'

Mention of his nan brings back the sacrifices he had to make for rugby.

When she passed away, he was in New Zealand getting ready to play Wales in the 2011 Rugby World Cup.

'There wasn't even a discussion – I wasn't coming back for the funeral. When my brother was getting married, I told him I would be there – provided I didn't make the tour down to New Zealand. I did make it and I missed the wedding. I'd say most of the time my family thought I was a bit of a bollox.

'As I say, the player was different to the person. And the sport I was in created a bit of a monster.'

He offers another example. O'Callaghan is as friendly as anyone you can meet, but he references a Lions tour from the past as an example of being clinical too.

'We had to go to one of these leaving dinners at the end of the tour and we were dreading it because you were supposed to talk to corporate people, sponsors, officials, whoever. We went in, formed a tight circle with our backs to everyone and stood in such a way that no one was getting through. If someone got picked off the circle was formed even tighter. It was ignorant enough when I think back on it but as players you didn't want to be talking to anyone outside the camp.

'Except Joe Worsely that is. Joe went in and we didn't see him for the evening. He came back to us at the end of the dinner with a stack of business cards. I roomed with him and he spent the rest of the night messaging the businesspeople he had just met. "Hi X, it was great to meet you today." "Hi Y, lovely to meet up. Stay in touch."

'"Joe why are you doing all that stuff?" I asked.

'He replied, "Well, I am going to do a testimonial at Wasps in two years and I am going to link in with these people and you never know when in life you might need their help either."

'Joe, and a lot of the English players, were way ahead of us in that regard and it often comes to the fore now in my mind.

'Getting that side of things sorted, having more time with my family, that's what I am focused on now.

'So much of you is tied up in what happened over the previous 20 years. That's who and what you once were, that's what people knew you for.

'It's up to me now to change the perception.'

10

VALUES SYSTEM

Donncha O'Callaghan didn't want a fuss around his retirement. He was ready for life after sport and had planned well for it. Long before his last game, he was thinking about possibilities that lay ahead. And he's largely thrived since.

His case supports Dr Stephen McIvor's belief that the nature of an athlete's retirement will effectively be determined by what effort they made in pursuits outside sport.

McIvor, who like Tony Og Regan, has competed at a high level and works as a sports psychologist, traces a lot of the difficulties that sportspeople face in retirement back to when they were kids.

He feels it's becoming increasingly difficult for a child who is good at sport to identify with anything else in their lives. He says knock-on effects linger even when they move on.

McIvor played professional rugby for Munster and Ireland, winning three senior international caps for his country during the 1990s, and laments the lack of balance in young people's lives.

'Take a young kid of 17. He or she is constantly asked, "How did you do at the weekend? Did you come first or second?"

'Turns out the kid won and can't wait to relay the news. All is good.

'What happens when they don't win, and the same question is asked?

'Think of having to reply with inner disappointment, perhaps devastation, a feeling of failure. In this case the answer certainly will not be positive because of the weight attached to the question.

'What creates that environment?' he asks. 'It's the expectation. The tone of the message. Facial signs. Throwaway remarks on social nights out. Hence there is no relaxation and kids are not allowing themselves to enjoy what they are doing.'

Down the line, McIvor reckons, that pressure tells.

'From the start it's always been about how many they scored. How many tries? How many first serves did they make? It seems nonsensical that people would be judged on that basis, but they have been all their lives. But we don't live in a sensible world anymore,' he shrugs.

This could help explain why so many are left high and dry when they leave their sport. They know nothing else.

'Essentially a lot of your post-sporting life depends on how much of your identity was wrapped up in that position you held,' McIvor suggests.

'Retirement is connected right back to any person's identity. How much they invested in their athletic life versus how much they invested into their social identity. Those are crucial aspects straight away.'

McIvor says that retiring can leave a multitude of layers to peel back, depending on whether they left through injury, deselection or of their own accord.

'No matter what, though, they need to have an outlet too. I look after elderly, I write books, I paint.'

'A purpose is massive,' he says. 'So too are structure and schedule. We are such a complex species that we feel the need to pigeonhole things – we'd be overcome if everything came at one time. So, we break things down and structure is massive.

'Human beings are also a community-based species. We need interactions. The best tool to have in retirement is the tool to communicate and be able to be comfortable in an environment, constantly integrating and mixing. If we are over-stressing about things that's another added thing we don't need to do.'

He also wonders why sports fans elevate athletes onto such lofty pedestals. And he offers the example of an Australian rugby player who is more deserving of such plaudits – for his actions away from sport, that is.

'We really put our sportspeople on a pedestal. Why? Because they run fast. Or that they can score goals?

'A fantastic quote from one of my few heroes in sport, Dave Pocock, always kept me grounded,' McIvor adds. He always says, "It's just a game of rugby."'

McIvor delves deeper into Pocock's background. He was born in Zimbabwe, grew up on a farm owned by his family, as a kid he hid under a bed one night when the house was raided, with a machete, trying to protect his sister. Eventually, the family fled the country during a period of heightened unrest owing to the Zimbabwean government's land redistribution campaign. They migrated to Brisbane, Australia, and Pocok went onto win 78 caps for the Wallabies. Outside of sport he had strong beliefs – he wouldn't marry his own partner until there was marriage equality in Australia, for example.

'Now there is a proper hero and role model,' the psychologist states. 'Look at the beliefs he had, in his own life, outside of sport. What is really important in life? He showed what is.

'We need to follow suit here in Ireland. Are you a nice person? Do you get on well with friends? If so, sport becomes less pressured. Life is simple until we come along and complicate it.'

Through daily contacts within his professional role, McIvor is increasingly concerned that some kids who focus heavily on sport carry stress all through their lives. 'Even though they are young, sport is really important and serious in their lives. That is not useful.

'We need parents to counterbalance that. How? By good parenting in terms in terms of putting emphasis on other things in their kids' lives – outside of sport.

'I see every day in my job that athletes doing swimming, playing rugby, GAA, or tennis, they are completely wrapped up in it. I can see the stress in their faces, and I tell them, "You're not a rugby player."

'But they look at me quizzically.

'So, I add, "You're someone who plays rugby and you have brilliant skills which let you smash it out of the park. But you are not a rugby player. It is just one of the things you do."'

He concedes it can take some time for that to sink in.

'There is a really fine line in terms of identity, but I would say that you can actually see these kids smile in front of you, and the load start to lighten on their young shoulders, when they eventually recognise that they are more than just a tennis or rugby player.

'Up until then, because they attribute so much of their character to the sport they play, things can become shaky if their form dips. That's when you have to have people around who see them as more than just an athlete. They need people who see them as a person first and foremost.

'Kids really need external factors in their lives, or they fall off a cliff otherwise. They need other parts in their lives. You will find that they carry less weight and baggage if that is the case because their whole identity is not linked to that next performance.'

McIvor feels that, when left alone, young sportspeople are conditioned to show the best of themselves.

'Nowadays there are two messages we are sending to kids. The first is that sport is serious. The second is that sport is important. Neither are true. It's not serious and it's not important. It's an escape from life.'

PART THREE

WHEN THE ROAR DIES DOWN

NO REGRETS.

Niall Quinn played his last game for the Republic of Ireland in their 2002 World Cup second round defeat to Spain at Suwon Stadium. "I found it very emotional at the end, but it's not anything I want to labour. Better players than me have been through that. You just take your leave. Walk away."

THE LONG ROAD BACK.

Former Irish Premier League footballer, Paul McGee with Nottingham Forest's Gary Charles in 1991. Injury destroyed his dreams and a harrowing time ensued before McGee found a way back. "I was looking at myself in the mirror," he recalls. "I didn't look well. I wasn't there. It wasn't me. Something took over me."

HIS OWN MAN. Shane Supple, playing here for Bohemians in the SSE Airtricity League, quit professional football at just 19. It took a move back to Ireland to rekindle the flame. "I will miss Friday nights in Dalymount," he says. "The atmosphere, flares, banners and Johnny Logan's 'Hold Me Now'. Nothing will replace that."

BUSIER THAN EVER. Former Ireland striker Kevin Doyle retired after two concussions in 2017. He now breeds horses. "You see players really struggling," he says. "I've been so lucky to come home and I'm not in England in a house, sitting there twiddling my thumbs."

SECOND LIFE.

Ex-Ireland prop Marcus Horan is currently player development manager for Munster, preparing athletes for retirement. "As a player, every weekend you had a purpose," he reflects. "And when you stop playing, you're nearly trying to recreate that. You've got to try to get your excitement from somewhere else."

END GAME?

Just the beginning, actually. In March 2009, Tommy Bowe scored a try and later celebrated with the RBS Six Nations trophy after Ireland beat Wales in Cardiff. In retirement, Bowe has excelled in the fashion, business and broadcast worlds. "My time was up," he says. "And I think I was quite content in knowing that."

HOGAN'S STAND. Former Irish lock Trevor Hogan achieved much in his career before injury intervened. "I spent a lot of that time reflecting on everything and, gradually, I started to come to terms with it."

MAXED OUT. Donncha O'Callaghan quickly developed a successful media career with RTÉ and Eir Sport after he retired in 2018.

REDISCOVERING LOVE OF THE GAME.

Gary Murphy endured a variety of emotions trying to keep his pro tour card. "Golf takes us on an emotional rollercoaster from start to finish," he says. "It's the delusion that brings us back out every time."

HIGH ACHIEVER.

Dublin's Paul Flynn retired having won everything Gaelic football had to offer. Off the field he blazed a trail as well, becoming CEO of the Gaelic Players Association. "I have memories that I will cherish forever. I move on now with gratitude to the next chapter of my life."

© Cody Glenn/SPORTSFILE

Darren O'Neill, representing Paulstown Boxing Club, Kilkenny, celebrates his win over Ken Okungbowa, Athlone Boxing Club, in their 2015 bout at the nationals in Dublin. After calling time on his distinguished amateur career, O'Neill is still harbouring hopes of a professional bout. "That boxer's itch is still there," he says. "It's as simple as that."

© Matt Browne/SPORTSFILE

GENIUS LIVES ON. In late December 2004, a delighted Paul Carberry celebrated with trainer Michael Hourigan, left, and Kay Hourigan after winning the Lexus Steeplechase. "In 2016, I saw my surgeon who advised me to stop. I was gutted." But Carberry's legend lives on . . .

© Paul Mohan/SPORTSFILE

TIME'S A HEALER.

Nikki Symmons, seen here in one of her 208 appearances for the Irish senior women's hockey team, struggled with retirement initially. "The goal was always to qualify for the Olympic Games. I dedicated my career to achieving this goal but, unfortunately, we didn't quite make it. I would never give any of the years back, I enjoyed every moment and did it really for the love of the game."

© Brian Lawless/SPORTSFILE

ROLE MODEL.

Wexford's Gráinne Murphy took silver in the Women's European 1,500 metres freestyle event in 2010. Murphy was one of the brightest stars in the sport at international level until injury and illness forced her to retire at just 22. She handled every setback with as much dignity and class as she did her successes. "I have had many amazing memories and experiences during my years as a high-performance swimmer and I will treasure them for the rest of my life," she states.

© Brendan Moran/SPORTSFILE

IRELAND'S GREATEST.
Sonia O'Sullivan, crossing the finishing line to claim the silver medal in the Women's 5,000 metres Olympic final at Sydney 2000, is one of Ireland's greatest athletes. Little wonder the idea of not competing at the top level didn't sit easy with her for quite some time. "I was never really comfortable with the idea of retirement, so to slow down and put things in another life perspective has never been easy."

© Dan Sheridan/INPHO

NOT YET OUT. Lindsay Peat is the most versatile of athletes with an All-Ireland medal with the Dublin footballers. She also captained DCU Mercy to National Cup and Super League wins and co-captained Ireland's basketball team. Peat played for the Republic of Ireland U18s footballers and won Irish Women's Rugby Player of the Year in 2017. "There were a lot of stumbling blocks and proving people wrong, including myself."

11

GARY MURPHY

Gary the Golfer

BORN: Kilkenny, 1972.
Won the Irish Amateur Closed Championship in 1992 and turned professional three years later. Won the Asian Tour School in the Philippines in 1997 and played in Asia for two winters, keeping his card each time. On the European Tour from 2005.
Stepped away from top-level golf in 2011, aged 39.

He watched it all vanish in the burning sunlight.

The tour card, a professional career, and with it, his hopes for the future. It was mid-October 2011 in the southern coast of Portugal when it all came to a head for Gary Murphy as he made his way from the golf course and headed for his apartment nearby.

The Portugal Masters was in town and Murphy needed to take centre stage there, get near a podium and hope for an encore in the coming weeks to sustain his career.

Overhead, as he left the course, the outline of a darkening sky seemed to draw clouds of wind, and as evening pressed ahead the sun slowly became more obscured. There was a hint of winter in the air, but Murphy noticed very little of his surroundings as he walked towards the digs he shared with his caddy, Bo Martin, fellow Irish pro Damien McGrane, and a few others.

He had turned 39 that day, though his mood was anything but celebratory. Back in the apartment none of his friends needed a degree to cop that. 'I just said that I would pick up a few things down in Villamoura – we had agreed to eat in the apartment and maybe have a glass of wine, but that would be it,' Murphy recalls.

'Villamoura was only three miles away,' he adds, taking up the story. 'There is a dual carriage roadway that takes you down there. I wasn't long on the road when I saw a lad walking. A pure Paddy. Legs like toothpaste, the suncream stinging his eyes out and the head burned off him,' he laughs.

Murphy took pity on him sweltering in the scorching heat, pulled over and enquired if he wanted a lift. In hopped Paddy and they made their way down to the port. The chat was gentle and before long Paddy pressed him to see how his day was going.

'How are you doing yourself?' he asked, grateful for the lift.

'Not great to be perfectly honest with you,' Murphy replied. 'I've had a fairly shit day.'

'Well, it could be worse,' Paddy quipped. 'You could be Gary Murphy – he shot 82 today!'

All Murphy could do was smile.

* * *

Unofficially, the 2011 Portugal Masters in October signalled the end of his battling professional life. Over the course of the next 12 months he did gamely plough on, availing of sponsors invites here and there, looking to find some sort of flint to draw a spark from. He tried both the Asian and Challenge tours but couldn't find any fuse to light there either.

Murphy looks back now and reckons all he did was torment himself by prolonging matters.

It hadn't always been like this. Across a decade and a half on tour he had amassed almost €2.2 million in career earnings, a considerable amount. During a spell in the noughties there was a period when he would bring home between €300,000 and €400,000 for a season's pay. But that was an all-too-brief juncture and, with the associated costs of life on tour, nowhere near substantial enough to secure his family's long-term future.

As time passed and the stakes increased, Murphy went in search of that magic ingredient that might guarantee security for the years ahead. He joined masses of golf pros in the hunt for the same mystery component. Every book he looked up, every variable he tried, seemed to point him in different directions. Try this club. Try this technique. What about this coach?

As he joined the flock, he discarded the natural flair and style that had put him on the map in favour of a more mechanical, manipulated approach. His contemporaries were all going down that route, so it had to be the way forward, right?

One size does not fit all, however. Murphy was something of a maverick and recognises now that he made the wrong choice by opting to follow ground that others had broken. He would have been better served staying within his own terrain and trying to better cultivate it.

As he abandoned his instinctive style, it wasn't long before warning signs flashed alarmingly. In 2010 his earnings dropped to under €20,000. He played in 27 European Tour events that season, missed 20 cuts and picked up just €19,152 to finish 227th on the money list. His biggest cheque that year was €5,800 for tying in 43rd place at the South Africa Open.

He's not sure if he earned anything at all in 2011. By the time the Portugal Masters swung around he knew he was in golf's torture chamber, inflicting most of the pain himself.

'I had received an invite to that particular tournament from Oceanico, who had been sponsors of mine,' he recalls. 'The deal I had with them suffered when the economic crash hit home and, though I was tied in a contract with them for five years, I didn't get to see it through because the property scene went tits up, and my arrangement with them was affected.

'They owed me a bit of a favour and, as I had no full status on tour by 2011, I needed an invite to try to finish top two or three to get my card. They got me on the roster and I immediately contacted the former Ryder Cup golfer, Des Smyth, to see if his son, Greg, would come and caddy for me. Greg had just won €9.4 million in the lotto and had gone public on his win. No joking, I asked him to come down to Portugal to carry the bag so he might bring me a bit of a luck.'

Greg's lucky charm seemed to have an instant impact. Murphy shot a first round of 67 and his second round was decent. As Saturday loomed, he approached his 39th birthday with something that resembled enthusiasm. It had been so long absent from his mindset that he wasn't sure what it was. It was a beautiful feeling to have that eagerness back.

'As a resort golf course, it was pretty easy, and I was going well,' he says. 'But on the third day I hit 82. Horrendous. That was curtains then. I went to dinner with Thomas Bjorn, who I was friendly with, and he asked what the plan was for the future. There was no mention of continuing to play golf. We both knew I was done.'

The conversation fleshed out different options but deep down the finality and, stigma, even, of retirement scared him.

So, while he unofficially quit that night, he allowed a wild eye to wander east and coerced himself to play two events on the Asian Tour some weeks later, to hopefully pre-qualify for mainstream European tournaments in 2012.

Taking up the story, however, he tells how fate had different ideas. 'My wife, Elaine, was pregnant with our second child Daniel, who was due at the end of December and Elaine had a tough pregnancy. Late on she was confined to bed rest for six weeks and it meant I couldn't go to Asia to play those events.

'That also meant I wasn't going back to tour school.'

Now was the time for a complete stock take.

'My full European card been gone since 2010, I was playing rubbish on the invited slots I did receive and, when I dropped back to the Challenge Tour, I played rubbish on that too. I had no status anywhere,' he says.

'I had been bleeding money for about two years at that stage. On top of that I lost heavily with some investments. A perfect shitstorm.'

Yet, an eternal optimist, when he looked into the darkness, he could still make out dim light quivering, fighting the gloom. That was his mental resilience; an unshakeable sunniness that one lucky roll could yet deliver. One decent tournament and he'd be back with the big boys.

In March 2012, that flicker radiated when David Williams, tournament director with the European Tour, called Murphy as he dropped his eldest child, daughter Hollie, to school one morning.

'Do you fancy a knock this week, Murph?' Williams wondered.

Murphy assumed Williams was in Portmarnock and wanted to play a few holes with him there as part of a recce for the Irish Open to be held a few weeks later.

'No problem, David,' he replied. 'Give me an hour.'

But Williams was in Italy, preparing for the Sicilian Open and they were a man short. He rang Elaine. They decided there was little more to lose.

Worst-case scenario, he would get a week in the sun which might help brighten his days, lift his mood.

'I didn't get there till Tuesday night meaning I couldn't play a practice round,' Murphy remembers. 'And there was no Pro-Am, so I just walked the course and got a local caddy.'

Two rounds later, as he stood on the 36th tee, it seemed as if that roll of the dice was finally going to land on a six. He tore it up, stood just four shots off the lead. If only he could make the cut it would be a massive boost to his earnings and potentially re-establish his status on tour.

As he came near the end of his round, he noticed the *Irish Examiner* golf correspondent Charlie Mulqueen looking on. Knowing of Murphy's predicament, the journalist boasted the incomparable beauty of a smile of pride as he almost willed the Irish golfer home. Mulqueen had been following Murphy's career for years, and was good friends with his father, Jim.

'I would say making that cut was going to mean as much to Charlie as it was to me,' Murphy insists. 'And I was looking forward to being able to give him some positive copy for a change.'

But dreams can turn savage in a flash. With pressure steadily setting in, and so much on the line, Murphy chose a six-iron into the 18th green only to suffer the yips at the end of his backswing.

'Pure fear,' he admits. 'The head had gone.'

He ended with a double bogey at the last and waited in dismay as the remaining golfers on the course lit it up. He missed the cut by just one shot. It was just the latest in the litany of hits that rained down.

'It was the lowest cut ever in the history of the European Tour,' he smiles wryly. 'Only five shots between the lead and those who missed the cut.

'I was six shots off.

'I decided finally that day I genuinely just couldn't hack any more. It was absolute trauma dealing with it all. I was well done then.'

One chapter was most definitely at an end. But the magnitude of retirement was still to hit home.

* * *

Murphy is asked how he coped in the early stages of retirement and he laughs.

'Red wine.'

'Go on?'

'Well, I didn't cope, really. It was car crash stuff. I knew nothing – only golf. That's still the case.'

The explosive fury of the small ball whooshing off the tee first captivated him at ten years old when he caddied for his father, JD Murphy, or Jim as he was better known. Jim was a friendly face to all, a respected golf coach and a great sports enthusiast. Gary, his only son, was a serious soccer player too and at one stage his coaches penned him down as the top prospect in Kilkenny. He was good enough to be called for Irish under-13 and under-15 soccer trials, but later lost interest in the game.

Golf had turned his head at this stage. For one thing, it allowed him to be around his dad a lot more and he also had a gift for the game.

At 16, he played a big soccer match on the day before a regional golf event and mid-game he found himself racing into a 50-50 tackle. Normally, this was where he would excel. Throw himself in, dig the ball out, pass and go again.

But he checked back just as he was set to make contact.

'In case I'd hurt myself and would miss the golf the next day,' he smiles ruefully. 'I knew then it was curtains for soccer.'

From there he shifted his entire emphasis to golf and just 12 months later he became a scratch golfer. As they watched him sweetly caress the ball around the courses of Ireland, those on the circuit exalted his natural ability. He played on instinct, made the game look effortless at times and looked primed for the amateur circuit. But could he dedicate himself to going professional?

Murphy had no hesitation on that score. He won the Irish Amateur Closed Championship in 1992, spent the next three years refining his game, and turned professional three years later. He won the Asian Tour School in the Philippines in 1997 and his card from the European Tour Qualifying School at the fifth attempt in 1999. He had achieved his goal – he was a sports professional.

'I guess I was so busy in the moment that I never took time out to appreciate the enormity of even getting that far,' he says softly. 'I had met Elaine as a kid – she grew up in golf circles too and we always got on well. Ten years later we met again and started going out. It was only when I was driving back from her place in Louth one evening, going back to Kilkenny, that I pulled in off the road and cried at the enormity of it. I guess I was just proud that I had made it onto the European Tour. It was a big landmark and that evening in the car, I think, was an acknowledgement of an achievement.'

Like so many others, the rookie wrestled hard with the pro game and it overthrew him more than once. He debuted in 2000 but dropped back to the Challenge Tour for two seasons before winning his card at the 2002 Qualifying School.

He took fourth place in the 2003 Barclays Scottish Open and netted €159,870. That 2003 season was his best on tour; he took home €386,420.

His form was sturdy over the next few seasons and, in 2008, he earned €301,792.

But in that same season the first serious challenge to his mental resilience manifested itself. When it arrived, it was wrapped up in a deceptive layer of anticipation – the promise of a tour win. But as Murphy peeled off its coating, all that unravelled was an agonising near-miss.

He wonders if he ever did recover from it.

'It was the Irish Open at Adare and I recorded my best Tour finish of the campaign, finishing in a tie for third,' he says.

'But coming into the last green I was in the shake-up for the tournament and had a seven-foot putt to sink on the 18th,' he states, just as clearly as it was yesterday. 'To my mind, that putt was to win the Irish Open. And I nailed it. I sat back with massive pride that I had held my bottle. I was almost convinced I would win. Home soil, a priceless win on tour meaning exemption status. Jesus, it would have been huge. People were coming up to me in the clubhouse almost celebrating but instead I watched Richard Finch from England nail a series of birdies coming down the home straight to win.

'I don't know if I ever did recover from that disappointment.'

He certainly endured a tough 18 months from there. 'Winning an event would have given me a two-year exemption towards retaining my tour card,' he muses. 'Can you imagine the pressure that would relieve? The security it would give you! I had to deal with the consequences of missing that. I was back walking a tightrope from week to week. I had been taking in around €300,000 per year but there were always bills at home and on tour no matter what I earned.'

Having come so close to lifting silverware and enjoying the spoils that go with it, Murphy went gung-ho in pursuit of a safety blanket to wrap around himself and his young family.

'In 2009 I spent 37 weeks straight on the road. My form was slipping, and I probably should have taken a couple of weeks out, but you always tell yourself to play on – that this next event could be the one to win and ease all the worries. It never was. My form dipped.'

Amber lights flashed on the dashboard each time he went to turn the key. He lost his tour card in Australia, came back to Ireland and took one week to gather his thoughts before he went off to Tour School again to recapture his European card.

After that, he headed to South Africa for two tournaments before Christmas. Murphy just freewheeled through the festivities. His mind was still on tour. He had seven days at home with his family before he was gone again.

'I didn't even think twice about it,' he admits. 'I was in that totally selfish bubble. "Don't tell me I'm not going because I am." That was my mantra.'

Mentally, he was shattered. He laboured early in the 2010 season and never shook the malaise that clouded him. His graph went totally downwards.

'The big crux of the whole thing was the financial aspect,' he maintains. 'It was catch-22. I was trying to get out there and make enough to provide for my family for the future. But near the end I was losing around €100,000 a year. On tour, no matter how you fared, you spend €3,500 a week paying caddies, flights, accommodation, the works. I would miss four cuts in a month, and I'd be down €12,000. On top of that you had to cover what it cost for the family to live back home.

'I was still willing to keep at it. That's the selfish side. It was what I loved to do. Yet, I knew that once I went off the Challenge tour, the next route was the third tier and there is no money in it. I had nowhere to go and even if I had, my game was shot to pieces.'

By this stage his son Daniel had just arrived, while Hollie was five and a half.

'I knew it was time to get off the road,' he admits. 'Still, I was panicking. I had basically tried to be sensible when I was making decent money. I had a reasonable enough loan to cover the property I invested in and at one stage my properties were worth three times what I owed. Add that to the decent money I was making on tour and I was "quids-in".

'But I went from €350,000 a year to earning €20,000, to then earning nothing in a short space of time. You have a certain lifestyle, but when you see your game going, house prices halving and your investments going through the floor, though, you know that's fucked.

'I found it next to impossible to walk onto that first tee and brush it all under the carpet. You just can't do it. Here's the stupid thing – as a kid I never played golf for money. I just loved the feel of a club, the smell of my mother's golf clubs, the grass, the gloves. But now here I was totally consumed with the money side of it. Obsessed. It dominated every minute of every day. It turned the game into a completely different sport for me. When I was playing into a flag, the hole on the green would get smaller than a mouse's ear.

'I knew deep down I needed to take weeks off to get back and "decompress", as G Mac (Graeme McDowell) would say, but when you do that you feel closer to the fire than further away from it.

'I was in the mode of being a selfish prick. I am just lucky that my wife grew up around golf, understood the game and all that goes with it. She was a great support structure for me. She tolerated that for so long.'

Near the end, however, following that competition in Sicily, Elaine looked at her husband as he weighed up one last shot at the dream.

'Really, are you actually going to keep doing this to yourself?' she asked.

'Elaine was right to call me on it,' Murphy recounts. 'I was bursting my own brain.'

* * *

Now eight years retired, Murphy hasn't yet come around to feeling pride at the measures he took to sustain his professional status and provide for his family's future. He shoots a look, almost of disdain, at the mere suggestion that he would.

But in time he will surely reflect with great warmth how he tried everything to stay with the game; the only thing he knew.

When he lost his ticket to play with the big boys on the European Tour, rather than rest on his laurels, he instead looked to the Far East to resurrect his playing career on the OneAsia Tour. There is honour in such valour.

It was a far cry from the European top table, but it was a punt in the hope that one win there would change everything. This came on top of seeking new coaches and methods and forgoing his unpretentious style for a more technical conformity that had gripped the game.

'I can't bring myself to feel proud of anything really, but I can honestly say I tried my heart out just waiting for something to click. Through it all I felt I had to keep playing. When that was eventually taken away from me, I just didn't know what to do.'

Off tour he tried to keep up appearances. He'd drop Hollie to school for 9.30 a.m. and try to keep busy after that. He started running four times a week; sticking on the iPod and hitting the road. It helped maintain stress levels.

But there were huge structural changes to make to his lifestyle, his home and his marriage, as he echoes.

'Elaine was used to me being away most of the year. And suddenly I was under her feet all day every day. That didn't help. Our marriage came under pressure because of that. I remember trying to help around the house one day, just doing a bit of hoovering, and she gave out to me for helping. It sounds mad but I could see it from her point of view – sure she had her own system and was used to me being away doing my own thing.

'The hardest thing was maintaining things with Elaine.

Imagine being away all the time and then being at home all the time. And being like a bear with the worry.

'The rate of divorce is massive among professional sport-speople and it would have been easy just to be another statistic in that regard. But while I'm not religious, I do think when you get married and have kids you have responsibility to them. You have to work at things.'

Retirement brought further challenges. His sponsors TaylorMade, Doonbeg and Kartel hung around for a while but soon there was nothing coming in. His self-esteem was shot to bits.

'I was always Gary the golfer,' he said. 'That's what I was known as. But after Sicily, I knew I was done. I pulled away completely. I didn't even wear golf clothes for three to four months and, for anyone who knew me, that was unusual because I had grown up wearing golf gear. I'd never have jeans on or anything like that. It was always golf clothes. I was no other person and would not pretend to be.

'I just didn't feel a like golfer, and I couldn't put those clothes on because it just was not me anymore. This whole thing of stopping playing, emotionally and physically, it was like falling off a cliff. I was 39 I didn't have another plan because I didn't think I'd ever need one.

'So, there was a triple whammy. Career gone, investments shot, and loans still outstanding as the economy floundered. Around that time, 2012 and 2013, I had no real nixers or gigs to turn to either. There wasn't much on.'

Two of his friends, Brian Quinn and Dwyer McAuley, were also big into golf and were involved with the Irish television station, Setanta. They asked Murphy to hold six fireside chats with Irish professional golfers. The series would, ironically, be called *The Cut Line*.

He embraced that series, enjoyed it, and took on a few other bits of media work. Around the time he was due to meet Padraig Harrington for their by-the-fire interview, his dad suffered a triple tear to his aorta valve and was admitted to intensive care at James' Hospital for two and a half months. While Jim initially recovered from that blow his strength was never the same again and the next couple of years were worrying for the family.

Murphy is asked what other support channels existed to help him and he ponders the question quite quizzically.

'None,' he replies.

Did the other Irish pros help out?

'Padraig Harrington got me a spot in Singapore out of the blue one time when I really needed it. Listen, we all got on well, the Irish lads, we were close enough, but they all had their own stuff going on too. It is a very individual sport. That's universal on tour, lads have all sorts of stuff to be dealing with.

'One or two of the lads maybe kept in touch with me for my first year away from tour to see how I was going but, look, after that nobody really cares.

'It's professional sport and, as I say, everyone is busy doing their own shit.

'In many ways, on that circuit, while we all got on really well, you are only friendly with these guys because you all have something in common with each other at that moment in time.

'In lots of cases there is no real substance to any of it, or many real and lasting relationships to come out of it – that's the hard part. People who say there are, in my opinion, are faking it 100 per cent. Now I'm not talking about camaraderie, or

Irishness, or maintaining that lads wouldn't help you out while on tour – of course lots of lads would be there for each other. I guess I'm talking genuine friendships. Lasting ones.

'And that's the hard part. All these people that you were so friendly with, and soldiered with, suddenly they were gone out of your life. Like I said, I fell off a cliff.'

Murphy knew he had to make things happen for his family all over again and so he circulated DVDs of *The Cut Line* series to other TV producers hoping to get some commentary work. It was a slow burner, but it worked. Eight years on, his reputation as a sharp and insightful analyst is still growing.

'Shortly after retiring I did some studio stuff with Sky and did commentary for the 2013 Irish Open and it went okay.

'I did a few more in 2014 and a few more again in 2015. That's been a huge help because, as I say, I had no plans.

'Was I going to get a real job? I'm not qualified do anything. And I wanted to stay in sport. To supplement things, I started doing bit of coaching and I enjoyed that. I started a newspaper column with the *Irish Daily Mirror* and got work as an analyst with the 2FM *Game On* show which kept me in touch with things.'

He began to teach at two different courses and enjoys helping young professionals who, he reckons, make all the same mistakes he did.

'I only know those mistakes because I made them as well,' he points out.

'I tried the management space too, but I actually found it to be very corrupt, a bit like football with the various agents knocking around. I picked up a few brand ambassador roles too, so the variety of my life is wide now, but, like being on tour every year, you are only ever a short space away from having to win your card back each winter. That's the glory of being self-employed. Huge diversity but no security.'

These days he's on the road 12 weeks a year with his commentary work. He'd happily step that up to 15 weeks but wants no more than that because of what he'd miss out on with his family. That's a far cry from the 37 unbroken weeks he spent on the road in the midst of his playing woes.

He won't scream it from the rooftops because he is still dealing with the trauma of a broken career, but eight years on Murphy is in a better place, though there is still an aftershock of retirement to cope with.

'No weight was ever lifted off my shoulders when I retired and it probably will never be fully lifted,' he concedes.

'Playing sport, you always naturally feel that you should do better, and the truth is that I never really had the career I wanted to have. I never really got to dance with the best-looking girl in the hall.

'But I have learned to compartmentalise, and time is a big healer. It has really helped being involved in commentaries and tournaments in other roles. Had I just cut everything and stopped going to events, it would have been even worse.

'At least by being there and watching golf live you can still smell the place and get a feel for it. It makes you forget that your own career was just pushed aside.

'I guess looking ahead I would love to deal with more younger professionals and mentor them. The truth is that everyone has issues and, with the exception of Padraig Harrington, very few players are able to move through the tour unscathed.'

How come Harrington is the exception?

'It's brilliant and it's astonishing,' Murphy smiles. 'Padraig is still so oblivious to any possible downside of his golf game. Even at the moment, when out on the course he's nothing like the player he was. Yet, I see him on the range and he's actually as good as ever he was. The form is not transferring from the practice range to the course and that would destroy me. But Padraig is as happy as Larry. He sees no downside. Now, in fairness, he does have a licence to be carefree in that he is exempt from having to qualify for a lot of events, he's a legend of the game, and he can tee up anywhere he wants. There is comfort and almost security in that and Padraig has that for life.

'He's earned it all. He's developed a psyche allowing him to just walk through fires and never get burned. I admire him. Watch the way he plays some days. He will come in after a poor round but will never articulate real disappointment. Instead he has this curiosity to get better. He could win a Champions event at 54 and say that he has just found the secret. That's an amazing place to be.

'For most players, trying to find the secret destroys them. It ruined me. But Padraig is happy to get worse in order to get better, he seems to have that wonderful relationship with himself which helps greatly.'

Slowly, Murphy is also getting back to better terms with himself. He is genuine and warm, and people know that.

In January 2013, Murphy's dad and chief confidant passed away. He was only 68 and Murphy's mam Ann and his siblings Jean, Hilary and Orla were left to plough on.

Gradually, though, there has been a shifting of the dark clouds, an end to the blanket of darkness that shrouded his life.

He jokes that nowadays he can almost enjoy a round of golf again even if he plays poorly.

'That's a major departure because for five years going out to play a friendly fourball with my pals destroyed me,' he adds.

'Down through the years the lads had never taken money off me, although they are more than at that level now. But it took so much out of me to be playing bad social golf. My whole mantra was always: "Watch me do this."

'I would pick up a club, express myself and show off with a trick shot or something – golf was something I was good at but during the worst times I couldn't even do that because I was playing so bad. I remember coming in from a round with the lads and thinking, "I can't do this anymore." It was absolutely heartbreaking.'

It's still hard to believe there was no one to talk to about all of that?

'I tried a few therapists here and there,' he states.

And?

'Look, there was no one to help, really. Think about it – Elaine was too emotionally involved and deep down nobody really understands the pain bar yourself. You are a busted flush. You are on your jack.

'Dad was a rock for me, a great supporter of mine, but he was gone.'

Jim would have been proud, though? Even if you weren't.

'Hopefully.

'Maybe I can help others now. Shane (Lowry) says he got the best golf advice he ever got from me and it was simple – I just told him to go and enjoy it.

'Even though I tried to enjoy myself I don't think I did.

'I would say to young fellas now to go and find out about the history of game, embrace yourself in the spirit and history of golf. That's something I'm going to do now – use the rest of my days as a curiosity. See what worked for people and what didn't.

'The whole golf industry is set up as a marketing exercise, all about the sale of equipment and merchandise. I fell into that bubble, off chasing new clubs trying to find form, it was all nonsense. At the end of the day golf is an art form. You are in the business of trying to beat yourself every day – that's essentially what it is. Keep it simple. I'm not saying go out and smoke a load of dope and laugh every day. But I would stress not to get hung up. Golf should just be a journey that lasts forever.'

Not complicating things is a cornerstone of his life these days.

'The main thing now is that I really enjoy seeing the kids grow up,' he says. 'I have some class days with my kids. I'd rather earn €70,000 a year and be there home the whole time than earn €200,000 and be on the road 50 weeks a year.

'I like going to Daniel's training and Hollie's Gaelic matches. My kids and Elaine are the most important people – they helped me – and watching them grow up is the number one thing now.

'As stressful as things have been, I am still eternally an optimist. To play sport for a living you have to be. I still have that mindset "maybe next week".

'While things were shite, we still got by. When you are not on tour you don't need much to get by. Once there is a roof overhead and food on table everything is grand.

'To the kids – you a hero to them. Saying that sounds mad because for the first few years after my retirement there were stages when I didn't want to live anymore. I could easily have killed myself.

'Easily.

'I don't say that lightly but a couple of times I reached a fork in road. And I could have gone down a wrong path. I didn't but it wasn't easy.'

Were he to do it all over again he says he would try to give himself a lot more credit.

'Feck coaches and agents, I would just go out and play,' he maintains. 'I spent so much time trying to conform to type rather than being myself when, in fact, the individuals are the ones who sustain the longest.

'The average lifespan on tour is 3.2 years, can you believe that? It's mental. So, I was actually above the norm and I had to go back nine times and fight for my card – I know some day I will take solace in that. Looking back, I played 400 tournaments on the main European tour and other events. That's just 400 weeks, only eight years of your life. I can see now, finally, that eight years is nothing.

'There is a lot of living to be done. It's taken me while to realise that.

'The only person I would take on if I was going again would be a mentor. You need someone that can see the wood for the trees – but this time I would listen to them. So many of us hear but we don't listen.

'I would trust myself. I had that natural ability at golf, but I went chasing something else. That's how daft the golf world is. It feeds insecurity. But when you are in the business of failing all the time, you finally succumb to it. Take Tiger Woods, the greatest of all time. Brilliant as he is, he has only won 22 per cent of the time on tour. Ben Hogan was 21.7. They have both won one in five. It's taken me years to figure it out, but this is golf in a nutshell – you are losing all the time.'

Murphy is finally ready to move into the next space.

Nothing will ever replace playing but he has other strings to his bow. Would there be a better mentor out there for young professionals? His insight as an analyst continues to be well received by golf spectators.

'Well, I'm finally now starting to call myself a commentator,' he smiles.

'I've been trying to shed a skin really. And it's taken about eight years to do it.'

12

PAUL FLYNN

Breaking Away

BORN: Dublin, 1986.
25th on the all-time Dublin scoring list with 13-89 from
122 appearances, winning 6 All-Ireland titles and 4 All Stars.
Stepped away from top-level GAA in 2019, aged 32.

Leaving the Dublin senior football WhatsApp group. That was the toughest part.

For all the boxes that Paul Flynn ticked on the road to announcing his retirement from inter-county football, he never figured leaving a messaging app would be the most difficult task of all. But so it proved.

It was the end of May 2019 when he sat down to thumb out a farewell text; his last contribution to a platform that he had interacted with for years. He kept it simple; thanked his teammates for all they had done for him, relayed how it was an honour to have gone to battle with them, informed them he was retiring.

And then he left the group.

'It hits you immediately,' he says, shaking his head.

'I had gone through all the hurdles. Chatted with my wife, Fiona (Dublin Ladies footballer, Fiona Hudson), spoke to my family. Sat down with Jim Gavin, and all this after weeks of assessing whether my body could stay going. I put together a few words for the press release, told a few others, and I was able to manage it all well enough.'

But when it came for the grey tick appearing to say his message had landed, and pressing on the icon 'leave group', Flynn's eyes started welling up.

'It was the one time my heart sank during the whole thing', he admits. 'It made me wonder what I had done. That's a funny dynamic isn't it?' he asks as he looks into the distance. 'In this day and age? To get upset over leaving a text group?'

Yet, upon speaking to others who had recently departed from the front line, Flynn discovered they felt exactly the same.

'Seems it was tricky for a lot of us. That was probably more to do with losing an affinity or connection with a group than missing the banter or anything. Knowing I wouldn't be part of it again.'

There is something almost brutal about the bluntness of it.

'There surely is,' Flynn concurs. 'Michael Darragh Macauley actually made the point that the team WhatsApp should rotate every year. It would make the process of retiring, being dropped, or having to leave the group a bit easier because from year to year guys would turnover anyway. Reviewing it in December might bring a bit more detachment to the whole thing.'

As delicate as Flynn was, he wasn't spared by those who had gone before him.

Just two hours after he quit the team's WhatsApp, he received a notification of being added to another gang.

You have just been added to the Dublin Rejects group.

Flynn laughs heartily.

He thinks it was Eamon Fennell who hauled him in alongside the old hands, transporting him from perhaps the most sought-after social media medium in the city into a virtual retirement home for grizzled old warriors.

'*Dublin Rejects* exposed me to a whole new facet of the market altogether,' he adds, still laughing. 'Almost straight-away you were back in touch with so many you had soldiered with. We were all back together again. And it definitely helped me.'

As a footballer, Flynn made an impression in so many big games and won countless trophies, but those are not necessarily the highlights he replays in his mind. Instead the endeavour and preparation for battle is what he laments most.

'I knew that if you wanted to play a game of football the most important aspect was your preparation,' he states.

'Gary Keegan always maintains that preparation is nine-tenths of performance law and he is right. I lived by that creed. Once I knew I'd ticked all the boxes going into a game it was just a case of producing that last tenth on matchday. With the work done I could nearly go out, perform, and actually enjoy playing.

'I think it's the same with retirement. If you can prepare for your transition after playing, then the changeover should be lot easier. People who don't do that, either through having no choice by being dropped out of the blue, or by being ignorant to the challenges of not playing anymore, they are the ones who struggle more when they finish.

'In that way I like to think I prepared well for retirement. It didn't make it an easier to leave a stage like being a Dublin footballer, it's just I was able to cope that bit better.'

Flynn, more than most, worked exceptionally hard to ensure that it would be the case.

* * *

In 35 championship outings with Dublin, he scored 3-33. He was quite often the hardest toiler on the team too, regularly clocking up distances of 12 kilometres-plus per game.

While the slog was severe, the return was rich. Ten Leinster titles, six All-Irelands and four consecutive All Stars. The gods were kind to him too; he arrived on centre stage with an ensemble who would become the greatest football team of all time, holding September residence on Jones' Road for the best part of seven years.

From day one those at his club, Fingallians, knew what he was capable of. Former Dublin hero Ciaran Duff, known as 'Dully' to his friends, spotted an edge very early on.

'Dully always told me I had a raw talent; a bit of bite, and a really hard work rate, but skills were what I had to develop to become a proper player,' Flynn says, 'so I just focused all my attention on that aspect of it for my formative years, always working while I was in college on my skills and speed.

'There was always another challenge to be met along the way. I spent hours upon hours training, it was pure repetition, kicking off both feet, working with the ball.'

With tedious monotony Flynn built up his skill levels off left and right and on game days it stood to him. He developed from an honest, athletic powerhouse into an accurate shooter, graceful and poised in front of the posts.

'You learn and grow too,' he insists. 'Work-rate is one

thing but scoring two or three points a game really makes you stand out. That's what I aimed for, to chip away with a point each half at the start of my career and then the bar rose to almost two points a half. But if I came out of a game after only scoring two points, I would still be content because it would be a given that I was after working hard in defence too.

'So, while a really good game might lead to three, four or five points, as I grew, I learned that having just 0-1 after your name didn't necessarily mean you played bad either. I was at ease because of all the preparation I had done. Let me explain it this way – some days you wouldn't get a shot at goal for the first 45 minutes, but I knew the work I had put in, the extra work, would count and I learned to back my body. If I was man-marked I knew the opponent might be able to stay with me and cover me for 45 minutes, but I knew I would have the last 20 because of the work I had put in. I was confident about that. I felt I'd have a stronger finish than my opponent and maybe the amount of times I clipped over a few points in the final parts of games was no coincidence.

'It was a tough role I played, half-forward but always getting back, breaking and counter-attacking but I never doubted myself when I was really motoring.

'Then at the tail end of it all, as I got older and the body wouldn't do what I wanted it to do, I wasn't able to back myself as much. Near the end I was worried I would be taken off in games and that had never ever been part of my thinking. Toward the end it all slipped a little for me.'

Flynn had spent so many years working relentlessly and repetitively on his shooting and skills – and just as much time building his body to sustain 12-kilometre outputs at high speed on match days for up to 77 minutes.

'I had worked really hard on my physical shape and I want to maintain that in retirement,' he insists. 'It's not a vanity thing but when you work hard to be a high-performance athlete and have a certain muscle mass and shape it can be hard to see that change or decline. If I felt I was putting on weight or losing my shape I would struggle with that.

'The rugby and NFL players have that quite often. As players, they take in 5,000 calories a day in some instances and, when they leave sport, they are conditioned to keep up that intake. Yet, they obviously don't train as hard because they don't have that purpose or necessity anymore and can easily put on weight and lose shape. They look in the mirror, see their body is changing and people don't know how to deal with that either.

'For me, that's really challenging. I weigh myself every day now since I have retired. I didn't even do that when I was playing. My fighting weight was always 91 kilos, I could never really get down to or stay beneath 90 kilos for long and I was always onto our nutritionist about it, but I was told my muscle mass was perfect. And so was my weight.

'When I retired, I crept up to 94 kilos at one stage and it rattled the hell out of me. I hardly ate for the week and went training five days in a row,' he laughs. 'But I'm glad to be like that because I would hate to let myself go.'

Flynn is full sure too that if he didn't have a meaningful career, post-playing challenges would be much more traumatic. He worked hard to transform his life off the pitch too, switching from being a plumber to going back to college, to getting a role in the commercial sector with Aer Lingus before joining the recruitment business.

'I realised in the recruitment sector, especially, that the harder you work, the quicker you rise and found that to be the exact same in Gaelic football.'

His next role was to be appointed as Chief Executive Officer of the Gaelic Players Association. A big job, but he makes an interesting point that while his former Dublin teammates have cemented their legacy on the game, they are all heavily invested in their careers too.

And he is certain that professional motivation and the ability to bring some balance into their lives, to counteract the tight grip that the inter-county game exerts on players, has been a key driver behind Dublin's success.

'I followed that template too, made a change in career, and just focused on my strengths. On the pitch I was never the best footballer at underage level, but I went on a relentless pursuit to be the best I could. I did the same off the field.'

In fact, Flynn grew so used to that elite, ferociously driven environment, that even when he retired, he hired a personal trainer to work with him.

'People might look at that and ask, "What the hell?" But I felt I had to do that to push myself the way I want. That was so hard – leaving a training dynamic where so many other lads were pushing you on. I still need that. And why wouldn't you want to pay for your health anyway?

'You'd pay at least €50 if you ate out these days or spend nearly as much on a couple of cinema tickets and some sweets, so to pay €30 an hour to a personal trainer and make an investment in my life and health is more valuable. I need to keep focused and push myself. There always has to be a challenge in life.'

He overcame many of his. When his injuries mounted and game-time greatly diminished, Flynn became a little perplexed with his sport.

At the end of the 2018 All-Ireland final, he was among five long-serving Dublin players who had received no game time in the decider. He stood awkwardly, away to the fringes, as the rest of the team and subs whooped it up in front of Hill 16, having worked their unrelenting, unforgiving magic on Tyrone. Those senior players had once been mainstays of the side but had succumbed to the acceleration of youth that had infiltrated the starting 15. It hit Flynn hard.

'When I didn't get a run in that final of course I was pissed off,' he admits. 'That's the competitor coming out and it would be only natural.

'I did something that night that I wouldn't be too happy about. I probably had a few pints too many afterwards, such was the disappointment. I tried to hide away from it. That was not a good idea and I regret doing that.

'I guess I didn't want an experience like that again. But now that some time has passed, I can look back and see that I had a great run.

'If I could peel it all back the highlight would be how my mam and dad and the whole family enjoyed the journey, and how it connected the whole lot of us, brought us closer. We have a big family and we have many different challenges, and this was something that galvanised everyone, brought us all together and that was one of most rewarding things. They were proud and I appreciate that now even if I didn't fully realise it at the time,' he replies.

'But, as regards the team, there was a new generation coming through and I knew I had to get out of their bloody way.'

* * *

As CEO of the GPA since June 2018, the Fingallians man has seen the issue of retirement, and the social and psychological challenges it raises, rear up with great ferocity.

He is currently looking at a pilot scheme introduced by the AFL Players Association in Australia, called Max 360. The project is being run by the AFL's wellbeing department and surmises that an industry that drafts young players directly from secondary school owes a duty of care to develop them off the field too.

'A player can be obsessed with his career and go the full 180 degrees with it,' Flynn says. 'Or they can be 180 degrees focused on their personal development. And the concept is that too many people only invest in 180 degrees – in one facet or the other.

'But the AFL programme maintains that they need to do 360 degrees to reach the maximum potential in their overall life. There are different strands to it, but it is something we are looking at closely with the GPA.'

Increasingly, however, his email inbox is filled with messages from former players looking for help. While the GPA have always had a main focus on current inter-county players, Flynn maintains they are now placing further scrutiny on past players because anecdotal evidence suggests that many need direction.

In his professional role, he has seen at first-hand the dangers that retirement brings. Gambling, relationship break-ups, depression – those are prominent themes that emerge when former players make contact.

'It's coming back to us every day, and some of the stories are very worrying,' he insists. 'Lads totally down and lacking confidence, lacking purpose. We have listened to them. At the start the GPA was very much centred on current players but not anymore. It's about past players now as much as anything else. These players gave it their all on the pitch, emptied themselves for the sake of the county jersey but they didn't have a balance in their lives.'

That's the critical cog, Flynn reckons.

'The problem is that it's actually too late at the end.

'What we are doing is trying to make them reshape and reset their goals long before they retire. Try to build some coping strategies so that when they leave, they have a worthwhile new life. We're remedying what should have been done at the start of their careers,' he explains.

The GPA has also adjusted their development templates for current players, identifying three pillars for players to consider as they represent their counties.

This first is physical – meaning that a player is fully informed and supported as he tries to prepare his body for the rigours of inter-county level.

The personal aspect recommends that players take time and space away from sport to have relationships outside.

And thirdly, the professional facet urges players to have a career that inspires them, so that when they do retire, they have something meaningful to turn to.

'If you take one of those pillars away, you can still replenish it with the other two,' Flynn states.

'But if one pillar is way too high – and it's usually the physical aspect with GAA players – it means the other two are very low. This suggests that they don't have enough time for relationships, or that their careers are not evolving sufficiently.

'If they neglect those areas, they're in trouble. It could lead to them losing everything, principally their own identity, when they stop playing as they haven't invested enough into making sure there are good people around them, or they don't have a fulfilling career to throw themselves into.'

Flynn refers to an academic paper entitled *Athletic Identity Foreclosure*. It refers to massive commitment to the athlete role in the absence of exploration of occupational or ideological alternatives and looks at the subsequent consequences.

'In other words, it shows the lengths players go to to be identified as an athlete,' he clarifies. 'We looked at it through the eyes of our membership. Currently, we have 500 student members and asked them if they identified principally as a student or an athlete. They nearly all identified as inter-county players first.

'That raised a red flag with us. What will happen these people if they are de-selected? They are young so that could easily happen.

'What happens if they sustain a bad injury?

'Or opt out?

'Think about that – they have just lost their entire identity. When you lose that, your purpose in life goes. The knock-on effect is huge. Your confidence vanishes, you don't want to get out of bed. You turn towards anti-social habits like gambling or heavy drinking. The walls close in.

'In the GPA, we highlight how players need a sense of something beyond sport. We are directing all our research findings at the younger ones but it's difficult to get the message home because they are so dead set on playing for their county.

'Guys have to retire – that's the nature of sport but if, along the way, we can develop them and show how useful a purpose beyond sport is, then we have a chance. It's a very formative time between 20 and 30 and these people should be building careers, relationships and professions. If at the end of it all you come out only playing hurling and football you're way behind.'

Flynn acknowledges that many past players never had access to this flow of information, support or direction. And that too many current players fit their education around their GAA lives.

'Nowadays, all of our guys are hyper-educated,' he says. 'They nearly all have degrees and masters. We're very good at getting our students into college but from there those students must also excel in taking meaningful employment and not just jobs they take up so they can devote more time to GAA.

'I fell into that trap myself,' Flynn notes. 'I was a plumber who went back to college to take a teaching degree just so I would have the hours to devote to making the Dublin team. It was short-term thinking.'

* * *

Back to the football. Just as Jim Gavin piloted the Dublin players towards a seemingly unstoppable approach to sporting immortality and an unprecedented five All-Ireland senior titles in a row, Flynn, who was a lieutenant of the team even before Gavin's arrival in the cockpit, made the call to parachute out.

He pulled the chord just as history called.

From the outside it was strange. Why not stay involved in the panel, especially in such a momentous year? Take the medal. Stay part of history forever.

'Those who know me understand,' he says, firmly batting that suggestion aside. 'All that matters is I am easy with the decision. My body was giving way, simple as that. I had an uphill battle to get back into the starting 15 and it was an insurmountable challenge especially when I couldn't go to the limits I once could.

'Don't get me wrong, I knew the enormity of what I was leaving, and I thought long and hard before leaving. In fact, I appreciated the magnitude so much that after I stepped away, I made the decision to go to every Dublin game for the rest of the season just to get used to the idea of not being involved. I was intent on making the transition from player to supporter quickly, but I was always conscious of the history that lay ahead too.

'But I was in decline no matter what way you look at it. That is a hard fact for all of us to stomach.'

When he tried to look for benchmarks to gauge his performance levels, he only grew more frustrated.

'All I ever did was compare myself to the 2014 version – a high-performance athlete buzzing around the pitch, beating opponents and kicking points for fun.

'But I knew I couldn't do that to the same level anymore. And I realise I will never be able to do that ever again. It's gone. Regardless of what I do in the future those days have passed. Time waits for no man.

'So, yes, I miss being at the peak of my powers. I really appreciate the time I had, and the fact that, when I left at the end of the 2019 national league, I self-selected to leave, rather than being de-selected. That made it a bit easier to cope too.'

The irony is he had turned up for pre-season in better nick than he can ever remember. With back surgery of 2018 complete and a December largely free of excess, he was fully armed for the Dubs' assault on sporting immortality.

He returned to training at 88 kilos and, though he looked drawn and gaunt, his times in the team runs were very impressive. Through the years his body fat percentages had ranged from 11 to 13 per cent. He returned to Dublin training in 2018 with a body fat percentage of 8.9. Premier League football level.

'I shed weight, as if to say, "Let's give this a real good lash,"' he recounts. 'I did the runs with the lads and won most of them: I was moving well.'

Yet, for all the sweat lost in practice there was no blood spilled in battle. On match days he was consigned to the trenches and saw little time on the front line.

'And that was the killer,' he concedes.

'After getting into that shape, having no time on the field during the League ultimately resulted in my effort levels going down and my mind began to switch off too.

'I had a couple of meetings with Jim during that league campaign. Now, I never once went in saying he needed to give me more time, or anything like that. It was more like, "Jim, I'm giving everything, and nothing is happening."'

Around then, old back problems started to flare up again and he felt a tingling sensation in his toes. With no sign of elevation back into the first 21 he decided he wasn't going to risk himself any further. The lack of pitch time reinforced his decision to step aside.

His heart wasn't heavy when he made the call, nor was he jumping around with relief either. The challenge, he knew, would not necessarily be seeking to replace the incredible kicks and highs he experienced with the Dublin team but more around finding another avenue for the training and preparation regime that had gripped him throughout his career.

As the end line beckoned, further meetings with Gavin confirmed that Flynn was still in the mix, still in the manager's top 25 pick, but he had a bit of work to do to get back into the starting 15.

Normally, Flynn would retreat, digest the feedback, sharpen the sword and return for the next battle with even greater potency but, as the spring of 2019 faded and the evenings began to lengthen, he just didn't have the energy for another fight.

'I had nearly come to accept I was finished so maybe in a way I did have a ramp to help me when the fall came,' he reveals. 'Even the psychological aspect of going on and seeing the lads win five in a row and not being part of it, I think I've dealt with it all quite well.'

He found the first 2019 championship game as a supporter, against Louth, very hard to handle, but it was easier to look on against Kildare and Meath. By the time the Super 8s came around, he felt well able for the changeover.

Or so he thought. Being in the stands for both the All-Ireland final and replay nearly ate him up inside.

'Two of the most difficult experiences of my life,' he admits. 'Especially the replay. I was working in the GPA suite at Croke Park and I watched the guys do a lap of honour at the end. I tried to keep it together but inside I was crying,' he reveals.

'It was really, really difficult. I was looking down at them, comparing myself to Con O'Callaghan and Brian Fenton, wondering could I have been out there with them. But here's the thing – I was comparing the me of 2014 to them as opposed to me of 2019. And they were different people.'

On the night of the 2019 All-Ireland final replay when Dublin claimed the first ever five-in-a-row in men's Gaelic football, Flynn watched that evening's drama unfold. He was grateful to have his brother beside him on an emotional night.

They had their sister's 50th birthday party to attend to straight after, another godsend that allowed Flynn to quickly bolt from Jones' Road.

'The best thing ever,' he says.

'It meant I could leave Croke Park in a rush, head straight over to party and that celebration was all about one person – my sister. I was just another face in the crowd at that party having a few beers. All my family was there, and my friends too, so it was a welcome escape.

'I definitely felt people were looking at me differently after I made the call to retire even though they most likely weren't!

'So many people were saying, "Why didn't you just hang in there?" But I didn't feel like I had to justify myself, I was very proud of what I done on the pitch. Anyone who knows me knows I would not hang around and just be a bystander. If I couldn't give 100 per cent, I wouldn't want to be there.'

The week after the replayed final things settled down again. Flynn was back in his own routine. As a player his schedule had been rigid: Monday night or morning in the gym, Tuesday and Thursday were pitch sessions, Wednesday and Fridays were either recovery or extra gym sessions. Even on those nights smaller groups of players would meet up for sessions. Weekends were all about games.

'In my first week away from the team I went to the gym but

there was no one to account to,' he laughs. 'That was so hard to get my head around. I had been so used to being pushed and pushing myself. Thank God I had the club, that saved me because I was able to give something back and have a target again. When you leave the inter-county stage but have a club to play for, the fall off the cliff is not as steep. You have a huge purpose and focus on the club and that's such a massive help after retiring from a county team. There are a whole new set of goals to aim.'

He looks back with nothing but gratitude. It helps that he can walk into his parents' house and on the mantlepiece there are four All Stars to go alongside the six All-Ireland medals he won.

'I'm so grateful for all that,' he says. 'People might harp on about not being there for the final leg of the five, but the truth is I got the maximum out of my ability and I have no regrets. Life just happens and the whole transition came when it did – but not before I had achieved all I ever wanted and all that I ever worked so hard for as a young boy.'

13

DARREN O'NEILL

Southpaw Slow to Slip Away

BORN: Kilkenny, 1985.
Represented Irish amateur boxing teams and captained
national team at London 2012 Olympics. Won silver at EU
and European Championships.
Stepped away from amateur boxing in 2019, aged 34,
with the intention to fight professionally.

Darren O'Neill sinks back against his chair and tells it straight. 'If there was one bit of advice that I would give to anyone coming into the final rounds of a sport or even facing into a new chapter in life, it would be this,' he says. 'Have something to do when you wake up in the morning. Or somewhere to go. Have a plan.'

O'Neill was a shining jewel in the crown of Irish amateur boxing and, while he wasn't a household name like Kenny Egan, Mickey Conlan or Paddy Barnes, he was one of the most respected boxers to ever don the green singlet. His success on the international stage was considerable, winning European Championship silver in 2010 and EU gold and silver as a middle and light heavy in 2009 and 2014 respectively.

He can look back with serious pride on his career. Olympic

boxer. Irish captain. National champion. European medallist. A natural leader and team player, he excelled in an elite, individual sport; a gifted southpaw who travelled a distance that saw Irish boxing escape a dark abyss for the bright lights of the world stage.

He was bright and educated too.

On his journey he encountered good times, packed arenas and loud cheers, won four national middleweight crowns and three Irish heavyweight titles. But, after picking up a hand injury in 2017, aged 32, he silently slipped out of the system. More worryingly, he was allowed to.

And he wasn't quite ready for any of it.

The former Kilkenny under-21 hurler initially left his stick and sliotar aside to pursue his dream of boxing in the Olympics and achieved that in the London 2012 Games where he captained Team Ireland.

He never formally left the 'Medal Factory' or the Irish Amateur Boxing Association (IABA) High Performance Unit, as it became known. But he did spend the bones of two years out injured, nursing a broken hand, and that injury ultimately called time on the career he'd forged. He stood out as all that was good about amateur boxing, and such was his love and passion for grassroots boxing and its ethos that the prospect of turning professional was unlikely. Instead it was assumed by many that he would be kept in the fold in a coaching role.

That was the thinking anyway.

But it didn't happen.

Now, as he maps out his story, there is an outline of unfinished business.

During that prolonged recovery from the hand injury in 2017

he found it hard to fill his days and stick to his fighting weight. He reckons he ballooned. In fact, he only went from 80 kilos to 87 kilos, but for a fighter who thrives on sharpness, both mental and physical, this was a near catastrophe. 'I had too much time on my hands,' he states flatly. 'The days were long. To put it mildly, it was not a good period for me.'

Reality hit hard that the good days might have passed but the usual suspects were around him and that helped. Ollie, his father, had trained him out of his Paulstown club. His brother, Aidan, was his cut man. Allison, his then girlfriend and now fiancé, was a constant rock of support. They had pillars of strength for him. Just like the people of Paulstown.

When O'Neill captained Ireland's boxers in the 2012 Olympic Games the locals on the cusp of the Kilkenny/Carlow border seemed to stand that little bit taller, their chests puffed just that bit more.

'I think they got as much of a lift from it all as I did,' he reflects.

And despite the frustration of 2017, O'Neill wanted to look ahead and give his people more to cheer, though he wondered where his next fix would come from.

'I never made a grand announcement,' he said. 'Never had an official retirement. But when you see the months passing, you tend to look back on what you did. The mind wanders. Like, I had won seven national championships and I started thinking how two years out of the sport had maybe cost me another brace of titles. You'd be on nine belts then and sure you'd have to go hunting for the tenth.

'There were other temptations too. As the hand recovered, I was asked to spar with lads to prepare them for the 2018 and

2019 Elites and I had this inescapable feeling that I could still step back into the ring and do a job.'

Ollie wouldn't hear of it, however. His dad's words were stern but kind, relayed with an earnestness that his son would remain healthy.

'His exact words were, "Leave it go, you don't want to be going back and be beaten by someone you shouldn't lose to just because you are not right, and haven't the work done."

'And as fresh as I felt after sparring, dad knew that I hadn't the work done. So, that was that. The two years kind of merged into each other then. I'd been used to an elite environment, major championships, training camps, some incredible hotels and facilities and some shit ones too. But I was also part of a team and that was massive for me, maybe it stemmed from my hurling background. I enjoyed being with other people. In a flash, all of that was gone. You're sitting home with a sore paw, the days have to be filled, and the hype and the adrenalin are things of the past.

'It's some comedown, I tell you.'

The bone that shattered in his right hand was troublesome but manageable. Or so he thought. By 2018, the problem still hadn't healed so he underwent surgery to remove fragments of bone that were floating in his hand.

Before he knew it, he'd been off-Broadway two years. The theatre of his sport, the roar of the crowd, those memories never diminished in his mind, but it became apparent that there would be no curtain call, no grand finale. The show had moved on without him.

The curious thing is how O'Neill still felt so pure and passionate about a sport that was rotting away, in some parts at least. Judging controversies, such as the jaw-dropping decision that saw friend and teammate Michael Conlan – and others – robbed in Rio at the 2016 Olympics.

In the immediate aftermath of his loss in Rio, Conlan gave a heated interview to state broadcaster RTÉ. 'AIBA (the international amateur boxing body) are cheats,' he fumed, referring to world amateur boxing's governing body. 'F**king cheats. They're cheating bastards, they are paying everyone... They're known for being cheats and they'll always be cheats. Amateur boxing stinks from the core right to the top.'

Conlan was world champion at the time and dominated his three rounds against opponent Vladimir Nikitin only to lose both the first and third rounds according to all three judges.

O'Neill had previously seen his own dreams of reaching a second Games dashed by a highly contentious points loss to Abdullayev Abdulkadir of Azerbaijan at a European qualifier in April 2016. He thinks he clearly beat the Azerbaijani, landing 54 punches to his opponent's 26. But it was his rival who qualified and went to Rio.

'I was completely all over the place after that,' O'Neill remembers.

In mid-summer 2017, he felt another lash of the judging process when he suffered a controversial split decision defeat to Ukrainian heavyweight Ramazan Muslimov at the European Championships in Kharkiv, Ukraine. O'Neill had already indicated it would be his last Europeans, and he lost a close battle on a 4-1 split to Muslimov when it appeared his opponent had gassed out in the third and final round.

O'Neill knew that decision would again cost him status, medals and money.

'I was so pissed off,' he says. 'It was another major medal taken away from me, more funding taken away from me too.'

Later that evening he tweeted, 'What to say? Everyone agrees I won but Ukraine gets decision AGAIN. Thanks all for supporting me over my 13 years boxing senior for Ireland.'

Throw in doping scandals and political manoeuvring right up to international level, and boxing remains in some disarray. O'Neill's love for the sport has always pulsed strong though he doesn't think its reputation has been improved in any way since then.

'It's a shame because at elite level preparation is paramount and you have to draw from your own pocket a lot too. The official funding is dependent on what medals you win, how you perform. The Irish Sports Council fund athletes so you train diligently, then you go abroad, and you are hostage to some judge's decision somewhere. You just hope you're on the right side of it. If you're not winning, the funding to allow you train next year could go somewhere else. That's the political side of it too – someone can just decide that the money is going somewhere else.'

O'Neill admits to being naive when he was younger.

'I saw no corruption,' he says, 'just the odd blip here and there but the more you were in it, the more you saw it. Dodgy decisions left, right and centre. Even in the feckin' multi-nation events, tournaments that don't really matter, you see things that happen. I was on the receiving end of a nice bit of it unfortunately and it sat me back financially as much as anything else. But I am not going to say I was the only one – we have seen in the Olympic Games and other events where we all suffered. We are not allowed to say the whole thing is corrupt, but you can decide for yourself what label you want to stick on it.'

Disaffected by what was happening in the amateur game, he hoped that the Rio Games would have been a watershed moment for the sport, that people would finally accept the sport needed to get its house in order.

'If anything, I think it has got even worse,' he states.

The 2017 split decision that went against him had huge ramifications for O'Neill. Athletes receive podium grants for performing in a major event like the Olympics which could have been worth up to €40,000.

'If you win at world class it would be €20,000 and then drops again to €12,000,' he explains. 'For years I was lucky that I was able to do a bit of work and make a few bob whilst boxing for Ireland. And when I was living at home it was manageable too. There were a few years when I was getting away with it because the IABA would feed you and put you up for camp and that, but you certainly don't thrive. You just make sacrifices that need to be made.'

Apart from funding, the injuries kept him out of the sport for so long that he knew it was time to forge another path.

'And two years on I am still forging it,' he states. 'I wasn't quite ready to give up boxing either because the passion never dies, I suppose. Once the hand healed and I was able to get back training again, even doing a few boxercise classes and hitting some pads, I instantly felt better about myself. Even training and getting fit helped my mental health.

'I was in good nick still. I guess you don't lose what you have spent a lifetime building up. That's what got me thinking again, "Maybe I still had something left to give?"

'That's the madness of it. As I had made no grand announcements about retiring I kind of saw the door as being half open still.'

That slight gap was just enough to encourage him to think twice about hanging up his gloves. He reacted with his trademark eagerness.

* * *

O'Neill often throws out the joke that he missed being punched in the face. But the smile turns to earnestness when he paints a picture of a sportsman who still has a curiosity for his art.

He moved with the uncertainty as best he could, went back to college, took a job in business in Dublin, bought a house and started looking ahead to marrying his fiancé, Alison McMahon, in 2021.

'It hits you more as you get older,' he says, 'the reminders that a life outside of boxing was needed.'

He listened to the calls. As his career progressed, O'Neill had taken the decision to spread his wings, in an educational sense, in 2010. He qualified as a primary school teacher and subsequently devoted the next year to getting his diploma in teaching practice. He was placed at Holy Trinity primary school in Donaghmede and loved working with kids, though he has his own ideas about the teaching system in this country. High Performance Coach Billy Walsh and Zaur Antia wanted him to train full time in the run up to the 2012 Games, but O'Neill needed balance in his life.

'I function much better when there is more than one thing going on in my life,' he says. 'From my college days I knew I was

215

able to combine boxing with studying and classes so I knew I would be able to teach and get my teaching practice done too. Billy and Zaur weren't overly delighted, but they facilitated me, and I made sure to make it work. In fairness, I had spent years getting the teaching degree and I wanted to put it to work. Billy recognised that because he is a great man-manager and while there were teething problems at the start, we worked through it.'

In 2016, he went back to education again.

'My form had dipped ahead of the Rio Olympics and I was struggling to make weight, I found it hard to always keep under 80 kilos and when I cut that weight too rapidly, coming down to 75 kilos for fight week, my energy would decline during the closing stages of fights. I sensed it would be best to start looking at going back. Right from the time I was a kid, my parents had always insisted that education came first, and I missed the 2002 World Junior Championships because my Leaving Cert was on around the same time. It was tough looking on, but I appreciate they made the right call.

'I knew going back to college the second time around that the business sector was now the next move because I wasn't in a rush to go back teaching. So, I took an MBA (master's degree in business administration) at DIT Aungier Street with a view to working in that sector.'

It was a part-time course over two years and O'Neill liked it. He never broadcast his sporting prowess, but it wasn't long before his classmates recognised that they had an Olympian, seven-time national champion and Irish captain in their class. They even went to see him fight a few times.

'Boxing helped me in college too,' he points out. 'When it

came to presentations, I had no bother stepping up and delivering one. Half the time I mightn't have had a clue of what I was talking about,' he jokes, 'but I was used to public speaking and that was a help.'

There was plenty to help ease him through a tough comedown from competing. He and Allison bought their house in Navan and he took a job working in Dublin for a company that is currently in liquidation.

Many column inches have been penned wondering why O'Neill and some of his peers are not yet back in the IABA family, coaching the next generation. While he would love to have stayed in a sporting environment, he says he simply had to take work – the household bills weren't going to be paid for him.

Keeping fit has remained a constant, however. And when he helped Gardiner and Browne tune up for the 2019 Elites, he couldn't ignore that his form was still good. At one stage, possibly because he was punching so well, Browne's coach, Steven O'Rourke, looked for reassurance that O'Neill wasn't going to make a comeback and oppose the men he was sparring with.

Maybe that confirmed O'Neill's view that he still had something to offer. He replied with a throwaway remark that there would definitely be nothing to worry about if O'Rourke managed to get him a few professional fights. O'Rourke didn't blink at the suggestion.

'Okay, leave it with me,' he replied.

That's when the seed was sewn for an unlikely comeback. That seed will need a lot of watering for it to bloom, though.

Ollie O'Neill was first to question the logic of a return to the ring.

'Dad advised me not to go there,' O'Neill says. 'But I told him I had unfinished business, that I still had something to offer, and that I was going ahead with it. Dad wasn't delighted, but when he saw I was serious he completely threw himself into it too. He actually went off and got his pro boxing coaching licence! Soon, Aidan, was back on board again as well.'

With the band now back together, there was the issue of a venue. Never has there been a tougher time to try putting together a professional show in Ireland. This is as a result of the 2016 Regency Hotel shooting which resulted in one fatality and serious injuries for others ahead of a WBO European Lightweight title bout. The incident hugely damaged Irish professional boxing and insurance costs for future events subsequently went through the roof, rendering future professional bouts here a rarity.

'That tragedy changed a lot and then money is a huge aspect of it too,' O'Neill explains. 'Shows are being stopped by the spike in costs which is a pity because we've loads of boxers trying to make a breakthrough.'

Nonetheless, O'Rourke, managed to secure a maiden professional fight for O'Neill – in Belfast on 25 October, 2019, against a Hungarian journeyman, Norbert Szekeres, on the 'He Who Dares' card.

Szekeres appeared to be the ultimate old hand. He was 33 with ten years' professional experience. But he had lost 77 of his 99 professional fights and his last win came three years and 31 fights ago.

Somehow, one of the main faces of Irish amateur boxing for the past decade and mainstay of the Irish Amateur Boxing Association's High Performance programme, was now pitted in the pro circuit with one of the sport's great journeymen. There was little romance to this one.

There would be no pay cheque for the privilege either. Until you make headway in the pro game you pay to compete. O'Neill was due to fork out €1,500 for Szekeres to appear. Any takings for himself would have depended on ticket sales.

Would he even have got a grand out of it?

O'Neill lifts his head and stares quizzically. 'Jesus, no, you'd be lucky to break even. And that's the one thing I said to Steven – I will fight once I don't lose money.'

For better or worse, the fight with his Hungarian opponent was ultimately cancelled, another frustrating turn for O'Neill.

'Still, I wondered what was there to lose?' he counters. 'Aside from staying healthy, I have nothing to lose. I will see what happens. You never know – one or two wins and you could then fight for something real. I just don't want to be sitting on a barstool down the line and wondering what might have been. I always remind Dad of one of his favourite sayings: "You'll be retired long enough."'

While he concedes he most likely won't be in the mix for world, or even European titles, a possible Irish cruiserweight title bout could be on the cards provided he managed a couple of wins first.

'I'll be disappointed if I don't get to give it a fair crack,' he says. 'I know the amateur game is totally different to this, and with my hand injury I don't have the power to drop people like I once did, but I am competitive. Allison has given me her backing, so too has Dad. And I still feel like I can do something.'

There is another angle to all of this. Speak to those around the sport and they'll insist that O'Neill really should be coaching with the IABA by now. They'll say the same about Kenneth Egan and Eric Donovan.

O'Neill, once Mr Irish Amateur Boxing, now has little to do with them, apart from sparring or sending friends the odd text before a fight.

'You'd have to ask them,' he says when pressed as to why that is the case.

'There is a raft of coaching talent and experience out there and I feel the IABA is overlooking it. The likes of Kenny, Eric, Andy Lee. John Joe Joyce has founded the Olympic Boxing Club in Mullingar and they have already been hugely successful.

'We have all experience. Eric and Kenny went back and got their education too. Even speaking to youth teams in recent years those lads soak up every word you say because you have been there and done that and they want to learn.

'I look at these kids coming up now, preparing for competitions and they are almost hoping to draw the world champion in their first bout. That's the confidence they have. Jesus, years ago when I was starting out, the world champ was the last opponent you'd want to draw.

'I guess that the group I was with, we tried to change things and the way Irish boxers were perceived. Now the young lads have confidence, that feeling of the right to win because they have seen likes of Eric and Kenny go up against the Russians and eventually break through. They have seen in the past decade that, as a country, we can be as good as them and that's their mindset. Those lads who have paved the way should be used for their experience.

'I thought I would be coaching by now,' he freely admits. 'I am a qualified teacher, I am very technical about things, and I get on well with people. But probably the biggest thing I can offer is that I was there when we were a poor side and was ever present on the journey where Irish boxing developed into world leaders. I feel I have a lot of information to pass on.

'But the opportunities are not there right now so I have looked elsewhere.'

When head coach Billy Walsh and high-performance director, Gary Keegan, moved on, the frantic rate of progression stalled.

'Things haven't been the same since,' O'Neill muses. Indeed, when he speaks of the two stalwarts who overhauled the health of Irish boxing, it's in a hushed, reverential tone.

'It was a huge blow to lose them and we are still seeing the ramifications. It still is a huge blow, never mind boxing, but for the country too.

'Billy was a sound man, great to us, he protected us from all the nonsense that went on in the sport. He and Zaur were like chalk and cheese. Zaur is the best technical and tactical coach in the sport. His game plans were the best in the world.

'Billy developed a lot, technically, too, because of Zaur, but Billy's people skills were second to none. His management skills were unreal.

'Both of the lads boxed themselves, but Billy came through the Irish system and, like me, dreamed of going to the Olympics. He knew the ins and outs, had a hand in local and national politics, and he shielded us from a lot of that.'

What was once a way of life to all of them is now long since faded into the memory banks. The Medal Factory that Walsh oversaw, which nurtured Irish boxers on the road to winning seven Olympic medals, in addition to European and World medals, has seen its production lines struggle to yield the same quality. Meanwhile, a year after taking up his position of USA boxing coach, Walsh was rewarded with the World Boxing Coach of the Year award for America's prowess at the London Games.

Quality people like former world champion Bernard Dunne are working hard to try and restore the good days but it will be a challenge get back there again and, ahead of the Tokyo Games, there are not as many medal prospects as in recent times.

It's hard for O'Neill and his old teammates not to look back with some nostalgia.

'Well, the High Performance Unit demanded so much of us,' he recalls. 'I had to laugh at the use of the word "amateur" so many times. How ironic? We were anything but. We were more committed, organised and determined than most professionals. Diet, regimes, nothing was left to chance.

'And when it ends there is a hole. After I came back from the 2012 Olympics, for instance, I was shattered. I didn't really want to be around anyone as I had nothing left to give. Those close to me said: "Hang on, we supported you for the last few years, you have to give something back." But after London I had some of the toughest few weeks I ever had, and people didn't understand.

'They just couldn't understand: "But you are just back from the greatest show on earth, why are you not buzzing?" I didn't have the answer, I just found myself narky and I actually just wanted to hang around people who were there competing at the Games with me. I felt they were the ones who understood me, they got me.

'Did they really? Maybe I just wanted to keep the whole thing alive – it was such a massive build-up and then such a huge anti-climax.

'We were such a tight unit for so long and then it all ends. And it's never the same again.'

As the chat winds down there is little definite about where O'Neill is at. His first professional bout was delayed, while Covid-19 put paid to so many sporting events in 2020 that even trying to promote regional boxing events was impossible.

But the Kilkenny man is establishing a business career, is still fit, is on the property ladder and has a wedding to look forward to. There may be unfinished business in boxing and maybe he needs to get closure on that front now.

'Who says there has to be a magical formula to all this?' he asks.

'Generally, sports people have short lived careers, but I had a decent innings; I had a great career. I've beaten some great guys and won important medals.

'Even though I have a real itch to get back in, I am happy with life too. I have a good education and a good job.'

Before fights Kenny Egan and himself would always look at each other, wonder why they had starved themselves to death to go out and get punched in the face. They'd compare nerve levels and wonder whose stomach was rumbling the most. Then they'd lace up the gloves, go out into a noisy arena and do what they were born to do.

'We knew the sport could bring you to crazy places,' O'Neill smiles. 'That could still be the case.'

14

PAUL CARBERRY

Staying in the Stables

BORN: Meath, 1974.
Champion Irish jump jockey in 2001–02 and 2002–03.
Won a host of big races on both sides of the Irish Sea
and rode 14 winners at the Cheltenham Festival.
Stepped away from racing in 2016, aged 42,
and turned to showjumping.

Balls of steel. Bravest of them all. Genius. Stylish. Thrill-seeker.

That's how his fellow jockeys described Paul Carberry when he stepped away. And the portrayals were fair enough. His career had more cliff-hangers, twists, and dramatic endings than a screenwriters' brainstorm session.

So, when you've lived your life on racing's rollercoaster circuit, and based on those testimonies Paul Carberry never got off, how do you come up with a sequel on the outside?

'I retired at 42,' says Carberry, 'not because I wanted to but simply because I had to. I didn't want to go at all, but my leg wasn't strong enough anymore. If I had I another fall I could have been in even bigger trouble.

'After listening to my doctors and the medical team I had to weigh everything up and, in the end, I heeded the advice of my surgeon. There was no other option but to retire. It was tough and it still is. If I wasn't injured, I would still be out there, no doubt about that.'

Carberry was no stranger to broken legs, having endured two of them. But they take their place among a catalogue of injuries he sustained over his stellar career. While resting and recuperating the final break, he cracked the steel reinforcements in his leg in a fall at home. He had to undergo further surgery for that.

'The second time I broke it, I smashed up along where the screw went in and with the last one, they said if I fell on it again, I wouldn't walk,' he said. 'That was it. I had to decide to stop.'

In typical understated fashion, the Grand National-winning rider made a low-key announcement that he was moving on in August 2016, quietly outlining his intentions.

He hadn't ridden competitively since he fractured his left femur at Listowel the previous September when falling from Rich Coast, so he had almost got used to the idea.

'I had,' he admits. 'When you're not competing, there is a lot of time to think so I kind of knew what was coming down the tracks. If I fell again it didn't really bear thinking about the consequences, I suppose. There was only one call to make.'

It was a hammer blow, no point in saying otherwise. Carberry's whole life has revolved around horses. Hailing from a legendary racing family, his father, Tommy, was a top jockey in his day while his sister, Nina, and brother, Phillip, are also in the family business and very good at it too.

At two years of age Paul was already riding around on his dad Tommy's ponies. As he tells this story, he is out working in the stable yard again. This is where he is happiest, whether it's preparing to race, go hunting, or showjumping.

His earliest memories are attending the races with his dad. The Irish Grand National at Fairyhouse always stood out from the rest. Tommy started training horses soon after he retired, so the bug was inescapable. Training is a route that Carberry may yet take, though he's not sure if it will be financially sustainable, but, as a kid, all he wanted to do was emulate his father's achievements in the saddle.

'I just wanted to be around horses all the time,' he recalls. 'Others have different sporting interests, GAA, rugby, soccer, whatever but I'm happy when I am on a track, arena or in a yard.

'It was always the plan to be a jockey and I did that for a long time, so I know I am one of the lucky ones.'

He was given his first pony, Jack, at the age of three and that was it then. Deal sealed. 'From that moment on the saddle was where I wanted to be,' he laughs. 'There was nothing else really to interest me like horse-riding and nowhere along the way did I ever stop to think what I would do outside of it either. It was just one of those things – future mapped out and I was delighted with it.'

The thrill of the hunt always appealed too. Flat racing held little appeal for him.

'Maybe it's the buzz of not knowing what you're coming up against next or what you have to jump,' he said. 'The uncertainty and challenging yourself every day when you go out is huge.

'It's something I've had all my life and I often found that if I was after having a bad day's racing I could go hunting and kind of forget about everything. It's great from that point of view.'

Naturally enough then, Carberry was always going to favour jump racing more than the flat simply because of the drama and risks involved.

The Meath man is regarded as one of the most natural and bravest champion jockeys there ever was. He will forever be known for his poise and style on the horses he rode too, the tightness of his relationship with trainer Noel Meade, and the risks that he often took on racecourses, regularly leaving it late to surge past the finishing line, infuriating and thrilling many punters and observers along the way with his daredevil style. On the track, he had few peers. His waiting tactics, which were invariably clinically executed, much to the dismay of fellow riders, led to him being nicknamed him 'Alice' because his calling card for pouncing on his fellow jockeys was a verse of Smokie's classic, 'Living Next Door To Alice' as he crept up on their shoulders before cruising past them and roaring to yet another victory.

On the track Carberry struck up beautiful partnerships with a number of horses.

His win on Frenchman's Creek in the 2002 William Hill Trophy Handicap Chase at Cheltenham was sweet and Carberry made his job look so much easier than it actually was, that skill being reflected in how he led a horse that didn't always deliver to cruise home by three lengths.

Two years later, on Beef or Salmon, in the 2004 Lexus Chase at Leopardstown, Carberry's craft was enough to see off three-time Cheltenham Gold Cup hero Best Mate.

Winning with the sublimely talented but unpredictable Harchibald in 2007 at Newcastle was another landmark. Noel Meade's hurdler gave Carberry a real test in that race but Carberry got the best out of him as he did with Monbeg Dude in the 2013 Coral Welsh National at Chepstow, when they denied the AP McCoy-ridden Teaforthree to snatch a thrilling victory in the Welsh marathon. In this race Carberry exuded patience and calmness.

Style and bravery won many other Grade 1 events, but the jockey himself is in no doubt what the height of his career was.

'There were a few,' he smiles. 'There have been lots of other great moments on horses like Doran's Pride, Harchibald, Solwhit and Florida Pearl. But I suppose my favourite and most memorable horse of all time would have to be Bobbyjo.'

Bobbyjo won both the 1998 Irish Grand National and the 1999 Aintree Grand National and was trained by Carberry's dad which made those wins all the more special.

A close second for Carberry was that relationship with Harchibald. In the 2005 Champion Hurdle, they were narrowly beaten by Hardy Eustace right on the line, with many observers questioning Carberry's tactics on the day, when he left it right until the closing seconds of the race to surge.

Both Carberry and Harchibald were thrilling to watch when in full flow, and both delivered a performance and ride in the 2005 Champion Hurdle that is still talked about today. Harchibald was box office and the sheer drama of what unfolded in that race is never far from discussions and chats among racegoers.

The horse had all the ability that one could hope for, but he still couldn't manage to win the Champion Hurdle. The theory was that the 2005 hurdle was the one where he could eventually do it.

That race was brimming with talented horses, and the two-mile contest was seen as a symbol of a new-found Irish swagger at Cheltenham. Held at the height of the Celtic Tiger, the event came in the year that a new record of ten Irish winners was set at the course. And the first four home in that year's Hurdle were all Irish-trained.

In one of the best Champion Hurdles ever run at the course, Carberry and his horse looked to be absolutely cruising. Rarely has any horse moved as well and still been on the bridle with just a few yards to run – the demands of the race just don't allow it. It finally appeared like he was going to get past the line first, beating Hardy Eustace, who was looking to defend his title, on the way.

Carberry had done a great job in putting his horse to sleep for most of the race but when he finally did ask him for his effort, and it was at the very end of the race, there was nothing in response. He went down by a neck.

It was hugely disappointing but, with the enigmatic nature of the horse, many observers maintain to this day that Carberry's approach was correct – and point out that few knew Harchibald better.

Carberry himself is not one for looking back much, but does reflect that if there was one race he would go back and strive to win it would be the Champion Hurdle or Cheltenham Gold Cup, having come second in both over the years.

Still, a riding career that spanned 25 years and yielded 14 Cheltenham festival wins leaves little to be recovered. In addition, he won numerous big races on both sides of the Irish sea, being crowned Champion Irish jump jockey in 2001–02 and 2002–03.

'Sure, there were plenty of good days,' he says. 'Some testing ones too.

'But when I look back, the pride would be not only helping the good people I worked with, but also sustaining a living and career in an industry and sport that is very tough. It's not easy to stay going at times but I suppose I have managed that.'

Carberry is very much to the point when he answers questions. Not a word is wasted, and he is not one for getting away with the highs or lows that have visited him over the past five decades.

Pleasant and courteous, he is not one for small talk at the same time.

When he reflects on his career, he knows better than anyone that it certainly wasn't a straightforward ride. For a start, his career was dogged by injury all the way through.

'It was very hard to deal with those injuries especially when you would think you had recovered but then might meet a setback along the way. Staying put and resting was something I found very hard.

'But the only positives I can think of from all those injuries over the years were that they gave me a fair indication of what retirement would be like. When you are out so often for long periods of time, retirement is actually the last thing on your mind but all those days by yourself and not competing, it gives you a taste for what life is like after sport. So, there are few positives to be found in any injury setting for a sportsperson but without doubt they helped me prepare for when I had to step away.'

Another of the injuries saw Carberry having his spleen removed while there were countless rib and shoulder complaints too.

He frequently found himself in the headlines away from the track too. Sometimes visits to pubs and nightclubs didn't leave him in peak condition for racing the following day. The patience of trainer, Meade, was truly tested at times.

An episode aboard a plane from Spain to Dublin in 2003 saw a two-month stay in prison looming before the sentence was reduced to community service. But all who know him testify that there isn't an ounce of badness in Carberry. He made the call to give up alcohol for the remainder of his riding career and that helped deliver further success before he called time on jump racing. Right up until his last injury he was riding winners in big races.

His final Grade 1 winner came aboard Gordon Elliott's Don Cossack in the 2015 Punchestown Gold Cup. When he finally did retire, he was considered by legends like Ruby Walsh, AP McCoy and Barry Geraghty to be the most naturally gifted horseman of his generation.

Carberry was close to Walsh, Geraghty and Robert Power in particular, and while he misses seeing them on a daily basis, he still keeps in touch with a lot of that gang.

'I still have the same friends that I always did,' he says. 'It's a small country and you would bump into them quite a bit. So, there is no issue there in terms of moving on or feeling isolated from the lads and people you were once so close with. I still see them out and about competing, see them in yards. We would still speak a lot too.'

His initial plan was to keep busy and break a few horses. He targeted getting involved in showjumping when the strength in his leg returned.

As time passed and his leg healed, Carberry found it increasingly difficult to stay out of the saddle, eventually taking very well to showjumping and competing in the Dublin Horse Show in the RDS in 2017, just a little over a year after retiring.

Carberry had long been a fan of the sport and dreamt of

competing in the Dublin Horse Show. His unexpected career change was fully vindicated after winning his first Grand Prix that year.

'That win gave me an awful lot of things,' he says.

'If I was to be straight and tell you the one thing that I miss most from racing. it would be the buzz.

'I miss the adrenalin coursing through me and missed the big days. That's a great feeling and it's hard to find after you leave sport. Maybe I went looking for it again, but I definitely found it at the Horse Show when that Grand Prix went to a play-off. That feeling was unreal, and it was great to have it once more because you don't know will you ever find it down the line.'

Carberry and his own gelding, Brandonview First Edition, paired up to win that horse show event and last year they combined again to deliver Carberry's his first SJI Autumn Grand Prix win, which has been described by racing pundits as a truly staggering achievement and a result of his excellent horsemanship.

'I'm happy enough with where I am but I want to improve and do more,' Carberry says.

'As I said I got a huge rush from that Grand Prix and it definitely showed me I was on the right track.

'It's the complete opposite,' he says of the switch, 'you're trying to sit and wait for a stride whereas in racing you're trying to get a long one and jump quick and flat. It's taken me a long time to get the hang of it and I'm slowly getting there.

'It's a lovely way of staying involved and staying competitive but it's a completely different discipline and there is more I want to achieve there too. But overall happy with the progress made so far.'

A popular figure on the racing circuit, he says he has ambitions to achieve more in showjumping, and beyond that feels he might consider training.

'It's a hard business but I might take a further look at it,' he says.

'There is very little money to be made in it these days but it's something I may well consider going further into in the future. For now, I am happy enough with the progress I am making in showjumping and I have enough to keep me busy.'

Carberry is asked what advice he would give jockeys who are coming near the end of their career.

'Just to have a plan. It's tough going so have something lined up but that would be a big help. I would say to people to listen to their bodies too. I would have stayed going as long as I could only for the medical advice, but the truth is the body wasn't able for it anymore and you have to listen to the experts too.

'When I was out injured, I got that window into what life would be like after sport and maybe there's a chance for jockeys to look outside in that instance too, when they are out recovering from injury.

'But maybe you don't want to hear any of that either,' he laughs. 'We all just want to be around horses, fit and competing – that's the bottom line.

'I suppose when I look back all I can say is I was lucky that I got the chance to do what I loved for so long. And lucky too that I can still be involved in some way, still getting a buzz all these years on. To have had that from the age of two, when I went on my first pony, well that is special too.

'In life you have to love what you do,' Carberry finishes. 'It's not like work then. That's the key, really. And thankfully I've managed to keep doing that.'

15

PEOPLE BEFORE PRODUCT

Gary Keegan would applaud how Paul Carberry navigated the fences that fate put in front of him and took ownership of his retirement.

There is something admirable in what he has achieved, purposefully striding ahead in another discipline when it was clear he could no longer race. Indeed, Keegan wishes more sportspeople would follow suit. He remains bemused at how many of them wait until the final furlong before lifting their heads and realising the final post is upon them.

'The chances are the sportsperson will have been an incredible asset for their manager, club or administration for a long time,' Keegan surmises.

'Ideally, then, the organisation should sow the seeds for a conversation, to go like this, "You have two to three years left with us. Start thinking about your future. You're still a big influence on what we do here, but as the contract draws to an end, your influence may be more off the pitch, track, or course. You will still get action and game time, but we need to give those emerging the chance to breathe too. This is the road ahead, we will support you, but you need to be aware of our vision and make a call on whether that's right for you."'

Keegan reckons most athletes would respect such honesty. He encourages them to be ready and prepared for such a conversation and then to act on it.

Most of the time, however, he fears they are not willing to engage.

'And because they're not agreeable to that talk, managers don't want to broach the matter either. No one wants to. All you are doing is pushing the issue further down the track and that is how managers are seen to terminate players careers. What transpires in the end is usually not something to be proud of and there can be bitterness at how a player is discarded,' Keegan remarks.

'This is Ireland where we have way more amateurs than professionals, but I would still argue that a parting of ways must be done right no matter what your status.

'The organisation should say, "We are giving you another contract here, but that will be the last. We want to hear from you in two months on your plans for the future. What are they? What road are you going down? Can we help you with anything? Can you help us going forward?"

'Retiring is rarely easy but if an organisation and an athlete start communicating well in advance, trust and respect can be fostered. They may see mutual ground.'

Having worked with as many organisations and coaches as athletes, Keegan knows most are more pressed with team development and success rather than the welfare of players moving on. That's the ruthless but realistic nature of the business of sport.

Still, what about the duty of care owed to an athlete who has served so well?

'The organisation must really bestow that because a manager always has to look detached,' Keegan replies.

'Managers have to be able to select you today and maybe not tomorrow and they cannot be getting emotionally upset as they do their job. If they do, it will affect their decision-making process. Which is not good.

'Managers are usually concerned with many other things. So, it's up to the player or competitor to find out where they lie within the overall plan and maybe dialogue should start then.

'There is definitely a role for someone else within the backroom team or club to start that ball rolling, and management could facilitate that. As part of our care for these players as actual people, are we going to be proactive and deliberate about how we approach this issue in the future? Or are we going to continue to say and do nothing?'

Increasingly, it seems that whether you retire with or without success or glory is irrelevant – you could still be cut loose in a flash. In February 2020, a special *Daily Mail* report laid bare the scale of the mental health crisis affecting Great Britain's Olympic and Paralympic athletes when they retired.

A number of medal-winning athletes opened up about their struggles with depression, anxiety and suicidal thoughts since quitting and many have raised concerns about the lack of aftercare offered by governing bodies when they finished UK Sport funding.

Craig Fallon, Britain's 2005 judo world champion who competed at Athens 2004 and Beijing 2008, took his own life at the age of 36 after suffering severe depression. Track cyclist

Callum Skinner won gold and silver medals at Rio 2016 but also suffered from depression after retiring and now leads campaign group Global Athlete, a campaign for positive progress in sport.

Here in Ireland there is an after-care service for those athletes who were once Olympic-funded but have moved on.

Eoin Rheinisch is the Head of Performance Life-Skills at Sport Ireland and a three-time Olympian. A former top canoeist, he retired from competition in 2014 and his department at Sport Ireland look after many needs of athletes, including strength and conditioning, physiology, psychology and all the various aspects geared towards performance.

Rheinisch and his colleagues in the Performance Life Skills department, Niall O'Donoghue and Emma Saunders, focus on three pillars for overall development – education, performance and career. They help their competitors during and after their time at the coalface.

'We also want athletes to have a good performance when they leave sport,' Rheinisch stresses.

'Even when they finish up, we are still here to help. We have had a couple of athletes come back to us after retiring because they are still not sure what direction to take or are struggling with the emotions they are feeling. And it's not just in a career sense that the institute has helped athletes after leaving sport. Depending on the needs of each individual, other services are offered like conditioning, nutrition or physio to help an athlete wind down the right way.

'You have to be conscious of the challenges out there,' Rheinisch says. 'I read the article on GB Olympic medallists with high depression rates after the Games. It sounded like support was only in place for six months after they decided to call it a day. We don't have that hard stop here. If athletes need us after they finish, we are here to help.'

The organisation stays with them. How reassuring must that be for someone about to walk away from the sport they love?

PART FOUR

TRAILBLAZERS TARGET NEW TERRITORY

16

NIKKI SYMMONS

Who Am I Now?

BORN: Dublin, 1982.
208 appearances for Irish Women's Hockey team between
2001 and 2013, scoring 31 goals. Won Irish Senior Cup and
Irish Hockey League with Loreto. Inducted into European
Hockey Federation Hall of Fame 2015.
Stepped away from hockey in 2013, aged 31.

In the summer of 2013, Ireland failed to qualify for the women's hockey World Cup and Nikki Symmons cut a frustrated figure.

She had been injury-ravaged for years but by the time her team bid for qualification her hamstrings were overcompensating for weakened hips. 'I couldn't play to full potential in that last game which we needed to win to get through and that hurt more than anything,' she remembers.

Missing the World Championships pinched badly, but a pick-me-up loomed with the Euro Nations Championships in Belgium also on the horizon.

Although they didn't win the tournament, Symmons regained her best form there and, when the hooter sounded in their final match against Scotland, she walked off the pitch, stopping only to hug Scottish coach, Gordon Shepherd, and cry in his arms.

For five years, Shepherd and herself sparked off each other. They were two fiery characters, neither partial to a backward step. But this time they came together in the most humane way.

'We always fought,' she says, smiling. 'He knew I was a threat because I always scored against them and he was always yapping away, trying to wind me up, just little things to try and put me off. He'd get onto the referee if he thought I made a foul, or try mind games, but I guess when people did that over the years, it only inspired me to work harder.

'He did annoy me a bit. But the 2013 game, my last, was different. I walked off the pitch and he came over to me. That's when I started crying. I think he quickly sensed the significance of that occasion – that it was my last game as a hockey player. There I was in his arms – crying on the shoulders of a guy who had been giving me grief for years. Mad.'

That it should mean so much won't surprise anyone who knows Nikki Symmons. For almost a decade and a half she stood in full bloom as an Irish hockey player, perhaps our best ever.

Her youth was spent preoccupied with building a career of unbending purpose and she loved every minute of it.

'People would sometimes tell me that I had no life such was my fixation with sport,' she laughs. 'But I think they missed the point. Sport gave me the best days of my life.'

Deep within her lay an obsession to break new ground for Irish women's hockey. She had a wild longing to be an Olympian and she extended herself fully to try and achieve her dream.

In any sport becoming a centurion is a milestone of magnificence but, impressively, Symmons managed to hit that landmark twice. Between 2001 and 2013 she played 208 times for the Irish senior team, scoring 31 goals.

The journey began long before that.

As a teenager her heart was initially set on being a professional tennis player. She pushed hard on that front, perhaps too keenly, because she remembers being angry with herself during games and losing discipline and focus. Leaning towards team sport she eventually settled on hockey.

She represented her country at under-16, -18 and -21 level, and all through her transition from underage to senior athlete she faithfully turned out for her club, Loreto. In all Symmons played for Ireland at six Women's EuroHockey Nations Championships and played in three Olympic and World Cup qualifying campaigns and, regarded as one of the finest exponents of the game anywhere in the world, she was inducted into the European hockey federation's Hall of Fame in 2015.

Somehow, along the way, she found time to represent the Irish women's cricket team for a year too.

When the winding road she covered finally straightened out to an end point, and her arthritic body called last orders, Symmons' iron-willed mind rebelled at the prospect of retirement.

'I gave so much of my life to training and playing games that it was always going to be so difficult to walk away,' she says.

'My friends were right in one way – I was a creature of routine. Up at 5 a.m. for gym-work or yoga, off to work for the day and back training that night. That was my schedule.'

Everything is finite, however. One day the alarm didn't need to be set for the crack of dawn, nor was there a need to leave the warmth of home for an evening training session. Time caught up with her.

'And for the next three years I scarcely did any exercise at all,' she reveals. 'Hardly broke a sweat. If I saw stairs in front of me, I would look for a lift instead.

'I had given so long to training, preparing my body and exercising that I wanted to do anything but for the next few years. Simple as.'

It's easy to see why that was the case. She had tailored her entire existence around being an elite athlete.

She played on a team that started paving the way for the promotion of women's sport long before the 20x20 movement, the campaign aimed at changing the presentation and perception of women's sport in Ireland, was ever considered.

Very few cared for their efforts at the time. Women's sport was largely unsupported and unheralded with traction of no more than a sidebar in national newspapers. There was very little commercial interest or sponsorship and minimal financial support, and the players regularly had to raise funds themselves, a practice which continued right up to 2018.

The ground they broke may never be properly appreciated.

'Leaving home at 5 a.m. In a gym for 6 a.m.,' Symmons remembers. 'A quick breakfast and off to work. I was a teacher, so it was a day in the classroom with kids, maybe out coaching school teams too. Training again in the evenings – either with the club or the Irish team back at UCD.

'More sessions at the weekends, and club matches too. It was very intense.'

If anything, near the end of her time as an international, Symmons rose the stakes even higher, undergoing bespoke recovery programs, taking pool and bike sessions to help her aching body, anything to keep nimble and supple.

From a long way out, she had seen her career shrouded in

doubt. She underwent two hip operations, one at 26 and the other three years later, but still made it back in time for the 2012 Olympic qualifiers. Medics urged her to consider throwing in the towel, but she didn't listen.

Mr Tom McCarthy, a consultant orthopaedic surgeon at the Sports Surgery Clinic in Santry, operated to remove a big lump of floating cartilage from her left hip and after the procedure, revealed how scans had shown the onset of arthritis, a condition that was hereditary. All this came at a time when the words 'high performance' started to enter the lexicon of women's sport, words that were music to the ears of Symmons.

With even greater determination, Symmons recovered, finding that regular physical activity was key to relieving pain and inflammation and reducing stiffness.

'It took a while but eventually I started more training on an individual basis,' she says, 'and that meant more modified work to keep the body right just to get onto the pitch.'

Like Paul McGrath, who was plagued with chronic knee injuries, she performed to an excellent level long after she was expected to. Unlike McGrath, however, she didn't just do her own training – she also trained fully with the team and took extra sessions to recover quicker.

It was on 24 August, 2013, however, that life was thrown upside down, and all routine cast aside with it. The pleas for purpose which had always driven her started to be met with a flagging spirit.

No trumpets sounded when she walked away. Nor was there any fanfare for a true Irish sporting great.

Earlier in these pages Eoin Rheinisch detailed how Sport Ireland stays with the athlete in retirement. Very few were there for Symmons, however, when she stepped away and that's because she scarcely uttered a word to anyone.

Perhaps if they did, she could have talked things through, got stuff off her chest. Instead, she kept to herself. That was a mistake.

Not long after that Scotland game, Symmons began yearning for the world she had left behind. She hadn't bargained on retirement affected her so instantly.

It wasn't long before she questioned her identity.

Her confidence levels dropped.

She lamented the lack of purpose.

She missed the bit of fuss around her.

And she lost complete interest in exercise.

'Yeah, all of that,' she muses. 'It's all crazy. All that training and then nothing, no exercise, no gym. My mind flipped completely. I realised I was able to do what I wanted, eat what I wanted, and I didn't have to train anymore. It was all very strange.

'Friends would go to the gym and enquire if I wanted to come along too. I had no real interest. It never even came into my mind to get out and do a bit. I think some part of my mind or body was trying to tell me something.'

* * *

If Symmons played the game with fire and brim, Harry Booker was the man who lit the spark.

Harry was her grandfather and both she and her mum, Melanie, lived in the Booker household with him and his wife, Rhona, until Nikki was six.

Symmons' parents' marriage broke up when she was still a

baby and, while initially estranged from her father, she slowly re-established contact with him during her teens. But her grandparents were a constant and steadying influence on her through her formative years and beyond.

'Especially because my dad was not always there,' Symmons says gently.

'Obviously that has an effect on you too. In my teens I probably used sport as an out, a chance to put my own stamp on things.

'I am much more open about all this than I was back then, I have been to therapy a lot, talked about it a lot, and I am comfortable now.

'But at the time I kept a lot in, never wanting to upset my mom. Sport was my outlet. I got very angry with myself at times and I think that's why I had to stop playing tennis but then I discovered the glory of being on a team, training, the challenge of winning. The thrill of playing for your club, province and country, all of that gave me a huge purpose in life. And it helped me with my identity too.'

Years later, Symmons revealed on national TV that she was gay, but she acknowledges that her sport was extremely inclusive, which had been a huge help. Her close friends and family knew by then, but she appeared on RTÉ's *Second Captains* show, and chatted about her sexuality, in the hope that it might even help one person feel more comfortable with themselves.

'I had great support after that interview,' she says.

'Not only about the LGBT side of it but just people in general liked the interview and it felt great that I could show how sport was a place for everyone. And the end of the day it is your performance that counts, not who you sleep with.

'And during those times when my dad was in and out of my life, a lot of other issues were offset because sport was such a constant. Having a regular fixture like that was so important for me and the family. It made Mum so happy to see me involved to such an extent. After my grandad, she was my number one fan, with my granny right up there too. Both of them would drive me everywhere – they came to all my games – they were amazing. There are lovely pictures of them up in the Loreto clubhouse with me.

'At two and a half they had me playing tennis and Grandad would always say, "Nikki, you're going to be a star." He had me in every sport possible. Our summer holidays were spent in caravan parks playing tennis or something else. He had the best saying for us as kids: "chin over the plate, eye on the ball, and close the door".

'I am not afraid to admit it, I was the golden child.'

She offers this little anecdote as evidence.

'One evening I was in the house and there were Leinster trials the following day so we were all a bit nervous.

'Everyone was told to be quiet so I could rest. But our house flooded that night and, before we knew it, we had a river running through the kitchen. They all took shifts to hoover up the water overnight, but Mum wouldn't let me near it. It was all about focusing on the next day and being right for that. So, while things weren't exactly straightforward in my life that's the support I had.'

Harry, an accountant in Trinity College Dublin and an official with the Irish Rugby Football Union, was 92 when he passed away. A governor of High School, Dublin for over 50 years, he was a tireless community worker and a man of infectious enthusiasm, energy and organisational ability. Many that he came into contact with marvelled at the pace with which he attacked life. It was remarked at his funeral that the tempo he maintained would have floored a man a third his age. He had a belief that life was like riding a bicycle: 'You won't fall off unless you stop pedalling.'

With that tsunami of energy driving her on, it's not hard to see how devout and obsessed with the sport Symmons became.

'I wanted to make them happy and proud,' she reflects. 'They instilled the importance of preparing well, to give myself every chance to play elite sport, and how to handle setbacks as well.'

When the end came, however, having spent the bones of 25 years at relentless pace, it was always going to be extremely difficult to adjust and transition.

Especially when she hadn't fully acknowledged the end herself.

* * *

It's a definite regret that there was no official retirement statement because it denied her of the chance to formally close that chapter of her life. The knock-on effects of that have been considerable.

When the Irish team tried to qualify for Rio a few years on in 2016, Symmons sat in a park in Belgium, unable to watch. More recently, when the side finally made it through to the Olympics, via a thrilling 2019 play-off with Canada at the start of November, she wasn't up to taking that in either.

It's partly because she never reconciled her own parting of ways. The current Irish women's squad are a bunch of gritty individuals who lack any sense of when they are beaten. The infusion of new blood into the team has, at times, set pulses racing in this country and made the players a marketer's dream. For paving the way alone, Symmons should be a constant source of inspiration to them.

Maybe she is but, instead, while they were dogging it out with Canada in front of a sell-out crowd at Donnybrook, finally prevailing after a two-legged qualifier, she was alone, receiving match updates from a work colleague. And even at that, her colleague had to check if it was okay to send on snippets.

Deeper inspection suggests that the success of the class of 2019 roused old ghosts for Symmons. Three times her own team were well down the road towards Olympic qualification only to find insurmountable obstacles at the end of each trek. Failing to make the London Games caused a particular type of deep, raw pain – one she never really got over.

On that journey, Symmons and her team sometimes played in front of decent crowds – though more often they performed for hardly anyone. The promotion of the games was up and down, at times poor and occasionally very strong. She remembers playing the Irish Cup final live on RTÉ, which is not the case now, and recalls TV crews following their qualifiers. Thanks to sportswriter Mary Hannigan, there were even two-page spreads in the *Irish Times*. But they were constantly fighting for recognition and hoped they would finally turn a corner with Olympic qualification.

That didn't happen. She wondered why the hurt still lingered all those years later when the 2019 team finally qualified and senses it is because she gave no closure to her own experiences. She never officially closed that chapter of her life. Back it came to haunt her.

'I guess the truth is I just ran away from it all. I didn't officially retire – I just disappeared,' she explains.

'People didn't understand what was happening in my head, but this was my personal battle. My battle with losing that whole identity I had grown up with.

'I will be blunt about it. I had many panic attacks after retiring. I was angry, sad and disappointed that we hadn't achieved more. And yet my body was relieved that I was no longer competing. That was the dilemma I had.

'It's a bit of a blur now as I look back, but I had a massive mix of emotions and I wasn't always able to control them, especially when I had a few drinks. Everything changed. I totally eased up on my nutritional intake and, as I said, exercise went out the window.

'It wasn't as if I went back to friends and family because I moved to Switzerland. It was the right move to make but I ran away a lot back then. Whatever story I had created, I didn't close it out properly. There's a message here: after devoting so much of your life to something you must acknowledge what you have done. I didn't. That's one regret.'

She is proud of the current Irish team, admires them, and feels almost guilty that she wasn't able to watch their games with Canada.

'Their success is so deserved, and it was such a long time coming. I got a few texts afterwards telling me that I had been part of that journey, but it took quite a while for that message to really sink in, to be honest,' she says.

'I know in my heart I was part of it. All I ever wanted to do was play hockey for Ireland and to be an Olympian. Even when I was sounded out to play for another country, and it happened a few times in passing, Ireland was my heart and soul; I felt we could qualify for major events and I went out of my way to make it all happen. I went to Germany to play for a club there (Eintracht Braunschweig during the 2006–07 season) and to experience training with different clubs. To get specialist training. My grandad and mom driving me around the country for matches and extra training, that set the dial. You work all the way up trying to make the highest level you can.

'When it all ended, I should have taken a bit of time to reflect. Maybe that would have helped the transition from playing to retirement.

'But I never did that. Instead I looked back and saw how complicated our road to the Olympics was – we had intricate round robin sections to get through before we could even make the crossover games. It was harsh. For instance, the London 2012 Games involved a round-robin format with five teams, all played within one week and we had to win every single game to qualify. Whereas in 2019 we had one one-off games to make it through.

'This stuff goes around in your head . . . the fact that we didn't qualify ourselves . . . it led to heartbreak for some time. And there is still heartbreak there that we never got through.

'While I couldn't watch the girls playing against Canada, it had nothing to do with them at all. I was delighted for them but there is also a big gap for me, looking on and wishing I could be part of it. That's just me being honest.'

Symmons had identified the 2012 Games as being the pinnacle of her career and would gladly have disappeared into the sunset had she made it there. Once that didn't transpire, she endured a massive struggle to get going again.

By then she was also bearing the repercussions of those hip operations and struggling fortunes at club level. It was a strain to keep the show on the road. After one club game, her brother came over to commiserate after they had lost and, as they chatted, she started crying again.

'"I don't want to do this anymore." That's what I told him. I couldn't bear losing again. So many times, I had been living up to this dream, but I was getting no closer to it.'

Her brother reminded her nothing was compulsory. She was starting to come around to his way of thinking.

With no official retirement marking the aftermath of the Scotland game, Symmons was basically allowed to slip away from the public conscience in August 2013.

As she surveyed the landscape, new horizons emerged in the distance. A position on a Sports Management masters in Lausanne, Switzerland was grasped and accepted on the athlete scholarship programme. She travelled over alone, but also to be with her girlfriend who was already there.

From that Masters, she got a job with the International Hockey Federation (FIH) in its digital communications department. Her job specification was to help raise the global status and popularity of hockey, leading their online and social media strategy.

In some ways it was the perfect job. In other ways it was awkward.

'I avoided some of the FIH events because it would have involved meeting teammates, people I had played with. That was nothing to do with any of them at all. It was me. I can see now that there was just stuff in my head at the time.'

Symmons commentated at the World Cup qualifiers and the Rio Olympics for FIH and found that especially awkward.

'Because I had so desperately wanted to be there as an athlete,' she explains. 'But I guess I did manage to get some love back for the game whilst there at these major events – even Rio, where I saw at first hand the values of the Games. I had to steel myself for all that.'

As challenging as being in Rio was, a new episode of her life story had started. She didn't immediately recognise it, but the narrative was changing in front of her.

* * *

As she details the transition from playing to retiring Symmons admits she almost had to form a new character.

'I was a different person when I was an athlete. When I was playing, even if it was fake sometimes, I had a swagger about me. I was really confident. I felt good running out in front of lots of people or empty venues. To me, whether you were singing the anthem in front of 300 people or 3,000 people, the honour was huge.

'Even when I was retired and working for FIH, I remember going to a tournament in Argentina where there were thousands of people at the games. Those I met saw that I had an FIH badge on and many of them came over, chatting away, and it was great to have that interaction. You know what, I miss that bit of limelight too.

'It's like your uniqueness in life disappears. I did try to keep it all going, doing some commentary work and then being part of the RTÉ series *Ireland's Fittest Family* soon after I stopped playing.

'In an overall context, though, it was too early in the evolution of female sport to be able to stay in Irish sport in a meaningful way.'

The journey continued when she joined multinational company, Philip Morris, which is based in Lausanne.

'I joined for a few reasons,' she details. 'I needed a break from sport, and because I saw the company at the start of the biggest transformation ever seen in the business world. The department senior vice-president is also a trailblazing woman, Marian Salzman, and it is an equal salary certified company with a diversity and inclusion drive. That was all very important when deciding my next move, as the sports world is still very uneven regarding gender balance and equal pay issues and sports in general is not doing enough about diversity and inclusion.'

It took some time, but she started to identify that many skills from her sporting past were transferrable to the corporate world. Not that she ever sung from the rooftops about her past life.

After three months working at the company, one of her colleagues came over and chastened her, 'Hey, you never told me you played hockey for Ireland! Or that you got into the Hall of Fame. You need to be much better about telling people stuff like that. You need to show off your achievements.'

Symmons took note. She had noticed how other athletes who had performed at Olympic Games commanded a certain status and reached positions others found more difficult to access. Olympians are hot property in the corporate sector and being part of that elite was something Symmons always desired.

'In that respect, part of the issue of dealing with retirement was the fact that I wasn't an Olympian either really hit home. And even now, would I be a better proposition to a company or organisation had I qualified for the Olympics? I probably would. In my own head anyway.'

She knows she can't retain that mindset forever. Nor should she. Things are working out fine. At Philip Morris, Symmons is now looking after operations of content and digital channels for a business that spends billions in research and development.

'Gradually, I have been able to find myself again, though. I've been able to refer back to how hard I worked in sport. How we communicated with each other. The discipline and determination. The resilience.

'That made me remember when coaches of mine would remark that I was often the temperature gauge of the team, saying that how I played helped determine how we would do. I realise now it could be the same here at work. If I am having more productive or communicative day, you help the team around you too.

'In the corporate world you see things that upset others but, really, they are things not worth getting stressed about. I always go back to hockey when you might be under so much pressure to score the last penalty to win a game or run a hundred yards to make a last-gasp tackle. Those are pressures you can't learn everywhere.

'As an athlete I find that you turn up for a job in the workplace and you are able for pressure and ready to go. Obviously, not everyone – in any company – will be highly motivated all the time but I find that, as a sportsperson, you come in and don't usually mess around.

'You have an instinct. You are a good team player, good, too, on the communication side of things. Had sport not helped me with all of that, and helped me to make bold choices, I'd never be here in this country or company.'

* * *

The readjustment is ongoing.

By the time the Covid-19 pandemic forced the postponement of the 2020 Olympic Games, Symmons felt that she was finally ready to sit down and throw herself into watching the Irish team. She felt ready to take it all in, content that while she endeavoured hard to make it herself, she was also thrilled for those who did manage to get to that level.

'Some of the players were pretty young when I played with them, but I always tried to help out with tough training sessions, dealing with being dropped, that kind of stuff.

'A few of the Loreto girls are now starring at national level and I fondly remember passing on skills and drills from the Irish team to them. Knowledge-transfer is a key aspect of development of new and old generations alike. And it's something I really try to bring to my new working environment too.

'Players like Nikki Evans, Anna O'Flanagan and Shirley McCay – these girls are amazing and deserve all they get.

'When I was a young player on the national scene, people like Arlene Boyles, Clare McMahon and Jenny Burke helped me make the step up from youth to senior player and that's something I will forever be grateful for.'

Away from home, having forged her own path, Symmons is now open to reflection.

'I plan now on continuing my education, like taking courses in diversity and inclusion. I want to use my platform and background to help in this area in the future and become a leader in this space.

'I know I had more confidence when I was playing, but I am slowly getting that back too. I think the hardest thing for me was losing my identity. It was so perplexing that I actually did my final college project on the subject.

'But I'm now starting to feel proud of what I did, the road I took, the journey I had.'

Resilience. Determination. Bravery. Learning and evolvement.

Harry Booker, when he looks down on her, surely smiles with great pride too. He taught her well.

17

GRÁINNE MURPHY

Forever Young

BORN: Wexford, 1993.
Former European silver medallist, holds three senior Irish records,
in the 800m and 1,500m freestyle and the 200m individual medley.
Stepped away from competitive swimming in 2016, aged 22.

Sunday, 29 July, 2012
Swimming
Aquatic Centre
London Olympic Games

She was there in name only.

In London, 19-year-old Gráinne Murphy was a pale shadow of herself, finishing last in her 400 metres heat in a time of 4.19.07 – a full ten seconds outside her qualifying time. She immediately withdrew from the 200 metres freestyle and soon ruled herself out of the 800 metres freestyle too.

'Once I dived into the pool for that 400 metres heat I knew things were not right,' Murphy remembers. 'I knew that was that.

'For years, I had done the same warm up to taper for an event,' she explains. 'It was generally the same routine from when I was

15, incorporating a three-kilometre swim. But we even had to scale that back because three kilometres was a lot for me with the circumstances I faced. The warm-up took place an hour and a half before the race started and my coach and I took a chance that race day might turn out to be a good day. After the warm up we both knew it would not be the case.'

The pressure to perform in London was huge. Murphy had established herself as one of the country's top sportspeple and was heralded as a geuine medal prospect in the eyes of many following her victory in the 1,500 metres freestyle at the 2010 European Championships.

Her coach, Ronald Claes, knew what she was capable of. In London, however, Claes' humanity shone like a beacon. He was both understanding and supportive.

'We didn't have to say anything to each other after the warm-up,' Murphy continues, 'because we both knew then it wasn't going to happen for me. The one hope we had was that I might be okay on the day. Very few others knew what was going on, very few outside my support team knew that I had contracted glandular fever. Afterwards people offered up all sorts of opinions, but, as far as I was concerned, they could say what they wanted. They didn't know the full story.'

It would have been easy for Murphy and her team to come out pre-Olympics, reveal the contraction of glandular fever, and reduce expectation. But she was a private person in the first instance, and not one to lean on the excuses either.

'Instead we tried to tweak training the best we could, keeping things to ourselves,' she says. 'I guess things came out in the public domain after the 400 metres heat and people were surmising. When I finished that race, I was so weak I could barely get myself out of the water,' she admits. 'It was a struggle to do so.'

Distraught at seeing her Olympic dream dashed, having seen five years of rigorous, full-time training go up in smoke, the 19-year-old Ballinaboola girl had to face the nation. Such was the expectation on Murphy's shoulders that she was deemed a feasible medal prospect and that drew in a more general television audience for her heat. This led to her failure to qualify being played out on a very public platform. For a young athlete who always kept to herself that was tough. Much worse, though, was the fact that she hadn't been able to do herself justice.

She shuffled quietly back from the pool to her changing room, and that walk is as clear in her mind as if it happened yesterday.

'John Kenny from RTÉ was in the mixed zone waiting for an interview,' Murphy remembers. 'I get on really well with John and never once passed him after a race but this time I just said, "John, I'm going to have to come back to you." I needed to be by myself; I was absolutely devastated.'

Kenny was completely understanding.

'No problem,' the reporter replied, empathising with the situation.

Murphy picks up: 'For a journalist to say that's no problem to an athlete who is after competing for her country in the Olympics is very understanding. The media were all waiting on the story of why I hadn't qualified but he was very respectful even though it was his job to get my reaction as quickly as he could. Maybe it helped that I had never passed him before and there was respect between us. But I was lucky because it gave me time and space to go to my coach and reflect on what had just happened. And that's all I wanted there and then, just to be with a familiar face from my support team.

'There was an awareness that many people back home were looking in, so after a little while my coach urged me to compose myself a little. From there I went back to talk to John. But I was so raw.'

At the time a national newspaper repored that political pressure was then applied for Murphy to swim in the 800 metres heat amid reports that her future funding might be affected if she didn't perform. Murphy, however, knew she simply wouldn't be able to race again. To get an outside standpoint she spoke to Billy Walsh, the Irish Boxing High Performance head coach, and a fellow Wexford native. She also consulted Sonia O'Sullivan, who was chef de mission for Team Ireland at the 2012 Games and in charge of the national team.

'They gave me a different perspective. I listened to their advice but, ultimately, I knew I wouldn't be able to do myself justice and decided not to swim. I didn't watch the heats of the 800 metres event, although I did watch the final.'

Not only did she take herself out of competition, Murphy went back to the Olympic Village, collected a few bits and pieces from the apartment she was sharing with Melanie Nocher, and then flew back to Ireland, both for her own peace of mind and to give her flatmate every chance to prepare for her own specific events, the 100-metres and 200-metres backstrokes.

'I knew that getting out of there was 100 per cent right for me,' she insists. 'I do put on a very good front at times and so no one really knows what goes on behind the scenes. But it was tough dealing with the fallout of London; one of toughest things I will ever face in my whole life. Apart from what happened to me there was a lot of politics going on in the background and I didn't need to hear about any of that, not only for my mental health, but for my health in general. I was lucky my parents were there, so I was shielded and able to move out and do what was best for me.'

Aside from the fears for her funding, other internal issues, such as the selection of coaches, were emerging at the same time. Outside forces were starting to invade her space more and more.

On home ground Murphy had more bloods taken to ensure her condition hadn't worsened and, a few days later, she, somewhat unexpectedly, decided to fly back to London for the closing ceremony. Possibly to close out the Games and the painful memories that came with it.

'Going back to Wexford in between did a lot for me and it just felt like a safe place; that's the best way to describe it,' she says. 'I come from small village where everybody knows everybody and no one there was wondering what illness I had or hadn't – they just wanted to know was Gráinne okay.

'That was really nice because I saw everyone just pulling together around me. They tried hard to get me comfortable with being back out in the public again. My family has a hotel so even though I had lots of things built up in my head, about what people might think of me, it was the best thing I ever done to come back and just be around people. To be able to front up. Maybe that's why I went back for the closing ceremony too.'

At her young age, having invested so much time and sacrificed so much for what could have been the pinnacle of her admittedly callow sporting career, she instead spent the aftermath dealing with trauma, both physical and psychological.

It was a dark time.

Murphy readily admits the full extent of the experience didn't hit home for some time.

For a start, she continued to struggle with her condition, glandular fever, long after the Olympics.

'I could never keep my body 100 per cent right for a long time after it,' she admits. 'From 2012 to 2016 there was never a run of two months where I didn't get sick. It is very hard to train to the level you want if you constantly get sick and see the progression you want suffer.

'As I speak now my health is getting better and my immune system is too, but would I say I am as healthy as I was prior to ever getting it? Probably not.

'To this day, I am still conscious of not over pushing myself and that can be challenging at times. I am just about managing now and that's what I have been doing since it came.'

* * *

She stepped out of a lane for the last time three years later, at just 22, with her identity tightly aligned to swimming.

'I did get people coming up to me until very recently asking how training was going,' she smiles. 'I would just reply that it was going well. And I am working for Swim Ireland now as well, so I am always meeting people involved in the sport and they are warm to me. I can look back and take a lot of positives from my time competing so I'm fine with being known as a swimmer,' she nods.

That sense of peace is the least she is entitled to after the monumental, winding journey she trekked.

The sacrifices were colossal. The serious stuff commenced following enrolment at Castletroy College, Limerick, at the age of 13, so that she could train in the University of Limerick international standard pool.

'I moved there when I was 13,' Murphy recalls. 'Looking back, I was so young it was probably easy enough for me to do without much hassle. It was all simple enough really; I moved there to progress in swimming.

'I had been in secondary school in Wexford, an all-girls school and from there I moved to a mixed school in Castletroy, so that was a bit of a change. But the transition went very smooth which I hadn't fully expected.

'My parents bought a house in Limerick for which I am very grateful, and Mam would spend every week with me. She returned to Wexford at the weekends and Dad would come to Limerick when Mam went back. They were there every step of the way with me. I am the youngest which made it easier. My sister was in college in Shannon studying hotel management and that was only out the road, so it all kind of worked.

'That's how it went until I was 18 and got a bit of freedom when I started driving. My parents would come down and visit after that and I stayed put until I was 22 or 23.'

The roads from Limerick over to Wexford, and those arduous treks for two hours and 40 minutes across country trails, would test Eddie Irvine's navigation skills but it wasn't until Murphy got behind the wheel herself that she fully appreciated the mammoth effort her parents had made, the energy and commitment they had invested in a shared dream.

'It's funny,' she laughs. 'At the start when we were going back home, I used to sleep a lot and mum did the driving. So, I didn't really know a lot about the trek, only that we would stop along the way for a toilet break and where the stops were. Aside from that I was asleep for the majority of those journeys. But when you drive yourself, it's a different story! You realise exactly how bad it is.'

Education was part of the plan, but she was essentially there to swim. Some like-minded athletes linked up with her and she nestled nicely into the school, ran by its understanding principal, Martin Wallace.

'There were stints when we missed four to five weeks at a time, away at some international event, and some schools wouldn't really support what we were doing, but Martin was great in that regard,' Murphy remembers.

It was hard to invest so much into training and then head off to the classroom.

'I kind of just coasted through school,' Murphy says, 'I did enough to get through and when I got to sixth year I split my Leaving Cert over two years, three subjects the first year and three the second year. That helped too.

'But I needed to do it. We could be gone out of the school Mondays to Thursdays, competing weekends, often outside of the country. So splitting it into three and three worked.'

Rising time came at 4.30 every morning over the next eight years, and straight to the classroom afterwards, getting through study and winding down at 8.30 in the evenings.

That dedication and commitment saw her first sprang to the attention of the Irish sporting public at 16, winning three gold and a bronze medal at the 2009 European Junior Championships in Prague. That success catapulted her into the glare of the Irish media and placed her at the top of sports bulletins.

More glory followed when she transferred her success to senior level, winning a silver medal in the 1,500 metres freestyle at the 2010 European Championships. She went on to break three senior Irish records, in the 800 metres and 1,500 metres freestyle and the 200 metres individual medley.

From an Irish swimming perspective, her progress was much longed-for, and seemed to offer a rock-solid foundation on which the administration could build again following years of flailing through muddy waters.

As recently as the start of the last decade the perception of Irish swimming was tainted. Mention of its brand would evoke immediate thoughts of controversial gold medals at previous Games.

Mine deeper still and the revelation of the sickening child abuse scandals that rocked the sport, with subsequent convictions for those found guilty, were more troubling.

There were frequent rumblings behind the scenes with ceaseless discussions around the lack of a national 50-metre pool and differences of opinion on certain coaches.

Slowly, change came a brighter future seemed possible. Murphy quickly became a face for hope in her chosen sport, a role model for the new, marketable Swim Ireland.

In 2010, she drove it all onto a new level when she took silver at those European Championships in Budapest. The *Irish Times*/ Irish Sports Council pronounced her Sportswoman of the Year. Expectation was growing all the time.

'I had no problem with that because I had big expectations too,' she says. 'And while I would have been aware of the outside, external stuff that comes with winning medals I paid no heed to it either. Really, I didn't. After a medal or an event, I always quickly went back to train. I could control what I needed to – even if the anticipation was growing in public.'

Some things, however, were outside her jurisdiction. In 2011, she had her shoulder cleaned out and it took time to return to competition.

It was after that when she was struck by glandular fever, just as her entire backroom had tightened the focus on the upcoming London Games.

Murphy takes up the story. 'In March of that year I was competing at an event and training in Copenhagen with Lotte Friis, who I trained with and swam against, and at that event I didn't feel well at all.

'I flew back, got my bloods done, and the doctors suspected a virus, but it can be hard to find exactly what was wrong in those situations. By April, nothing had shown up but we still kind of knew something was not right. I got more blood tests and eventually found that I had glandular fever.

'Straight away we pulled back on my training and adapted as best we could. We knew it would be a massive risk going over to London, but we took that risk and I prepared as well as I could and eased off best as I could coming into the 2012 Games.'

Easing off for Murphy, however, would be someone else's idea of hell. A typical tough week's training meant distances of between 80 and 90 kilometres across six days. Even letting up on the throttle, she was still covering between 40 and 60 kilometres. Tiredness remained the key issue, however, and some mornings Murphy would wake up and just could not get out of bed. One-hour daytime naps could often stretch into a four-hour slumber. Something was way off.

She examined her entire schedule to find answers.

'We changed everything,' she said. 'We even tried herbs, albeit out of competition as we were aware of all the protocols with drug testing. The herbs helped but they didn't sustain.'

Murphy could have been forgiven for cursing the heavens and wondering why the gods had inflicted this upset on her at such a crucial juncture in her career.

For years, she had done everything by the book using UL as her hub of excellence, accomplishing so much across ten sessions a week over a number of years.

As the London Games drew closer, she tried to keep the illness at bay and even clocked up Olympic final standard times in training, but the crucial difference was that it was taking much longer to recover between sessions.

Her support team knew the risks of competing at the Games below par, but collectively they decided it was a gamble they simply had to take, given the work that Murphy and the team had invested.

'Take away all the medical science, all the tests, everything and in the end the hope in going to the Games was that we might just get a good day,' Murphy says. 'And I could go out and do what I knew I could do.'

Fate was nowhere near as kind.

* * *

Following London, and the harrow of it all, everything changed. Changed utterly.

Just a month after the Games ended, so too did Ronald Claes' time in Ireland as Swim Ireland looked ahead to the next Olympic cycle and sought to make organisational changes.

Though Claes and his support staff at UL were progressing steadily, the decision was made not to prolong his contract. Claes was coach to both Murphy and UL and the news came as a massive shock to all parties who had huge respect for and kinship with their coach. Tensions were high between all parties. Swim Ireland felt justified in their actions – they had set a goal of qualifying six swimmers for London but only four managed to make it through.

In London, the notion of entering a relay team featuring Murphy had been floated but Claes had felt it would affect Murphy's individual preparation and a team was never entered. That didn't go down well. Pressure had also been applied for Murphy to compete in the 800 metres despite her suffering so much with illness.

Now, just a few weeks after enduring the biggest disappointment of her career, Murphy was without her trusted coach too; a mentor who had been with her every step of the way in the previous five years.

Her world was turned on its head.

'There was a lot going on behind the scenes,' she says, most diplomatically. 'It took a long time for things to calm down.

'I went on holiday when I came back from the Games and was hoping I could turn a corner when I came back.

'But I suppose I just didn't know where to go. That was a worrying time for everyone. I really had to work hard to get through it.'

Murphy consulted her sports psychologist, Declan Aherne, who she had worked with since moving to Limerick, and they attempted to build her back up after the travails of London.

'I thought I hit my lowest point around September and

October, but it didn't really affect me properly until a few months after that because I had been putting on a brave face as well,' she reckons.

'I'd say it was probably only in February or March of the following year when I really came right. Our family went skiing after every Christmas and when I came back from that things started to click back into place again.'

With her coach no longer in tow, Murphy kick-started her comeback in local confines, joining Fran Ronan, head coach at New Ross Swimming Pool. Ronan immediately set about helping to rejuvenate the young star.

Once her confidence levels began to soar again, she returned to Limerick. Stronger, if anything, for the torturous year that was.

'I learned that the journey back is just as rewarding as the one you take to win medals,' she insists.

'Medals are great, but I learned that it's what happens between each medal and how you deal with the ups and downs that make it all more rewarding.

'I decided to strip it all back. When I first arrived in Limerick, I was the youngest, but when I returned this time, I was the one training with kids quite a bit younger than me, even though I still wasn't that old myself.

'But it was nice be in that environment once more.'

Murphy balanced the next year there, studying for a degree in exercise and health fitness and training at UL, before moving to France for a year to continue her preparation to qualify for the Rio Olympics.

In November 2015, during her stay there, the team broke away for a specialised training camp in Romania. She was fast regaining her form and working well under her new mentor, Philippe Lucas, the renowned coach to French Olympic champion Laura Manaudou, who had won gold in the women's 400 metres freestyle at the 2004 Athens Games.

'Approaching Olympic year in Rio I was all ready to go again,' she recalls.

'I was making massive jumps under my new coach that I hadn't done in two to three years and it was all really positive. I was excited.

'For two weeks before that trip I had felt wheezy and I went to see the doctors for a check. They thought it was a viral infection and bells began ringing in my mind again. I was worried. But I flew to Romania thinking it would settle down.'

In the early stages of that camp, however, she still didn't feel herself and knew something was not quite right.

Due to the language barrier, she couldn't clearly understand what the doctors were advising, so she came back to Ireland and consulted her own medical team who advised her to take time off.

'They diagnosed a lung infection and a bad one at that,' she says. 'I got tonsilitis and everything else came with it, there was fluid on the lung as well.'

The infection was severe and took a long time to clear. Long enough to have hindered her chances in Rio.

'By now I really had to start thinking of my own long-term health,' she admits. 'I knew the levels of performance that I could still get to, and I knew my times were good enough to qualify for the Rio Olympics, but when I got there would I do myself justice? Would I be just competing, or would I be able to perform?'

Deep down there was no way she was going to re-inflict the torture of London on herself again. While her resilience had been steeled, her mindset was crystal clear leading up to Rio.

'I knew what I had to do,' she says. 'I needed to look after myself, simple as that.

'I remember, following the 2012 Games, going up to Dublin and meeting different committees and people for reviews of my performance and, in hindsight, I should have said I wasn't able to go. I was only 19 and those reviews had a huge impact on me. They were not easy.

'I wasn't going to be able for them again, nor having another serious illness to contend with. And I could also appreciate that I had a full life left after swimming too.'

Two months later, once she had it squared off in her own mind, she publicly announced her decision to retire from competitive swimming.

It still doesn't seem right that the bright young star of Irish swimming faded before she even got the chance to shine further on the world stage; one she was born to illuminate. But her retirement statement reflected an athlete in acceptance of the wretched hand of cards she was dealt. Her farewell was classy, focused mostly on the good times, and only briefly hinting at a rotten run of illnesses and sicknesses. For her own peace of mind, and her wellness, it was the only one to make.

'But I suppose deep down there was an awful lot of anger there and frustration,' she reveals.

'And I had to work through all of that.'

* * *

From November 2015, when she knew her days as an elite competitor in the pool were finished, until the Rio Olympics began at the start of August when she was selected by RTÉ to commentate on their swimming coverage, Murphy didn't once go inside a swimming pool.

That's extraordinary – from going almost 15 years where a day scarcely passed without her being in water to not going near a pool for six months.

'I felt like I needed to stay away,' she says. 'But when I got the call from RTÉ to commentate in Rio, it was a good push for me to get back into it.

'After getting the call I had about three months to get myself ready to go back into a pool and talking about swimming.

'I used it as a really good opportunity. It was nice to get the call as a female athlete, firstly and, secondly, I knew I would be working with Andrew Bree and Earl McCarthy, two really good guys.'

The experience was positive. She used it to begin moving on with her life, learning to detach herself from the disappointments she had endured.

She threw herself back into education, finished her degree in 2017, took on the six-month internship and worked on PR and Media campaigns right across the sporting spectrum.

'That's when a job came up with Swim Ireland,' she adds.

'I was hesitant to apply at first, but I spoke to few people and they said I had a lot to give back.'

She certainly has. Murphy was successful in her job interview and is currently the national coordinator for the 'Get Ireland Swimming' programme at Swim Ireland. It involves leading a participation programme nationwide, travelling the country, encouraging schools to take their pupils swimming. Since taking up the position, over 6,000 have taken part in the programme.

'Would I work in the performance department of the organisation? Probably not, but this job was in the participation department and that's what I enjoy because you are getting out there, meeting grassroots and making swimming accessible to everyone.'

She delights in seeing people who had never seen the inside of a pool until the age of 12 growing to love the sport.

Sometimes she misses the madness of her former life and sometimes she doesn't.

'Physically, I would not be able to give 100 per cent and there is no point in me ever doing anything unless I can put the maximum effort in.'

She gets a kick from media work, doing commentary for Swim Ireland at the national championships, the Olympics with RTÉ, the Paralympics with TG4.

'It's just changing the mindset,' she explains, 'this is now what I can give 100 per cent to rather than being in the water.'

She's back in college again, now studying for a masters degree and she has been drafted onto the European Olympic Committee 'New Leaders Programme', one of two Irish candidates and 30 from across Europe.

And what about the loss of who she once was? Grainne Murphy, Irish swimming star, international medallist, Olympic hopeful.

'I think I am still Grainne Murphy the swimmer.

'Swimming will always be part of who I am and hopefully what I did manage to do will be recognised over time. The whole journey has made me more resilient and there is still so much road ahead and hopefully I can keep using skills I had in sport in my career.

'I know how to stand up for myself, for instance. I know how to handle myself.'

18

SONIA O'SULLIVAN

Racing the Sunset

BORN: Cork, 1969
Won 16 major athletics championship medals including gold in
the 5,000 metres at the 1995 World Championships, and silver
in the 5,000 metres at the 2000 Olympic Games.
Injury interrupted elite level competition from 2009 and moved away
from the international competitive circuit at that juncture, aged 40.

Running fast. Forever. Every stride driving her towards greatness.

It was always the way. Right from when she was just a schoolgirl in Cobh, wanting to be the quickest to get home every afternoon, racing between lamp posts.

Sonia O'Sullivan always wanted to be first, whether that was in the fields around her hometown or training with elite athletes on a US scholarship programme at Villanova, about a half hour outside Philadelphia – a world away from Cobh but somewhere Sonia went to refine her talent and reach new levels.

In retirement, all these years later, she is still intent on making use of every stride, keeping some purpose to it all, but it took time to reach that stage.

With her competitive days behind her it wasn't easy to recall and redirect the focus and motivation that had sustained her through the years.

In 2017, a report by the Irish Sports Monitor found that almost 300,000 adults run regularly in this country, more than those who play soccer and Gaelic Games combined. Running is huge here and, if you get hooked, it's a habit that can cling for life, the ultimate health pill. As the old saying goes, 'Once a runner, always a runner.' Place a pin on a map anywhere in the world, check out a local park run, ten-kilometre race or marathon and you will find ages of eight to 80, all running to their own rhythms. Focused, not on the competitors beside them, but mainly with their own time and tempo.

But say you're Sonia O'Sullivan, and running was not only your passion but your life and career too?

In retirement, do you just switch off and start running socially? Is that even possible?

Most of her life, Sonia fastened her shoes each morning and the haste, distance and destination of the schedule ahead was determined by what her coach said, or what the training manual dictated.

When those days pass, and the focus fades, how can you find a stimulus to stay casually invested in the sport you obsessed over for so long?

For O'Sullivan, it was a complex transition.

Firstly, the Irish media jumped the gun. In early 2007, reports circulated in the national press that arguably the finest Irish sporting career ever was nearing an end, that O'Sullivan was calling time on her competitive days.

Those headlines appeared ahead of an appearance at the Great Ireland Run in the Phoenix Park and the country prepared itself to bid a mass farewell to the Queen of Cobh and her magnificent innings.

This was all news to Sonia.

She was on her last lap, no doubt about it, but she still had own aims and goals to strive for. The tap couldn't be turned off just like that.

On the contrary, there were a couple more track races in her schedule, a cross-country race to compete in, and she was also considering running another marathon.

Maybe those events could have culminated in a lengthy farewell season being played out, but Sonia was never going to grind to an immediate halt.

For her, retirement is a strong word and even now it's not one she easily uses. In truth, athletes like O'Sullivan never fully give up. They continue to run every day because it's what they do. They stay going until they find a new purpose.

And here's the great thing: while others were wording her sporting obituary, Sonia, whether she consciously planned it or not, was eyeing up another career milestone.

As twilight set on her elite days, she made one last tilt at the Olympics – running in the 2006 New York marathon with the hope to hit the qualifying mark for Bejing 2008.

'I don't think that I woke up one day and was retired,' she deliberates. 'I didn't have an official last race. I think I just evolved into retirement from international competition. The hardest thing for me was when I couldn't run due to injury, when it was hard to put a plan in place due to a lot of stop-start training.

'I think my last international race for Ireland was the world half-marathon in 2004, but I continued to train at a high level for many years after and wasn't far off qualifying for Beijing.'

She was very close, in fact, following a time of 2.42.05 which was just five seconds off the standard needed to get to the Games. These minuscule margins dictate the future, and, for O'Sullivan, that narrow failure – and subsequent injuries – interrupted any further realistic shot at glory.

'It wasn't to be,' she says. 'After that I could never quite regain the momentum and miles required to chase the Olympic dream again. Eventually I did succumb to injury and gave up the drive for one more Olympic race.

'That's the biggest challenge,' she continues, 'being comfortable with yourself when, mentally, you still strive to be the best, but your body doesn't co-operate. You have to adjust to accepting a lower level and a different purpose in sport and life.'

When you've won all around you, blazed trails across the country, continent and world, that cannot be simple. Especially for someone strong in their conviction that they could still perform at a high level.

Those mounting injuries that she speaks of rendered training intermittent, however, and her body didn't let her do what she once did.

O'Sullivan at least attempted to get used to life without elite racing, but it was a test. Every so often she found herself revisiting old training manuals that she used as a schoolgirl, just to see if she could hit anywhere near past times, but it was difficult to match with the quality of that era, hard to reignite the spark that had once fired a furnace.

She recalls missing the energy and adrenalin that came with training at the highest level. For a long time afterwards, Sonia never wore a watch to measure her time, speed and distance in training as she felt she didn't want to know how slow she was going. There was no room for reflection either. She just decided to move on to the next stage of her life.

Part of that involved a period of detachment from the sport that had consumed her for so long. She may even have fallen out of love with it.

Just how difficult was that decision to eventually let go?

'I never really took the decision to retire so I have never been comfortable with this question,' she responds.

'I just got slower and less motivated, walked away from athletics quietly, and my only real connection with the sport was through RTÉ commentary work,' she reveals.

'This helped a lot around the Beijing Olympics because it gave me an outlet to be involved at another level, and let me look from the outside whilst still having a close insight as I was still familiar with the athletes that were racing.'

O'Sullivan accepts that it took a few years for her to fully embrace the fact that athletics could remain a big part of her daily life.

She dabbled in other pursuits for a while, enjoyed them too, but, ultimately, running was what she craved the most.

In that time a very important realisation dawned that she should stay connected to the sport she grew up with – only this time without being fully absorbed. Just to enjoy it on another level while she looked in from the outside.

The challenge was finding a way to stay running and still retain a purpose.

* * *

O'Sullivan writes a thoughtful weekly column with the *Irish Times* and it always makes for great reading. In those pages she revealed how it was only in the last decade when she understood that many people see running as simply something to be enjoyed and beneficial to their health.

For a long time after she stepped away, she was still trying to be competitive and wasn't content to join the social runners. Finding a direction was the ongoing challenge.

That's when she started to set more realistic goals for where her body was at.

She did that through looking for certain times in park runs, ten-kilometre races, whatever she chooses. She found that once she had some sort of target, and it didn't have to be one that breaks world records, she could enjoy herself.

Sonia looked beyond running too and tried trail running, cycling and swimming. Those pursuits have all become a part of her new routine. They supplement each other and she gets a huge buzz from them on non-running days.

She has also made great friends from those experiences and her immense fitness levels from a lifespan of competing allow her to target personal bests in the other sports, in swimming and cycling especially.

'I continued to train at a high level and have never really given up that structure,' she reveals.

'There was a period before those sports became so popular amongst everyone when it was difficult to be training – and not with any purpose.

'But around 2012, when I became involved with the Irish Olympic team as chef de mission, I decided to use sport as an outlet – something I enjoyed rather than competed at.

'I also adapted to compete on another level and challenge myself in those other areas, such as swimming, cycling and triathlon events, but again those were not so popular as they are nowadays so I kind of missed that window to compete in them when I was still training at a high level.'

It's not hard to see why she misses the single-mindedness so much.

In representing Ireland on the international athletics stage for a full 19 years between 1988 and 2007, she competed in four Olympic Games, only narrowly missing out on that fifth qualification, for Bejing.

Her versatility ensured excellence across a number of disciplines, putting her right up there in the debate over who is the country's greatest ever sportsperson. From cross-country to track to marathon running, she excelled, winning six world cross-country championships, six world track and field championships and five European championships.

Even though she never raced in the event in college, the 5,000 metres turned out to be her speciality. In the 2000 Sydney Olympic Games, she won a silver medal in that event, having taken gold five years previously in the same event at the 1995 World Championships. O'Sullivan also set an Olympic 5,000-metre record at the Atlanta Games with her 15:15.80 semi-final win.

But such was her range as an elite athlete that she competed anywhere from 800 metres upwards, setting a multitude of national records from the 10,000 metres distance to the half-marathon.

Finding new goals, having achieved so much already, is not easy but O'Sullivan says it is advisable to have a focus inside and outside of sport.

'Purpose is important in your life every day,' she says. 'And there comes a time when you need to change the course of what you are doing if you can no longer operate at the same level. The difficulty is when you have given up so much of your life and then need to find something else to do.

'When I retired I did have my two daughters, Ciara and Sophie, to look after and as much as there were times when I would feel guilty training and travelling when they were still quite young, when I was at home more I started to wish I had another outlet to look forward to and take me away from the monotony of normal daily life.

'The big change is going from such an extreme purpose in life to slotting into everyday style and being content with that.

'There is no feedback like you get from a race, no central goal to work towards, just general life activities that you still try to be the best at but don't really give you that buzz of a race or hard training session completed,' she surmises.

Such insight demonstrates why Sonia has been much sought after since her competitive days ended.

As competitive retirement beckoned, she filmed a documentary, *Sonia's Last Lap*, to give a window into the mindset of a champion athlete coming towards the end of her career.

She also authored two books. Her first was called *Running to Stand Still* and her second book was her autobiography, *Sonia, My Story*.

In addition to that, the Cobh athlete has been a familiar face on RTÉ Sport analysing European, World Championships and Olympic Games and, as alluded to, she also served as chef de mission for the Irish team London 2012, as well as writing her weekly column.

She has been extremely forthright and frank in giving her own experiences of retirement, considering it is such a taboo subject for many runners and sportspeople in general.

Sonia feels that outside forces can be a determining factor in how athletes view life after sport, and why many are so reluctant to discuss what is coming down the line.

'I think the media can put pressure on athletes to retire when they are not reaching the highs they are used to every time they go out to compete,' she suggests.

'I also think athletes can extend their careers with a more balanced approach, not trying to be at the highest level forever.

'There comes a time when you can pick and choose your races, when you can dip into the bank of years and years of training and use experience and strength to continue to compete.

'Maybe not the highest level but a still competitive and career enhancing level.'

Over the past few years, Sonia has definitely found that balance and perspective.

She has begun reading running books, trying to understand more about the art of training and finding out more about the little extras that can be done.

Studying those has been enjoyable and informative with nuggets on the benefits of gym work, plyometrics, nutrition, having regular check-ins with the physio, gaining the extra sleep. The research culminates in feeling fitter, stronger and having less injuries to contend with.

That has been one piece of learning – all of this is not just to run a faster time but to build a more durable and stronger self, both physically and mentally.

Sonia is asked what advice she would give an athlete at the

turn of 30 who may have limited time remaining in a top-class environment. The first thing she responds to is not placing an age limit on what is coming down the tracks.

'Why do you say 30?' she wonders. 'I think 40 is the new 30, so there is still ten years of life left in those legs if you manage things with smart training and racing. There is still plenty more to be achieved. As you get older and have been through many years of training and racing, the willingness to remain focussed and competitive is often as much mental as physical, especially if the body is willing to co-operate.'

Another learning has been not to look back too much. Last year she competed in a local park in Melbourne, where she lives, and set the target of running a five-kilometre race in under 20 minutes, something she hadn't done in four years. At her peak she would have covered that distance in 15 minutes, but O'Sullivan is done looking back. Life is about the present and these days she sets her goals accordingly.

19
LINDSAY PEAT
Departure Gate

BORN: Dublin, 1980.
*An all-rounder, Peat plays rugby for the Irish senior women's team
and previously played basketball for Ireland and Gaelic football
for Dublin at senior level, as well as representing the Republic of
Ireland at under-18.*
Now 39, Peat recognises she is in the autumn of her career but, as
of autumn 2020, she was still a key part of the Irish rugby squad.

Ahead of the 2020 Six Nations season, the Irish women's rugby
team held a Christmas challenge, an internal series of endur-
ance tests for their players.

When the final results were announced, Lindsay Peat, at 39
the oldest player in the squad, was top of the charts.

'It was a 24-day advent calendar and each window we opened
presented a different fitness test,' she recalls. 'Rowing machine,
one-kilometre time trials, five-kilometre sprints on the bike,
burpees, resistance, all of that.

'All the way through I kept looking at everyone's scores,' she
laughs, 'Jaysus, I should probably be beyond all that at this
stage, but while I am in the set-up I just want to be the best I
can be.'

Peat knows that some time soon she will have to call a halt to her sporting career; one of the finest of a generation. Or maybe her coach, Adam Grigg, will call time on it. That might not be fully within her control.

As she approaches 40, the task of meeting the demands and maintaining the lifestyle of an elite athlete will be considerable, not least an ongoing recovery from an ankle operation for an injury she picked up in their third 2020 Six Nations game against England.

The injury ruled her out for the remainder of the season; one which the Covid-19 virus destroyed in any case, but Peat was in blistering form up to then and is intent on recovering and going again in 2021.

'We have such a young squad that I want to open the girls' minds as to what working to capacity is all about,' she adds. 'I'm envious of the stage that they are at, some of the girls are 18 and have a wide road ahead, but they need to know what is required of them too.'

Before she was injured Peat had to pull back on an upper body weight exercise because of tightness in her neck. One of her teammates, Dorothy Wall, was beside her doing hip thrusts to the absolute max and Peat hated not being able to go full throttle alongside her. Wall is a full 20 years younger, but Peat wouldn't countenance using that as a crutch.

'It's just an environment I love,' she says, 'and it makes all of us rise to the challenge. We are not professional, which is a pity, but this is a setting I would like to stay in for as long as I can manage it.'

It will require some transition and change in mindset when she finally does leave sport. Look at this for a list of feats.

In 1998, she represented the Republic of Ireland women's

under-18 soccer team in the UEFA Championships and played against England, the Netherlands, and the Faroe Islands in that competition.

By then she was already an accomplished basketball player, having taken up that sport at 13. Between 2005 and 2015 Peat played as a point guard for DCU Mercy, helping them to win the 2007 and 2011 Superleague titles. She progressed to full international honours, making her Irish senior debut in 2006, and co-captaining the squad during the 2009–10 season.

Her ties with DCU led to also playing Gaelic football for the college while, at club level, Peat helped Parnells win the 2015 Dublin ladies Intermediate Championship. That paved the way to her representing the Dublin ladies senior football team. She played in three All-Ireland finals, scoring 2-2 in those games, losing twice, but winning the title in 2010.

An intriguing sporting odyssey was not yet complete.

For a long time, Graham Byrne, a strength and conditioning coach that Peat worked with in basketball, had egged her on to take up rugby. In 2015 she eventually accepted a long-standing invitation to try out for the Sandymount club and developed sufficiently to be considered for Leinster selection in the IRFU Women's interprovincial series.

Within months of taking up the game she was fast-tracked into the Irish team by then manager, Tom Tierney. On 14 November, 2015, just eight games into representative rugby life, she made her international debut, coming on against England in an Autumn International at Twickenham Stoop.

The 2017 season was a highlight – she played in the World Cup and was voted Ireland's Player of the Year in the Six Nations. She's on the 30-cap mark now, but still hoping for more.

Long before it became fashionable to push for increased participation in women's sport, Peat was on a court, field or pitch, quietly doing the business. She will bow out of sport at a time when the profile of women's sport is flourishing. It doesn't bother her that she won't be around to reap more rewards. She's more concerned how she will fill the gap when it's over.

'I'm under no illusions,' Peat admits. 'There will soon be a void in my sporting life. You're talking about having 25 years of competition to replace. But I am lucky, outside of this life – and it is so important for me to separate – I have a wife who has supported me every step I have taken and a son, Barra, that we adore. When the time comes to step away, I will be focusing fully on them. The transition won't be easy but, as a family, we have gotten through difficult times and we will again.

'These days my name is hardly mentioned anymore without the words "39-year-old loosehead" coming beforehand,' she laughs.

'I don't mind that at all because I wouldn't be there if the management didn't think I could do a job. And I still feel I can too. That's all that matters. I know full well I'm at the wrong end of my sporting career. I would love to be in control of how things finish up, and hopefully I will be, but that may not be the case either.

'My time is limited. I am just chalking the games off one by one.'

* * *

Peat is quick to admit that the competitions, companionships and challenges all helped her negotiate roadblocks she encountered along the way. Playing sport navigated her through uncertain times. It scares the life out of her that she'll soon leave it all behind.

In trying times, she could always channel her energies into throwing on her trainers or boots and playing a game. Sport always seemed to steer her to a better place.

'I'm not sure what teammates thought of me at certain junctures,' she admits. 'Coaches too. I could be quite abrasive and maybe in people's faces. But it was always for the greater good, I felt. And thankfully everyone put up with it until maybe I learned to challenge things differently.

'But I definitely went through a bad time where I was angry, aggressive and probably not a nice person until I could fully come to terms with myself,' Peat admits.

'I was an absolute A-hole at times but hopefully teammates and coaches saw how hard I worked for them and, even though my personality impacted on people at times, they knew I was genuine about winning. That's the value of sport.'

Coming to terms with herself, as she puts it, was a huge thing. She didn't publicly come out as gay until she was 30 years of age. While the end point of that was liberating, the road there unveiled periods when she didn't know who she was. She experienced panic attacks, self-loathing, weight loss and drank as she struggled with the prospect of coming out to friends and family.

'Well, we are in a world where being gay is not okay with everyone,' she says.

'And when you don't really know yourself, it can lead to great uncertainty and dark times.

'Eventually I thrived off the confidence that sport gave me. I was quiet away from sport and confrontational when playing or training. Anxiety was there. I felt at times that maybe people would be better off without me being around. All of this was swimming around in my mind.

'Ultimately, it all came back to my family – the hurt and pain it would cause for my family if I wasn't around anymore – I couldn't do that to them.

'But for so long, I didn't know what was wrong with me. I would lie to people; tell them I was okay. Mam always said that no matter how bad things were, I could talk to her; that we would sort it all out together. She gave extreme examples and said that even if I went down particular roads in life, they would still be there for me. I drew strength from that and from my grandparents too – that family bond was huge. With that support – and maybe the focus I had on sport – I got through it.

'To this day, while my sporting and personal lives are separate, I draw from both. If I have cross words or disagreements with a teammate in the lead-up to a game, that is parked on match day. If you wear the same jersey as me, and you are fully immersed in the same goal as me, I will have your back 100 per cent. That's a family in my book.'

Having come out nearly ten years ago, Peat is constantly aware of the vulnerability of young people in the position she once was in. In 2019, she felt compelled to speak out and reply, via the *Sports Chronicle* website, to former Australian rugby international, Israel Folau, after he posted on social media that 'hell awaited homosexuals unless they repented'.

Peat, who previously endured homophobic abuse in an All-Ireland ladies' football final, replied that if she had just two minutes with Folau, she would be direct with him. Her name was Lindsay Peat – proud Dubliner, proud wife, proud mother, proud daughter, proud sister and proud rugby player.

Then she would point out how she had also the honour to represent her country at the highest level. She would tell Folau that she was gay and extremely proud of the fact; that when he judged her, he made her more resilient.

'I will fight to not go back to that dark place that you will never understand,' she wrote.

'If someone was out there suffering with the uncertainty of their sexuality, I can't imagine how bad they would feel,' she says now. 'I only had those issues short-term, but others deal with them for much longer. And then someone comes out with those views that Folau had and makes those feelings worse. Well, that could be a straw that could break the camel's back.

'Was it the right thing to do to write that open letter?

'I was very open and, like wearing the jerseys I do, I felt I had a responsibility to tell my story. If it positively affected one person then it will have been worth it.

'Life is like Lego,' Peat adds quickly, 'you have a certain set of pieces and you try to build whatever you can. But you only get one crack at this and you don't need extreme views out there trying to shake your very foundations.

'That's why I wrote it.'

Without sport, Peat may never have had the assurance to inspire so many people who felt vulnerable at a point in time, just like she was.

Her own personal development mirrors how her sporting career has evolved; in both areas she has shown resilience with an indomitable spirit, demonstrated leadership and teamwork, shown versatility too.

While every training session, gym rep, deadlift and drill

helped hone Peat's skills, the truth is that the biggest achieve-ment was finding her voice and true self along the way.

* * *

Take this snapshot from her daily cycle and you might imagine she can't wait to get back to the real world.

Breakfast means a fruit protein shake with avocado and beet-root thrown in for good measure. There's more fruit for around 11, which she often munches in the Ballymun Civic Offices where she works for the Health Service Executive (HSE). Red lentil and coconut soup and salad for lunch, grilled salmon for dinner.

There's a lot of preparation in that, but Peat points out that her wife's support makes it possible to maintain.

'Claire is just brilliant in how she helps me prepare,' Peat says. 'She's home before me two days a week and vice versa. We cook up and prepare in advance; it's great teamwork.'

Still, she must be dying for a bar of chocolate or bacon sandwich?

'Nah, when I eat crap or have a breakout meal, I find myself hankering after good food again,' she replies. 'Proper food helps me perform better, to feel better. I am around 81 kilos at the moment, which is small for a forward in rugby, but that weight helps me play the game in a style I want. I don't want to be sluggish, to labour around the field, I want to be mobile, take that ball and crash into the opposition. And this is how I must eat to stay at this level.'

Training-wise, it's just as intense. When she played Superleague basketball, she travelled the byways of Ireland playing teams from every corner of the country. With Dublin, ahead of Championship, there were three pitch sessions a week and at least two weights stints, never less than five gatherings a week. One individual pitch session could last anything from an hour and a half to two hours, and at the gym Peat always prefers an intense hour to anything else.

Basketball was an average commitment of three nights a week, a game each weekend, with training normally lasting two hours. Rugby has added to that workload since she took up the game, though she wishes they had a full-time environment to operate in.

'Without it we still hold ourselves to account,' she insists. 'I would say we get through as much workload as other teams, but it is just so hard to balance everything. Be it recovery or family time. This is the area I struggle with most. When I finish up a Six Nations Championship and I am at home with Claire and Barra, I sometimes am not mentally present for a few days because I'm still in the rhythm of being in camp with the Irish team. That cannot be the case going forward and I know that.

'For the 2020 campaign I have worked on that aspect. I've come home from camp a few times at night to stay with my family and it means I am not feeling as guilty and can commit a little better to Claire and Barra and be present. When I am with the team, I am fully with them. As I keep saying they are two separate compartments so I try to give both everything I can. But it's not easy, I won't lie.

'Sport has given me a real understanding of the term "addiction". But there are always highs to be chased and with that comes tears too. It's why I am constantly looking ahead to what's coming when I retire.'

And what has she done about it so far?

'Well not a whole lot,' she says flatly. 'I just don't have the time. Like, where would I get the time? Seriously?

'I know what is looming and I have been in touch with Rugby Players Ireland about what might lie ahead but I just haven't acted on it yet. While I am playing it's a little awkward trying to look ahead and predicting what will happen.

'For sure, I know there will be challenges but I have Claire and Barra, mam and dad, my sisters, my community – the people I represented. They have always been there for me and I owe it to them not to fall to pieces when I do retire. That's in my mind as well.'

There will be options. With her wealth of experience and journey of knowledge, coaching is one.

'But would I have the time and space to upskill if I went down that road?' she asks. 'My family deserve to have me around and I want to be with them too, going to water parks and up on rollercoasters, being able to enjoy myself without worrying about something else. Would I be able to do that in coaching?'

Media work is another. She is an accomplished performer on radio, TV and in print. 'I do love talking about sport,' she adds. 'That really gives me a buzz, so hopefully that would be one way of staying involved.'

Barra was recently introduced to the local GAA nursery, and his mum has made sure to introduce him to all that sport can offer. Anna Caplice, one of Peat's Irish teammates, gave him a Harlequins jersey to add to his Irish and Dublin kits and when the family drive by Croke Park they sing 'Molly Malone' and other Dubs songs.

'It's an identity for him and it will be great for him if he chooses to stay with sport,' Peat says. 'But I won't force him either. As long as he has a smile on his face doing something that he loves I'll be happy. The only thing is I am a little jealous that he is only starting fresh while I am at the end of my playing days. That's terrible, isn't it?' she laughs. 'My own son.'

When she does walk from sport, she will leave as a trailblazer. Peat broke the mould for others to follow.

'The 20x20 movement has increased the exposure of women's sport, there has been massive progress. We have had live coverage of games, sponsors, big crowds and that's what we want – we waited a while for that.

'I mightn't get to see the full rewards of all that,' she accepts, 'but those who went before me hardly got anything in that regard either. At least I got to see some type of progress being made for women's sport. I was part of that.'

20
FLIGHTPLAN

Gary Keegan tells of a former sportsperson he knows who recently took a trip to New York City.

'He was four years retired when he flew over there,' Keegan recalls. 'And he was walking through Manhattan one afternoon when he suddenly found himself crying – completely out of the blue.

'He managed to compose himself but later that evening he sat down to try and figure out where the tears had come from. He reckoned it was because he'd spent three years going around, doing different pieces of work, but hadn't confronted the loss and grief in his life for the team he once played for.

'He hadn't gone through that process and it came back to bite him.'

That both saddens and worries Keegan.

'To anyone who might be in a similar boat soon enough I would say, "Hang on a second, you are much bigger than the game. To you and your family and the people who matter, the game is not you. You are the game. And without you the team could never have been what it was."

'My strongest message to athletes coming near the end would

be to take control and be realistic,' Keegan affirms. 'Their bodies have given them everything over the previous two or three decades and yet some are still looking for more. If they actually lift their heads and look beyond, they will see how ex-sportspeople are in huge demand from certain businesses and sectors. In more demand that college graduates, in some instances, because of what they have to offer.

'These people will be self-organised, self-managed, ambitious, they will be disciplined and dependable, capable of good communication and working as part of a team. Companies out there are looking for them. In fact, it's almost as if the corporate and business sectors see the asset within the sportsperson more than the athlete him- or herself does. The day of athletes rejecting everything that comes after sport as "boring" is over. If that's your view that will be your reality. You get what you expect.'

All the research and evidence at Eoin Rheinisch's hands suggests that being proactive and linking small pieces of personal development throughout a career, rather than doing nothing until the end, is the proper approach to retirement.

A plan is paramount. Preferably a practical one that works. After all, a goal without a plan is just a wish.

'I would avoid getting to the end and asking, "What now?"' Rheinisch agrees. 'Develop a plan early and then check on it at various points through your career – that's the key,' he says.

'If you can say, "These are things I have in place" and you have planned for the end while you are still competing, it will make it so much easier – be it a work placement lined up, return to education, or something to focus the mind.'

Rheinisch adds: 'The saying that an athlete dies twice is probably cliched, and "die" is a very strong word in any case, but I look back on my own transition and I can see where that expression comes from.

'I had a degree, a lot of support, I went into coaching, and then back to education and I still found retirement tough. After I left sport I still probably leaned on my identity as "Eoin the Canoeist" for long periods.

'When you step away, you're going to miss that identity,' he admits. 'It takes a couple of years to realise that a sportsperson is not all you are – there is more to you than that.'

There is little in life to match the intensity of competing but Rheinisch points out that having a vision for a new journey helps the athlete ease into the next phase. At Sport Ireland, the former canoeist draws on his own experiences to help others. He refers to his own post-games slumps, when his form and training dipped after major events, as a good template for dealing with retirement.

'I tell them that when I had no plan in place for after major events, I struggled. It will be the same for them if they retire with nothing to focus on.'

Rheinisch and his team have also established links with universities in Ireland and identified scholarship programmes to see where their athletes can best balance their sporting needs with academic requirements.

'We have a network established to help bridge the gap between the career and finding a job. It's called the Athlete Friendly Employers (AFE) network,' he details.

'We have 40 reputable companies like EY, AIB, Decathlon, Dell and many others who are athlete friendly companies. They understand the needs of an elite athlete and are willing to work with us to allow a degree of flexibility around a high-level athlete. If they take on athletes to work with them, they recognise that they may need some leave to compete or maybe a half-time contract, or different style of contract that will allow the athlete to work, but also prepare for upcoming championships.'

Tony Og Regan's final counsel is straightforward – develop other interests outside the bubble. Regan has now taken a complete break from club hurling and simply cannot get over the free time at his disposal; time he has instead redirected towards family and friends.

Some evenings he runs, sometimes he chooses to go out on a lake rowing. He likes to cycle too. Regan works hard but also takes time for himself. Balance is his bible.

'As a sports psychologist, I am always looking for lights flashing when I talk to athletes. Are they over-absorbed in sport?

'What are their hobbies? If they can't give name one, a red flag is raised.

'What do you do in your free time? If the answer is rest, recover or analysis all I see is the bubble. A pedestal when they achieve. A slump when they don't. That's what being self-absorbed in sport is, not seeing the bigger picture. It's the very same outside of sport. In business or in the marketplace there are workaholics who are complately absorbed with their jobs, and their roles. They are so obsessed that it dominates their life and takes control of their identity. Everything they do is measured by success or progress in the workplace.

'The truth is – in sport anyway – that success and failure are not something we have control over; it's a dangerous thread we are selling to people. Coaches have to be conscious that it is healthier for everyone if their players are more rounded. Players must have perspective on life outside sport.

'Volunteer at a homeless shelter for a few days or go into the Children's Hospital at Crumlin and they will soon see what pressure is. Sport is never life and death and yet we make it seem so, losing and winning does not mean success and failure, you just experience these things at times along the way.

'But that buzz of winning won't be there in 20 years' time so put it in perspective. Move on. Don't be boxed into one group – have different clubs, musical societies, theatres and gyms that you are part of. Be creative. It's important to stretch yourself and give yourself that sense of competitiveness and performance elsewhere.

'When you leave sport, it will hit you. Am I done as a person? Am I sad? Am I grieving?

'Find out what's causing all that. What's broken? What you will miss most? Only then will you learn how to heal.'

Practical advice but, of course, there is room for sentiment too. Gary Keegan is sure of that. He urges athletes to accept retirement with pride and reflection.

'Be rounded before you leave and be proud on you way out. Own your retirement,' he states. 'Show gratitude for what you had, but mostly for who you are.

'As Irish people we are only early in our development as a high performance nation, we are only two decades in this space. We were fumbling around the dark for the first decade but now, finally, we are recognising that life after sport is so important.

'It's taken some time, but we know now that the athlete's story does not need to end with retirement. There can be a new chapter, even a new book. The world is lot bigger than sport. We forget that sometimes.'

EPILOGUE

THE FIRST DAY

It took Paul McGee some time to realise that he could have a life outside of football but when he did see a chink of light amidst the darkness of that distressing night in late 2011, he worked hard to turn things around.

Firstly, there was the process of admitting that he had issues. That began with a stay at Connolly Hospital shortly after that fateful night when his friend Dave stepped in and saved his life.

Once he went down the route of opening up and speaking about his issues, it only drew more emotions from him. The cleansing process that ensued has given McGee hope.

And a new perspective on life.

'I opened up,' McGee says. 'And that was the start of it. There was a lot of shite in me, a lot of bad things. I spoke to the counsellors and the doctors about the injury firstly and what it meant for the rest of my career.

'Other things helped too, like going to the gym or getting out for an hour. Clearing the head. Looking after my diet too. That's important. Overall, though, treatment was the real key and the best thing,' he acknowledges.

'I talked to counsellors about more than sport as well,' he

elaborates. 'Like not having a dad around when I was a kid. Other bits came out too. For example, I'm from Ballymun, but I didn't grow up there because I was mostly in Finglas. Tracing back, I was always on the move – be it in Finglas or my mam's, or in England. I never had a place to call home. I was always travelling with no steady foundation.

'It's only now in the past ten months that I have that base now. I met a woman, Michelle Geary, and she has given me things in life that I always wanted but thought I could never get,' he says as his eyes well up. 'I thought that not being able to play football would be the end of me but it's like I have a whole new crack at life again.'

McGee loves working for himself. His days are spent as a courier, out and about. On every stop-off he pauses for a chat. Some of his clients know him as an ex-footballer, others just see a warm, chatty delivery man in their office or premises as he does his rounds. In both his work and personal life, he is now wrapped in the warm embrace of people he loves and trusts. He becomes very emotional as he reflects on his life.

'Over in England I was surrounded by people, but I was actually on me own at the same time,' he whispers.

'At home I have people to help. And, finally, I am proud of what I achieved. I can look back and see that even when the game had gone away from me, I still fought on. I played for the Republic of Ireland Masters team in a few charity games and even to wear that green shirt again was nice, having had it at underage level.

'I know what is important now. Mam. My two boys. Michelle. I'm so proud of them all. But my boys . . .'

He trails off as he dabs his eyes.

'Evan is playing at Tolka and hopefully will go on to have a good career. One thing is for sure, he will have a good dad behind him, advising him all the way. Ryan is flying it too. He's a sports psychologist. Great lads.

'I have one final message,' he says. 'Retirement hit me hard. When I was playing football, no one could touch me. No one could harm me. For 90 minutes, I could go and enjoy the game. I loved it. It's the stuff that happened off the pitch. The game has been good to me. But it's also been hard for me too. Shockingly hard.

'Yet I'm alive. There are poor unfortunates who are not.

'I've come through it, but you must have people to chat to and you must have other interests to lean on when it all ends. Even now I can pick up the phone and ask the doctor or counsellor if I can come in for a chat. I exercise every day. In work, I'm back out meeting people again, chatting away to everyone. I have a routine. All of that is important.

'But if you asked me what fulfils me most now, I would say it's definitely my two boys. I'm most proud of them. They are my heroes. And hopefully they can be proud of me too. I'm glad I came back. Just to be with them.'

* * *

Tommy Bowe's journey has been entirely different to McGee's, but he has overcome his own setbacks and adapted remarkably well. He's quietly content with what he has done too.

'Well, I am I suppose, but I don't sit back and reflect much either,' he says. 'Life is too short for that.'

Crucially, Bowe has found a way of replacing the buzz of

playing rugby, which is extraordinarily hard for athletes to rediscover when they stop competing.

'It's like this. When I am staring down the camera and a red light comes and we go live on air, well that's the new type of fear in my life,' he laughs. 'And I love it.

'It's sink or swim then.'

The 2019 World Cup was a huge test for him. His first day in the hotseat came just 15 months after leaving life as a professional rugby player. Almost in a jiffy, he was presenting live rugby coverage on Irish TV.

'It happened fast,' he nods. 'I did 38 games in that World Cup and there was a huge amount of preparation needed for it, to know enough to start meaningful conversations, but also to get the best from your guests. It's like anything else – put in the work and be prepared.'

That tournament challenged him right until the closing link on final day.

'It did,' he laughs again. 'After the World Cup final, we found out that the official computing licence that generated our TV feed was going to elapse almost immediately once the cup was handed over.

'I got a call in my earpiece from Jammers, (director Jamill Abubakar) telling me to stay talking to my guests until I was told otherwise. What was meant to be a short, snappy six-minute review turned into an 18-minute debate because the live feed was gone from Japan.

'Now 18 minutes in TV terms is like a month in real life so I was just lucky that I had Louise Galvin, Jerry Flannery and Peter Stringer beside me. Great panellists. They all know their stuff and they'd talk forever, and we got through it fine.

'But then just as I prepared to wrap up and deliver the finishing line, the closing link for the entire tournament, nearby builders started drilling.

'I was there trying to say goodbye and all I could hear was this drilling noise. Talk about a distraction! That's the sort of stuff that will replicate the match day fear alright,' he laughs.

Playing rugby was a huge part of Bowe's life, but he's not for looking back. The way he sees it, there could be as much adventure on the road ahead.

'That's how I'm looking at it,' he agrees. 'The playing days are gone. It was brilliant to have them, but I always had on eye on the outside. I'm only starting into chapter two of my next career,' he says.

And that's it right there. Every end arrives with the promise of a new beginning.

ACKNOWLEDGEMENTS

I would like to thank everyone who so graciously gave their time and energy to help me write *When the World Stops Watching*.

As a sports broadcaster and journalist, who has spent his career interviewing sports stars and athletes, I have regularly wondered what life on the outside was like for these people, especially having seen the pressure, adversity and adulation that go hand in hand with competing at the highest level.

I really wanted this book to offer a representative sample of what post-competitive life was like for our athletes across all levels, not just the ones who won everything.

The sportspeople who helped me craft this story of life beyond the tunnel were just so welcoming, helpful and cooperative. Their searing honesty and insight created a very strong narrative and drove the project forward.

Their stories are incredibly personal. They range from harrowing and traumatic to intriguing and uplifting, and they travel deep into the psyche of the retired sportsperson.

Thanks to Paul McGee, Tommy Bowe, Niall Quinn, Kevin Doyle, Shane Supple, Donnacha O'Callaghan, Marcus Horan, Trevor Hogan, Gary Murphy, Paul Flynn, Paul Carbery, Darren

O'Neill, Nikki Symmons, Lindsay Peat, Gráinne Murphy and Sonia O'Sullivan for all your help.

All of you were straight down the line and forthcoming, generous with your time, and genuinely interested in helping me cover this subject. It was a pleasure to meet you all.

To Gary Keegan, Dr Stephen McIvor, Tony Og Regan and Eoin Rheinisch, thanks also for your valued contributions from a personal, academic and educational standpoint. Your reflective approach, stories and observations helped me to link the athletes' stories and weave the narrative together.

I have friends and colleagues to thank too. As always, Pat Nolan and Garry Doyle were a great help, advising me all the way through the process and going through the chapters in some detail. I'm very grateful to you both. As he always is, Kieran Shannon was extremely helpful in discussing the structure of this book. Paul Rouse was another big support, full of ideas and feedback.

Thanks to Eddie O'Sullivan for all his help and assistance.

To Fintan Walsh, Ian O'Riordan, Ger Keville, David Sneyd, Chris Blake, Marie Crowe, Eanna Martin, Máire Treasa Ní Cheallaigh and Ciaran Murphy, thank you all for either suggesting or helping me link up with some of the aforementioned athletes.

To all at Black & White Publishing, it was a pleasure to work with you again. Thanks to Campbell Brown, Ali McBride, editors Emma Hargrave and Alice Latchford, and photographic editor, Tonje Hefte, for all your help and support.

Finally, to my own family, I want to say a massive thanks. My wife, Ruth, always supports me in any project I embark upon, whether it's writing a book, taking on a new job, coaching a

GAA team, or even going back to further my education and I couldn't have written this book without her help and encouragement. To our three children, Jamie, Chloe and Aaron, I promise to continue embarrassing you for as long as I am around.

I dedicated this book to my late father, John. He was a great dad and had me on a pitch and in dressing rooms from the age of four. I've grown up loving sport since. My mother, Mary, has always been there to help me too and still is!

ABOUT THE AUTHOR

Damian Lawlor is a best-selling author and sports broadcaster with RTÉ. He comes from Kilruane in County Tipperary and lives with his family in Naas, County Kildare. This is his seventh book.